THE BOOK OF CRAFTS

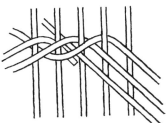

the book of
CRAFTS

edited by
Henry Pluckrose

GALAHAD BOOKS
NEW YORK CITY

Published by Galahad Books, a division of **A & W**
Promotional Book Corporation, 95 Madison Ave-
nue, New York, N.Y. 10016, by arrangement with
Henry Regnery Company, 114 West Illinois Street,
Chicago, Ill. 60610.

Library of Congress Catalog Card No.: 73–79819
ISBN: 0–88365–048–7

Manufactured in the United States of America.

contents

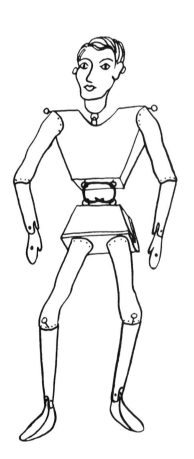

Henry Pluckrose

introduction

SOME TIME AGO I had a conversation with a professor whose first love was physics and whose sole aim in life seemed to be to make the nonscientific (of whom I am one) better aware of the fascination of Newton's law, the significance of light years, and the wonder of magnetic fields. The conversation was somewhat one sided, although finally I did manage to make the point that my interest was in the graphic arts. "Forgive me," he said, "I also care about the arts. I believe that our educational system is too geared to technology. We tend to forget that while new industrial processes give man greater freedom by reducing mechanical toil, educational programs have to prepare people to use their leisure purposefully. No, we must never forget the vital part that the arts still have to play in our lives."

A significant remark, I thought, for one whose life has been spent helping to produce a generation of technocrats who can put man on the moon, a spaceship round Mars, replace a man's heart or send colored T.V. pictures across the world. Wherever future developments may be in any of the many fields of human endeavor, man, because he is what he is, will always need to make, to fashion, to build, to create . . . and the implication of all this is that the child of today will have far more leisure time when he reaches adulthood than ever we thought possible a decade ago. Compare the lot of the Detroit auto workers, who hope to work a fifteen-hour week, with that of many of our industrial workers, for whose parents a sixty- or seventy-two-hour week was commonplace!

Educating for leisure, however, is no easy thing. The mass communications business—television, radio, piped music, tabloid newspapers—make it easy for us to sit back and do nothing until we become little more than automatons, working for the scientists who create the machines. If leisure is to be used purposefully, then from a very early age, children should be encouraged to develop their own skills and have interests of their own. These interests and skills will be quite different, even within the same family—for each of us is unique.

There has been, over the past twenty years, a growing awareness on the part of educators concerning the vital part the arts can play in helping a child to discover himself—by handling materials; by fashioning things such as cane, clay, and wood; by struggling to master the subtle skill of twisting a spindle so that the yarn grows like gossamer from the fingertips . . .

Yet, it is not only the young child who grows through activities of this sort. The adolescent, the young mother, the middle-aged housewife, the retired bank clerk—people of every age can gain an intangible something from struggling to master techniques that have evolved since the dawn of civilization. Many craft techniques remain unaltered since the very beginning, although the materials have become better and easier to handle. (We no longer need to dig our own clay; it comes prepacked. We no longer even need to fire it, if we buy it suitably prepared.)

The purpose of a book such as this is not simply to encourage everyone who dips into crafts to try working in glass or to fill their kitchen with empty detergent packs so that an army of dolls may be made for anxious little children. Rather, it is to serve as a handy reference book for all who feel that crafts should have a vital and important place in our own lives.

Teachers, craftsmen, youth club leaders, and the general hobbyists will find many useful and interesting techniques in this book.

Of course, purists may look at the contents and express surprise that this and that process has been omitted or is only referred to in passing It is, however, quite impossible to include everything or every craft. The aim has been to provide essential starting points from which a more detailed study of a particular medium can grow.

Rebecca West wrote: "Art is nothing less than a way of making joys perpetual." Art is certainly joyful, and the joys can be both intensely personal and shared.

In conclusion I would like to thank the experts who wrote the articles and who, unless otherwise acknowledged in the text, provided or found illustrations, besides giving freely of their advice; Mary Driscoll for the drawings and Maurice Brownfoot for the diagrams; G. D. Hales, who took many of the photographs, some of them under anything but ideal conditions; the staffs of museums and galleries and librarians, who gave such willing assistance and took such an interest; the manufacturers and suppliers of materials whose staff answered numerous letters and patiently dealt with queries. In particular, Mrs. V. Ellis and Mr. Barlow of the Singer Sewing Machine Company, Mr. B. H. Lewis of Enamelaire Ltd., and Mr. L. S. Ansell of Gemrocks Ltd. Their help has made the preparation of this book a much easier task than it might otherwise have been. I also should like to record my thanks for all the help given by Mrs. Margaret Rivers in the compilation of this anthology.

Leon Metcalfe

aluminum foil sheeting

ALUMINUM FOIL SHEETING should be of such a thickness that it can be cut with scissors and manipulated by hand. This ranges from candy wrapping foils to 26-gauge sheet metal, the whole range being readily available from a variety of sources.

MATERIALS

Grocery stores usually stock rolls of lightweight kitchen foil. Art suppliers often stock a medium-weight sheet foil in a variety of colors. Other sources of foil are milk bottle tops, pie trays, candy wrappings, and even empty cans, which can be cut down the seam and flattened into sheets for heavy work.

TOOLS

For working aluminum foil sheeting only very few tools are required, and these basically consist of a scissors, a ball-point pen, pencil, enamel and flat paints, and a regular white household glue.

METHOD

Generally your work need not be confined to one gauge of foil. With a little thought, finished objects can often be enhanced by adding decoration and detail with foil of a different weight from that of the main structure. The aim, when using a material such as foil, is to take advantage of its ability to pick up and reflect light. Therefore, painting on completed objects should be kept to a minimum. For color and image variations, rely on the reflective nature of the foil and the variety of light reflections that can be achieved through bending, curving, and angling the structure.

Perhaps the simplest work to attempt with lightweight kitchen foil is the production of figures. For this, no tools are required; all the modeling and manipulating can be done with the hands. A good preparation for this work is a play period. Crumple a small square or rectangle of the foil to be used and make a figure. In this way you can gain much valuable information about

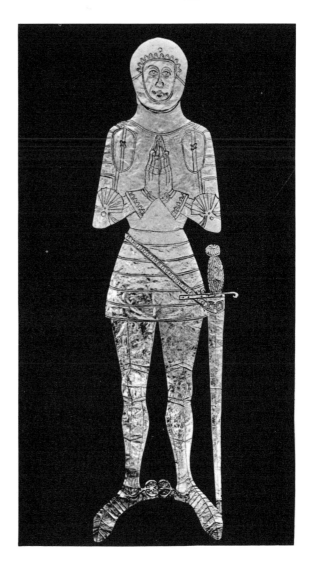

the nature and limitations of working in foil. With care and thought reproduction of almost any object can be produced in foil, resulting in finished works that are permanent and quite sturdy.

Heavy duty sheets of foil can be tooled by using a ball-point pen. First, trim the

1

Tall Christmas angels are made from tapered bottles, aluminum foil, and items found in most kitchen cupboards. Courtesy, Alcoa.

sheet to the shape and size required and sketch in the main outline of the design to be tooled; a soft pencil is useful for this. When the tooling actually begins, keep an even pressure and have a wad of newspaper under the foil. Remember, the work is being done in reverse, and the embossed lines are being produced on the opposite side of the sheet. Rubbings may be taken from either side of the completed tooled design.

A rubbing technique can be used with regular weight foil. Lay a sheet over any object that you want to take a rubbing from and smooth over the foil with a soft duster. Work carefully and with an even pressure to avoid tearing. An impression of the form will appear on the foil, and this can later be accentuated, either by following the lines with a dry ball-point pen or by using a colored felt-tip pen. With the rubbing com-

pleted, the figure can be cut out, using scissors or a craft knife, and mounted on to a paper- or material-covered board ready for hanging.

Any type of foil that is rigid enough to hold a form is suitable for molding, cutting, and decorating in the shape of masks or three-dimensional creatures. These can be left freestanding or used to decorate walls. Mobiles can be made from various types of foil, and the range of weights available enables the mobiles to be carefully and accurately balanced. Similar suspended work can take a more abstract form by basing the design on parts of circles, cones, or multiples and combinations of geometric solids.

H. A. de Coverly

bookbinding

BOOKBINDING BY HAND, as with other crafts, calls for an ability to plan ahead and to think and act quickly. Libraries can bind books for general use, but many people wish to have books bound to their own liking. Types of work that can be bound fall neatly into five broad categories:

1. Periodicals, which are bound in volumes when complete, and the regular publications of societies.

2. Paperbacks of a high quality may need to be preserved in stiff covers, and hard-bound editions of books may need to be rebound in a more advanced style.

3. Music always needs to be bound—particularly manuscripts.

4. Photograph albums, scrapbooks, and visitor or guest books provide exercise *par excellence* for the bookbinder in choosing paper and binding methods.

5. Portfolios for artists and slip cases for the preservation of valuable bindings and papers will add to your repertoire.

Do not take on, or even practice with, Victorian or any other poetry books; novels that are tattered, valueless, or dull; or worn devotional books. Be kind to the owners of the latter and encourage them to buy new ones for reading and preserve the relic. Repairing valuable books and sheet preservation should be tackled only when professional skill has been acquired through practice.

EQUIPMENT AND TOOLS

Catalogs for bookbinding equipment present a bewildering list, but very simple bookbinding at home or in schools may be undertaken with a comparatively small amount of equipment. The essentials are:

Lying press fitted with runners on one side. It should have a metal bar lever, termed a press pin, which is essential for obtaining correct pressure. The lying press will have to be on a stand, known usually as a tub, and must have a cutting device, known as a plough, with, preferably, two knives to fit.

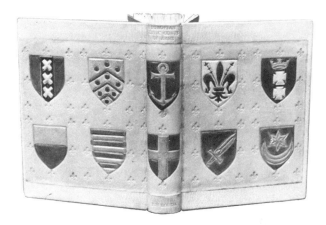

Book bound in natural Kano goatskin with inlay of natural calfskin, carrying tooled and colored coats of arms. It is constructed to give a flat opening, using the "meeting guard" principle.

Backing boards and cutting boards are both wedge-shaped and preferably made from well-seasoned beech wood. Backing boards must have their top edge beveled to an angle of $10°$, and, if they are faced with metal, they will withstand constant hammering and give long and accurate service.

Knocking down iron, when fixed at one end of the lying press, serves as an anvil for hammering surfaces level.

Sewing frame holds sections firm and level during the hand sewing process and is used with sewing keys for hemp and tape.

Nipping press or some form of clamp is necessary to give even pressure.

Letterpress, made of iron, is portable or fixed to bench and is used for temporary or prolonged pressing during any binding process.

Pressing boards, which can be made from plywood or faced with formica for refinement, are essential. These do not need to be fancy, and any other improvisation that will work can be used.

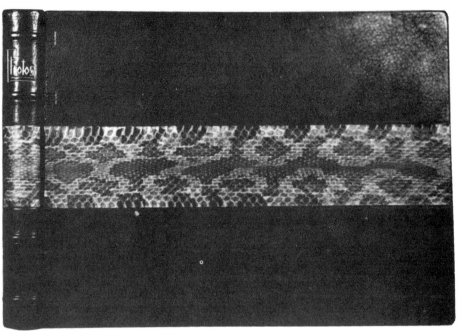

Photograph album made by the author and constructed to open flat, bound in black oasis morocco with a wide decorative center band of snakeskin vellum from an untreated python skin.

Small bench knife or strong card cutter used for cutting medium thickness strawboard and other card or paper (single sheets only).

Finishing stove (gas, electric, or butane gas) fitted with an outer ring for holding finishing tools in a heated area.

Finishing tools include handled letters mounted in wood consisting of complete alphabets with numerals and ornamental tools. Other tools to obtain will be a few line pallets for tooling straight lines across spines and some modern styled center tools of simple shapes.

Gold cushion is a prepared, level cushion covered with the rough side of suede or other leather and is used for laying out golf leaf.

Gold knife has a long thin-bladed edge for cutting gold leaf.

If work of a high standard is to be achieved, then it will be necessary to add the following equipment and tools to your collection at some later date:

Standing press is a large iron construction fixed to the floor and is used for applying even pressure over a large area.

French press is much like a standing press but made of wood.

Large bench knife or board shears for cutting large sheets of cardboard.

Guillotine knife, either bench type or freestanding, used for cutting quantities of paper, books, and cardboard.

Type fonts of brass in definite point sizes and in type-high dimensions made to withstand heat.

Type holder used to hold type in lines for tooling.

Blocking press electrically heated bench model, for blocking titles, designs, and dyes onto book covers.

Ornamental pallets for tooling across spines.

Fillet is a wheel-shaped finishing tool for making straight lines.

Roll is a wheel-shaped tool that gives a continuous line of pattern.

Gouges are single tools of ⅛ inch to about 1 inch across the curve used to tool continuous curved lines.

Spokeshave is supplementary to the paring knife.

Bodkin and awl are pointed tools for piercing boards and teasing out hemps.

G clamps are for holding down leather when using a spokeshave.

Paring stone is any smooth surface, such as a discarded lithography stone; sheet of

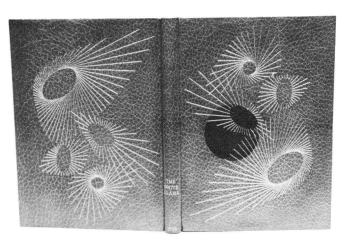

Book bound in purple levant morocco leather, inlaid and tooled in gold. The free-flowing linear gold tooling is patterned after the modern style of Paul Bonet of France.

Book bound in emerald green goatskin, inlaid in gold and blind tooled with a semirepresentational design based on fossil shapes.

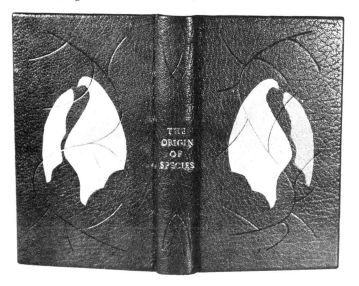

plate glass; or sheet of marble, such as a discarded marble-topped washstand.

Band nippers are used for forming the bands in flexible, raised banded work. Chromium-plated ones are sometimes available.

Hand tools to buy and make

Bone folders are used at every stage of bookbinding to supplement hand pressure. They can be fashioned from wood, discarded paper knives, or old bone toothbrush handles. Soak object in thin machine oil, shape one end with a coarse file, and sandpaper smooth.

Knives are required in abundance, such as a general all-purpose, wooden-handled cobbler's cutting knife with a broad or long point. Discarded power hacksaw blades also can be utilized for cutting. Avoid razor blades or gadget knives. A penknife is useful on some odd occasions, but it should be used strictly for bookbinding work and should not be regarded as a regular craft tool or the blade will soon become dull.

Sharpening devices of all kinds are essential to keep cutting edges clean and sharp. Oilstones, combination India, natural Washita, or Arkansas, if kept in boxes, will last many years. Strops can be made from plywood strips using brown twill aluminous oxide cloth, medium to fine, with strips of machine belting dressed with graphite mixed in with vaseline.

Shears and scissors of various sizes should be of top quality; those sold as binders shears are not advised.

A straight edge is a necessity; most binders use the usual metal ruler, which should be marked in inches.

Carpenter's try square together with small and large spring dividers will complete the tool requirements for marking up and measuring the backbone before sewing.

Binder hammer is a luxury. You can make do with a cobbler's hammer.

Saw, a tenon and dovetail, will be needed for making grooves across the backs of sections prior to sewing.

If you join a woodworking class and get some professional advice, you should be able to make some equipment, such as a lying press and tub, sewing frame, plough, etc. Have professional turning where needed, but metal bench screws can be obtained for the lying press. The metal fitting for the plough may present difficulties, so seek professional advice in this and in the purchase of any secondhand equipment 5 or tools. Simple basic finishing tools can be made from metal blanks (professional finishers make their own). Power tools make life easier. Handmade brass sewing keys work quite satisfactorily.

Adhesives are the most important commodity of all in bookbinding, and the success of the work depends on their correct use. Glue needs to be heated in some form of double boiler. Scotch glue, in pellet form, requires soaking until soft. Flexible glues sold in a glutinous state "ready for the pot" retain their elasticity and should always be used on the spine. Brush maintenance and a well-stirred, correct dilution make for even viscosity and enable the novice to attain confidence in gluing (many never do). Hot glue is being replaced by the introduction of cold polyvinyl acetate emulsions (PVA), which were developed to serve the speedy mass production of the paperback book industry. Paste, originally wheat flour and water, still has its place in bookbinding. It has a high degree of permanence without causing damage to material and is best for paper and leather.

Brushes must be of good quality and should be properly maintained for best results. Brush maintenance means overnight soaking and thorough beating out before each use. PVA on brushes is best removed with soapy water. The best brushes and the most expensive are made from hogs' hair.

Materials, expensive ones such as leather, should be used only for advanced binding and quarter-bound library style. Oasis morocco, which is the retanned, redressed, and dyed Nigerian goatskin, has for many years proved to be the most satisfactory for craft binding. Also, sometimes the native-tanned, natural, and dyed moroccos are available. These are much sought after for their natural markings and texture. The South African goatskin, known as Cape goat, makes a beautiful leather, but it is expensive and difficult for the nontrade craftsman to use until he has achieved a high degree of skill. Calf—sumac-tanned,

dyed, law, and natural undyed—is fairly easy to work with and readily obtainable. Skiver, which is the upper split of the sheep, is best avoided for binding except for thin, limp music or other light work because it requires great care in handling. Vellum of all kinds requires careful study before a novice attempts to handle it, and even the experts do not agree on methods for using it. Points to remember are that vellum is a stiff, dressed, slightly transparent skin requiring a backing of white or creamy white paper, which may or may not be attached to the underside of the vellum. The vellum will quickly react to moisture and to atmospheric changes, so complete control of the adhesive used during the drying must be maintained; even then, some movement will take place many days later.

Cloths, starched filled, such as Bancroft linen finish or buckram are the best for bookbinding purposes.

Boards, such as Davey Green or Red label, are used for stiffness.

Lining materials are used as reinforcements for spines and mounting:

Mull—an open weave cotton mesh fabric

Cambric — similar to mull but more closely woven

Linen—lighter and more expensive than either mull or cambric

Calico—coarser and heavier than mull, cambric, or linen, contains dressing

Holland — natural and dyed dark-colored blind material known to be used for binding before bookcloth appeared.

Paper to be used for endpapers should be only good quality cartridge or one of the handmade or mold-made papers that are produced in Europe. Handmade, marbled papers are expensive, but cheaper European makes are available along with a range of fancy printed papers, which may be used as endpapers, siding, or for covering boxes. Brown paper for lining backs of books should be the brown craft variety or can be obtained from odd wrappings. Thin,

Hand sewing method showing continuity of thread from head to tail.

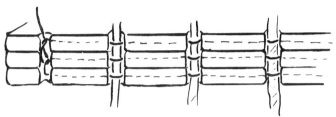

Detail of hand sewing method on tapes showing the formation of the kettle stitch, which is the most important feature of all hand sewing methods.

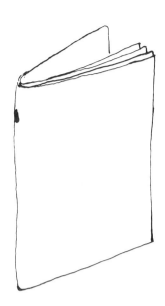

Uncut, 16-page (8 leaves) section of a book with partly cut head to avoid creasing. The collating back mark is also shown.

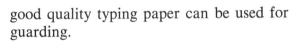

Method of hand sewing as used for some leather binding and also for thick section work (magazines, etc.). The hemp or cord used is recessed into the spine, and on the best work the cords are laced into the boards of the binding.

good quality typing paper can be used for guarding.

PRINCIPLES OF CONSTRUCTION

The minimum sequence of binding operations for all styles includes:

1. Preparation of section or sheets and pressing
2. Preparation of endpapers
3. Sewing or stitching
4. Forwarding, i.e., first gluing, cutting edges, and decorating them, shaping spine, forming shoulders, preparing and attaching boards, pressing, and cleaning off
5. Headbanding
6. Lining the spine
7. Preparing the covering leather or other material
8. Covering or making the case
9. Finishing
10. Casing in or siding and pasting down open, pressing
11. Opening up completion

When re-covering paperbacks, only items 2, and part of 4, 6, 8, and 10 are followed. The finishing consists normally of pasting the original paper wrapper onto the new cover.

Finishing

Lettering and decorating the cover require great concentration and attention to detail; practice is the only way to attain efficiency. Very briefly, the process is:

1. Plan the lettering (upper case capitals), symmetrical optical center, top center, lower center, or asymmetrical right or left. Variation in size of letters or use of lower case is not advised. Longitudinal lettering should read down.
2. Mark up the design or lettering on the actual material.
3. Prepare surface with dilute vinegar or distilled water.
4. Apply glair—the medium for making the gold in gold leaf stick.

7

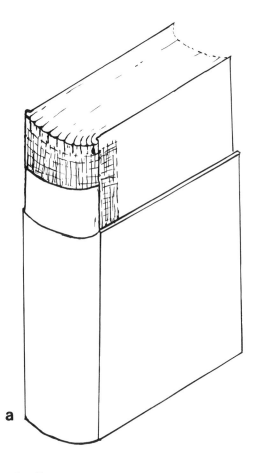

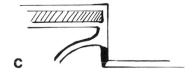

Construction of a cloth-cased binding. The sewn book is seen to have shoulders, a reinforcing mull extending over the side, a paper lining on top of this, and the case fitting overall. Note the extension of "squares" on the long (fore-) edge.

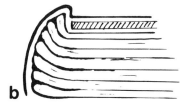

The fit of the case over the shoulder gives a ridge.

5. Grease the area to be tooled and apply the gold leaf.
6. Heat, clean the surface of the tool, and make the impression.
7. Clean off the surplus gold and examine the surface for defects.
8. Complete the removal of the gold and grease the area with a solvent (benzine).

The opening of (b) at the first endpaper shows the bend of the cloth above the shoulder.

Items 2 and 3 can be omitted when tooling cloth after you reach a certain level of proficiency. Items 2, 3, 4, and 5 are omitted when using foils that contain an adhesive element. The marking up of foil is difficult and is made on the carrier side with the impression coming through the foil. The fine detail of very small letters and decoration may well be lost by this spread of the impression.

Oasis morocco will always give good results if treated correctly, but cheaper cellulose-finished skins should be avoided. Some foils are not suitable for tooling on leather. Good quality linen cloths and buckrams also give good results when tooling, but art canvas and most of the paper-felted fabrics are difficult to use.

When paper is being considered for the substance of a book of plain sheets for use as an album or as a guest book etc., or when assembling materials for the endpapers, it is vital that the grain or machine direction of the stock be studied so that it will run parallel with the binding edge, i.e., from head to tail. Thus, the movement caused by the hygroscopic nature of paper is controlled or at least minimized. Also the pitfalls of cockling and creasing when using adhesives, which upon drying can be followed by

d

The French or American groove method of casing, note that the board is set away from the shoulder.

e

The free opening of (d).

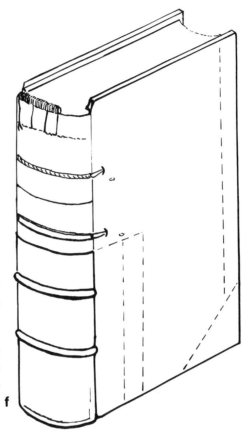
f

Construction of a leather binding sewn on recessed hemps, two of which are shown laced into the boards. A sewn-on headband is featured. There are raised bands across the spine. The dotted lines on the board show the proportions for quarter, half, and fore-edge strips covered in leather together with one corner.

warping and twisting, are also minimized if the paper is bound with the grain. And the final bonus for binding the paper properly is that it is easier to fold and to open the book.

Bookbinding is, of course, a craft that demands great patience and skill. Here you have the simplest methods and from these you can progress to more complicated work. Always carefully examine beautiful bindings when you come across them; you can learn a great deal just by looking. A wonderful sense of satisfaction and achievement can be gained from binding your own books.

g

Shoulder formation of (f) with detail of the position of laced-in cords. Note that the shoulder level is with the boards — without a ridge or a groove as in other forms of construction.

E. H. Blakeman

cane, rushes, raffia

CANEWORK, AS PRACTICED AT HOME, in schools, and in adult education centers, is generally known as basketry and, as the name implies, refers mainly to smaller baskets of all kinds used in the home. But in addition, canework includes mats, trays, and other articles made by the same methods.

Materials

The material used for canework is called pulp cane, or center cane. It is chiefly obtained from the core of the rattan palm that grows in tropical forests of the East Indies, although there are a number of suitable substitutes. The outer bark is stripped off (this is made into chair cane or flat glossy lapping cane), and the remainder is cut by machine to various thicknesses, which are referred to by numbers; the smaller the number the thinner the cane. For use in hospitals and by the disabled, there are certain types of cane that have been bleached after machining, thus making them more pliable and easier to work. There is another type of cane that is used in workshops for the blind and by professional basket makers. This is known as willow and requires more treatment than can usually be given either at home or in school. Willow is used for dog baskets, laundry hampers, and other containers that need to be rigid and durable.

Tools

For the beginner wishing to start on something simple the following tools are the most necessary:

1 pair 5-inch side cutters
1 pair round-nosed pliers
1 small knife
1 long ruler

It also helps the beginner to have an empty jam jar or similar type of container (the use of which will be explained later).

As most people do not have a work board to fasten the work to, it is necessary to provide some kind of weight to hold the

A basket made of the thicker cane used by professionals and in workshops for the blind.

work steady. This can be an old brick wrapped in paper or a piece of material. For smaller items, a kitchen weight suitably covered so as not to damage the work is satisfactory.

Terms

There are a number of technical terms that are useful to know because they save a lot of explanation when making a basket. The principal ones are:

Stakes are always the thicker of the two

*Woven bases are best left to
the more experienced weaver.*

or more different sizes of cane used in making a basket. They form the uprights around which the finer canes are woven.

Bye-stakes are placed on the right-hand side of the stakes after the upsetting has been completed; these add strength to the stakes.

Foot-trac is the method of fastening the stakes after placing them into the holes of a wooden base.

Weavers is the finer cane that is woven in various ways around the stake canes.

Upsetting is the method of using three weaving canes worked alternately and, as the name implies, it sets the work up to the correct shape required. It is most important that it be done correctly.

Randing is weaving with one cane.

Pairing is weaving with two canes worked alternately.

Waling is exactly the same as upsetting but is done at various intervals in a basket to give added strength and rigidity to the work.

Border is a means of finishing off the stakes after the basket has been made to the required shape and size.

Making a basket

Having decided on the type of article to be made, the next thing to decide is how long the stakes should be. This is worked out in the following way: take the height of the finished article plus three inches for the foot-trac border plus at least seven inches for the finishing border (this can be very much longer for some of the more complicated borders; the length given here is for the simplest ones).

For the beginner, prepared wooden bases can be purchased. (Experience is needed before a woven base is attempted.) When the number of holes in the wooden base has been counted, the correct number of stakes are cut and placed into the jam jar or similar container with about three inches of cold or warm water in it and left for about ten minutes to render the cane more pliable. As mentioned before, the bleached cane is softer to start with and, therefore, requires less or even no soaking before use. By placing only the ends of the stakes in the water, it will be found that they will enter the holes in the wooden base easily, especially if the dry ends are placed in first, and then the whole length pulled through to the wet part. When the cane is wet, it swells, and it may be necessary to enlarge the holes with the knife to enable the stakes to go through the base. Put only six or eight stakes in the base at a time; then work the foot-trac border. If all the stakes are put in, especially on a large base, they will be dry before all the work has been completed.

The following explanations and diagrams will make clear the different methods of weaving and making the foot-trac border. Weaving can be done either from left to right by a right-handed person, or from right to left by a left-handed person. The

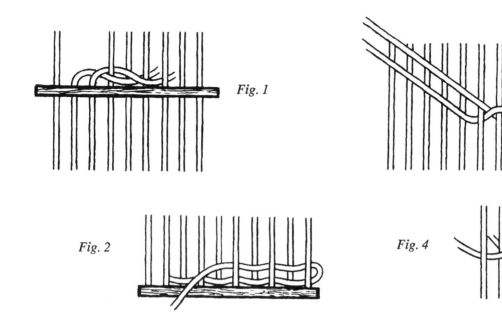

Fig. 1

Fig. 2

Fig. 3

Fig. 4

diagrams shown here are for a right-handed person.

Foot-trac. Leave about three inches of damp cane projecting underneath the base (it may be necessary to extend or reduce the amount left below the border since it will vary according to the size of the base and the distance between each hole). Working from left to right, bend down each stake in turn behind one and in front of two, leaving the end on what will be the inside of the basket (Fig. 1), all the time pressing the work well down onto the base. To work the last three stakes, thread them in order under the starting stakes, easing these up with the knife and at the same time making sure that the ends of the last three stakes lie on the base. Now go around on the other side of the work and pull the stakes up straight and tight to the base and follow the same procedure for that side.

Randing method. Using one length of weaving cane, insert it between stakes 1 and 2 with the short end pointing to the left on the inside (Fig. 2). The forefinger of the left hand is placed on the inside of the work at the back of the second stake to hold it in position and to press the stake outward if necessary; at the same time, place the thumb on the outside of the work, holding the weaving cane against the stake. Now

with the tip of the thumb place the weaving cane to the back of and away from the next stake; with the thumb and forefinger of the right hand bring it to the front of the work between the next two stakes. Repeat the stroke, pulling the cane through after a few strokes.

Pairing method. Place two weaving canes in adjacent spaces between the stakes, or take one long length of weaving cane, bend it in half and place the bend over one stake. Take the left-hand weaving cane and pass it in front of the next stake on the right, over the second weaving cane, behind the next stake and out to the front (Fig. 3). The second weaving cane is woven in exactly the same way. Continue working each cane alternately (Fig. 4). This is a stronger type of weaving than randing and is the one most generally used.

Waling, or upsetting, method. Three weaving canes are placed in adjacent spaces between the stakes (Fig. 5). Taking the left-hand weaving cane first, pass it over the other two weaving canes, in front of two stakes and behind one, bringing it out to the front (Fig. 6). Again using the left-hand weaving cane, repeat this stroke (Fig. 7). Using the left-hand weaving cane each time, continue in this way.

Joining a new weaving cane. Leave the

Fig. 5

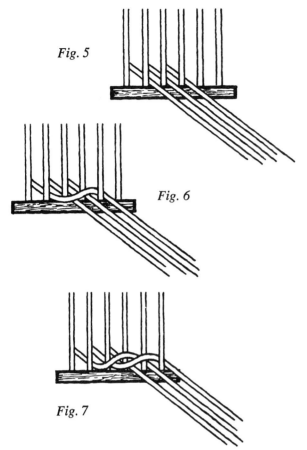

Fig. 6

Fig. 7

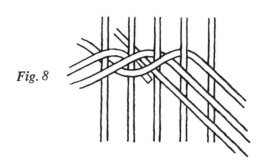

Fig. 8

(this is done to stop the cane from cracking when making a sharp bend).

The first stake is then bent behind the second and brought to the front; the second stake is bent behind the third and brought to the front; the third stake is bent behind the fourth stake and brought to the front.

The first cane bent down is now passed over the other two canes bent down, in front of the fourth stake and behind the fifth, and brought to the front again.

The fourth stake is now bent down with the first one and on the right-hand side of it —making sure that they both lie flat on the top of the work and not on top of each other.

The second and third stakes that were bent down are now dealt with in exactly the same way; at the finish there should be three pairs of canes on the front of the work.

Counting from the right, take the fifth stake in front of the next upright stake and behind the next and through to the front once again; bend the next upright stake down with it as before to make the pair.

Continue until there is only one stake left standing, then take the fifth weaving cane in front of this stake as before and, from the inside, thread it under the first stake bent down (this may have to be eased up a little with the aid of the knife). Now bend the last stake down beside this.

The right-hand weaving canes of the three pairs are now threaded through in the same way so that there is no obvious start or finish.

old cane on the outside of the work pointing to the right. Insert the new weaving cane on the right of the old cane resting against the stake (Fig. 8). The diagram shows the join in waling, but the same method can be used for all the types of weaving described previously. In this method there is one end finishing on the outside and one starting on the inside, and they will hold each other together when the ends are cut level with the work. It is most important to keep the weaving canes wet while working with them. They should be soaked for about ten minutes before starting work, and a damp sponge will help to keep them pliable while working.

After completing the basket to the required shape and size, the border has to be added. There are many types of borders, each suitable for different articles. However, one of the easiest and most useful is the three-rod plain border, which is worked as follows:

All the stakes should be squeezed level with the work with the round-nosed pliers

A selection of basketwork.

When the basket is dry, the ends of all the border and any joins made can be cut off close to the work. Should there be a lot of whiskers on the basket, they can be removed by singeing with a cigarette lighter, but care must be taken not to burn the basket.

RUSHES

For many years both freshwater and salt-water rushes have been used for chair and stool seating. Rush baskets and mats also are familiar objects. However, rushes are not particularly popular as a craft material for use at home or in school. First, they are somewhat expensive to use on one chair or stool. Second, they are rather dirty and often difficult to handle. Good results are not easy to achieve with rushes, the plaiting being difficult for the novice to keep to an even width.

There is, however, another type of material called sea grass, which can be bought ready for use. It is worked in the same way as rushes, and similar patterns can be obtained.

Tools

The only tool required for working with sea grass is a large steel sacking needle and a quantity of brown paper for packing. (When rushes are used, the odd pieces are saved and used for this purpose.)

Seating a stool

The usual method of covering a stool or chair is known as the rush pattern and is one of the easiest to follow, provided the work is kept tight and the same direction of working is maintained.

Begin by fastening one end of the sea grass (Fig. 9) onto the inside of the top left-hand cross bar "a" of the stool or chair with a small carpet tack; proceed by bringing the remainder of the seagrass over and under bar "b," then over and under bar "a."

From here, take it over and under bar "c," then back and over and under bar "d." Do exactly the same over bar "d." Continue in the same way, making sure that the work is kept tight and even and the miter in each corner is correct and in line.

As the work proceeds, work small pieces of brown paper between the two layers of sea grass at each corner. This will help to prevent overlapping and keep the miter straight, besides making it firm.

When the work is completed, the four miters should meet in the center of an equal-sided stool. The end of the sea grass can be tied off on the underside. The steel

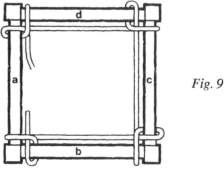

Fig. 9

needle will be required to make the last few rounds through the center.

Should it be necessary to make a join during work, it should always be done on the underside.

RAFFIA

Nowadays the use of natural raffia has been largely superseded by that of synthetic raffias marketed under various names and obtainable from art needlework counters and suppliers of craft materials. Synthetic raffia has many advantages over the natural product: uniform width, continuous length, repeatable and fast colors. It may be used in the same way as the natural material for making table mats, lampshades, handbags, hats, and many other articles. Another advantage is its suitability for knitting, weaving, plaiting, etc. Patterns may be obtained for raffia work, but if you assimilate the methods of use, it is not difficult to create original work.

Indian coiled basketwork is yet another form of raffia. Indeed, there are various materials and methods that cannot be included here due to lack of space.

Alan Lewis

clay and synthetic modeling materials

IN RECENT TIMES there has been a considerable increase in the variety of materials available to the modeler. This is probably a reflection on the shortcomings of the traditional methods in a situation in which the interest is growing more quickly than the availability of special facilities. Having made a model there is often a need to make it permanent, and it is here that the real difficulties lie and the answers are to be found.

To achieve permanence has always been difficult. The requirement to change a plastic medium into something hard and durable called for the use of a kiln or some knowledge of the casting process. Neither way was easy. Papier-mâché could be considered as a possible alternative, but as a modeling material it leaves much to be desired. But times are changing, and, although prices are rising, so are the options.

MATERIALS

The available materials can be divided into three groups. First, those that remain soft; second, those that start soft but can be persuaded by some special means to harden; and third, those that start soft but dry into hardness without any help or persuasion. Papier-mâché is a member of this last group, but its handling characteristics are so different from any other that it will be dealt with separately at the end of this section on materials.

Plasticine

The first group of modeling materials is typified by plasticine, a commercially produced substitute for clay or wax. At an adult level, this is an ideal medium for working out one's thoughts in the hands and for making little abstracted shapes that will indicate whether or not the idea is worth following up. It is also ideal for little experimental models, such as a small dog or cat. Move the head of an animal figure and note the complete change of expression that this action will bring about. Move the

Experimenting with textures by pressing metal shapes into clay or plasticine.

legs into a running position. See how the balance is changed if you wish to raise the front leg. Work out the mechanics of these problems, and you will begin to understand a little more about the nature of four-footed movement—and be a better modeler to boot.

There are, in fact, several materials in this first group of modeling materials, but they are the same in principle, and there is no need to dwell further on them here. Mostly everything that can be done with plasticine-like products was done some time ago. However, they are still enjoyed today. They have their obvious limitations in that size and scope are determined by the inability of the materials to withstand more than a limited amount of their own weight, and nothing made in these materials can

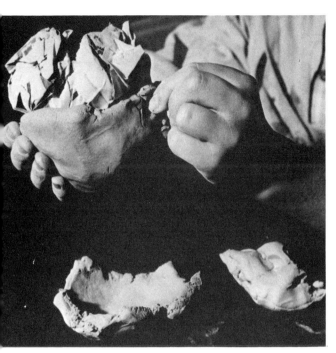

Making a ball around twisted paper.

Welding the joint together.

be retained. Nevertheless, within these limitations they are useful.

The newcomers

It is in this second group that we find the range of modeling and shaping materials has mushroomed. The qualities and techniques offered are so various that they cannot be typified by any particular one. Generally, they are sold by the pound and come in tins or neat plastic packs of some sort. All are carefully designed materials that remain workable for long periods and are either self-hardening through long exposure to the air or require some mild heat treatment in a domestic cooker. Normally, the usual degree of hardness will be adequate. Some can be recovered by breaking down and rewetting, but most are irretrievable.

The technique used in modeling a small chunky object is much the same as with plasticine. The object is developed from a ball. However, to economize, form the material round a lump of twisted paper. Alternatively, if the shape is to be long and lean, start with a wire frame. Any techniques peculiar to a particular material are covered in the instructions provided with it. Read them with care. These materials are

not cheap, but you will get your money's worth if you are able to use them properly and to some effect. Less common aspects of modeling, such as jewelry-making, are also described in these instructions.

Clay and reinforced clay. This last group of modeling materials can be considered as an alternative to the materials described previously. It includes two types—the common and prepared clays and the reinforced modeling clays. This group accounts for the majority of all modeling that is done. Hundreds, possibly thousands, of tons of clay are used each year. A small proportion is fired and turned into pottery, but much of it never is heated in a kiln.

Something about the nature of clay (aspects that are not vital to the modeler) is discussed in the section on pottery, but there are some points—particularly those relating to its handling properties—that should be mentioned sooner.

Clays are normally purchased in a plastic state ready for use. They become hard on drying. Unfortunately, they are much too brittle to be of use in a hard state. The

17

*A more permanent
"Willow Pattern" model
in reinforced and
hardened clay.*

modeler who wishes to retain his efforts must either have his model fired or cast it in some casting material. This could be a very real problem for the beginner, who may have no special facilities, but the problem has been largely overcome with the introduction of reinforced modeling clay. The reinforcing permits a hardener to be used when the work needs to be made permanent.

All the clays in the second group are cheap by comparison with the materials previously mentioned and are, in consequence, sold in quantities of 5 to 25 pounds. Twenty-five pounds of any of the normal modeling materials measure approximately 12 x 12 x 6 inches. One large pot or model can weigh many pounds, so it can be seen that cost is still important when purchasing clay.

Papier-mâché

In the third group of modeling materials papier-mâché is probably one of the cheapest to use. Personally, I find little joy in the making up of papier-mâché pulp, but it is an unfortunate and necessary prelude to working with this very useful, although not ideal, modeling material. In handling, it compares rather poorly with clay, but once the technique is acquired and the form

achieved, what a rugged substance it hardens into. I use the word rugged to indicate not just toughness but also the exterior texture—a smooth finish is really not possible with paper pulp.

We all have our pet way of making up the mash. Newsprint is normally the basic material, but egg cartons break down rather nicely. Tear up whatever you use into rather small pieces and let it soak for as long as you can. For any special finely textured material use an egg whisk to finish it off, but otherwise rub it through the hands. Drain off the surplus water, first by sieving it through a cloth; then give each handful a final squeeze. Now make up a concentrated solution of one of the white glues. Wait until it is clear and then mix it into the pulp. As quantity goes, the weekly newspaper will need about a dessertspoonful of the glue—plus water, of course.

This mixture could now be considered ready for use, but, in fact, it will be much improved by the addition of a filler of some sort. It must be realized that water adds enormously to the bulk of the mixture, and this will all disappear as it slowly (very slowly) dries out. Models based on bulk will fade away in large lumps as the drying progresses. A filler will help to diminish this effect, and the smaller shrinkage will

Preparing the pulp from egg cartons.

The proportions of papier mache pulp and clay prior to kneading.

Papier mache monster and tree.

also mean a smoother finishing surface although, as stated, the surface can never be really smooth. The greatest advantage gained by the addition of a filler will be in the handling properties. If to any given mass of paper pulp you knead in a quarter of its volume in plastic clay, much will be gained. There will be an increase in weight that will help to give it solidity. In assessing the value of papier-mâché, it should be judged on three counts: (1) the effort required in preparation; (2) the ease with which it can be modeled; and (3) the resulting end-product. It must be acknowledged that papier-mâché does not come out very well on the first two, but on the last count its claims are unique. The toughness/weight ratio of well-made papier-mâché is probably surpassed only by metal

alloys and fiber-glass. It is by taking advantage of these properties that we can expect to get the best from this material. Masks made over clay shapes for a start, puppet heads, thin spiny insects, models and structures made around wire, pendants, dishes, and jewelry all can be made successfully with papier-mâché.

TOOLS AND TECHNIQUES

The great beauty of modeling, when compared with almost any other craft, is that so few tools are necessary and very little technique. All you will need is a piece of wood sharpened rather like the blade of a knife (called a spatula), which you can buy for less than a dollar, a broken hacksaw blade, an old wooden ruler (or similar piece of wood), and a sponge. Rodin and Epstein probably had little more.

To make a start

As suggested earlier, squeeze your first little models out of a small ball of whatever

19

The early stages of modeling.

material you have chosen. If you are teaching children, then they too should begin this way, whatever their age. There will be no special difficulties except those that arise from your own inability to create the shape that you have in mind. If this is all new to you, you will enjoy the sensation. It is, as they say, therapeutic.

With some modeling materials, and clay in particular, you may find that there is a tendency for the surface to stiffen as it dries in the hands. Use a sponge to replace the moisture and proceed. Don't be too serious with your first efforts, but it will probably be worth your while to finish off each item with color or some other finishing medium, if only to get a better understanding of the types of problems that will arise later. Then pass on to something more substantial.

Let us consider the making of a four-legged beast such as a horse—one of those splendid draft Clydesdales—not because he is so splendid but rather because he has great thick legs that can support the mass of his body. Think of a racehorse and you will see the point. Even so, the body of a horse still may be too heavy to be supported by the legs if the body is made from a solid mass of clay. So, as already suggested, wrap the clay around a mass of twisted paper to make the body lighter.

With the body of the horse lying on the table, attach the legs. These will be rough coils of clay, quite unfashioned but with a good strong joint. This is best achieved by welding both parts together. Treat the welding as of first importance. It is always a sad sight to see good work develop faults in the later stages through initial carelessness.

It may well be that your model can stand on its own four feet already but, if not, put a support under its belly until the clay is "leather hard" and strong. Now add the head and tail, with the same care for the joints mentioned in the previous paragraph. The basic shape is complete. Now, using your fingers, supplemented where necessary by the finer edge of the modeling tool, begin the shaping and modeling. Develop the model in the way that you feel is right. This model is an expression of what, to you, is implied by the term draft horse. This may be in terms of solidarity, power, or even humanity. Yet there should be no need for you to be consciously aware of all this. Any serious piece of sculpture tells as much about the artist as it does of the subject.

Coiling

To achieve really large volumes with clay, you must learn to coil. This is a technique used by potters and modelers alike. Here let's discuss the making of a head. In the early stages it could just as easily have been a pot or any abstract form.

First, press out a lump of clay into a disc about three or four inches across and rather more than half an inch thick. Now pull off a piece and roll it backward and forward

A clay and wire bird.

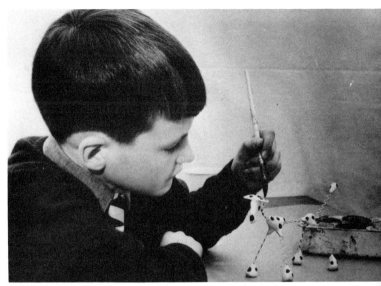

*Student adds finishing touches
to clay and wire dog.*

on the table pressing gently with both hands until it stretches out into a long rope the thickness of your thumb. One might expect this to be easy but you will find that your first efforts are rather bumpy affairs. It doesn't matter. Wind it around onto the edge of the disc so that it begins to form a cylinder. Smear over the joint between the coils on the inside and out as you work.

More and more coils are wound one on top of the other, enlarging the diameter as you get higher, until you estimate that the level would be about the level of the forehead on your head. Now wind the coils a little on the inside to shape and close in the top. Even at this stage there need be nothing about the shape that suggests a head, and you still have a hole in the top large enough for your hand. Put your hand in and with your beating stick knock some intelligence into it. Press out from the inside and beat in from the outside; a crude, rough shape to begin with, refined gradually stage by stage. Once it begins to take shape the top can be closed in. A little more beating, and then the modeling can begin, but don't be too disappointed with early attempts—portraiture is a very difficult art.

Modeling on an armature

A separate problem in modeling is the long attenuated figure that has little bulk and much length. The giraffe is a walking example of this, or the stick insect, but even cats and dogs can be interpreted in this way. The wire that you use to support the clay for objects with much height but little bulk will remain inside, for even on hardening none of the materials acquire sufficient strength to take the strain of all the height. Rule out normal clay for this work. The shrinkage will cause it to dry in a procession of cracks. Use reinforced clay or one of the specialized materials.

The thickness of the wire required to make an armature will depend to some extent on the model, but if you start with a coil of something a little thicker than 1/16 of an inch approximately, it will cost you only pennies extra but will last ages. Figures standing on one or two legs will require a base of some sort. Having twisted your wire into shape, model a base and push the bent ends of the wire into it. Bend the ends to enable them to lock more securely into the base. Now let the base dry a little and start working from the bottom up.

Something a little different and quite exciting can be produced using the new corrugated modeling wire that is a part of the reinforced modeling clay process. This wire

21

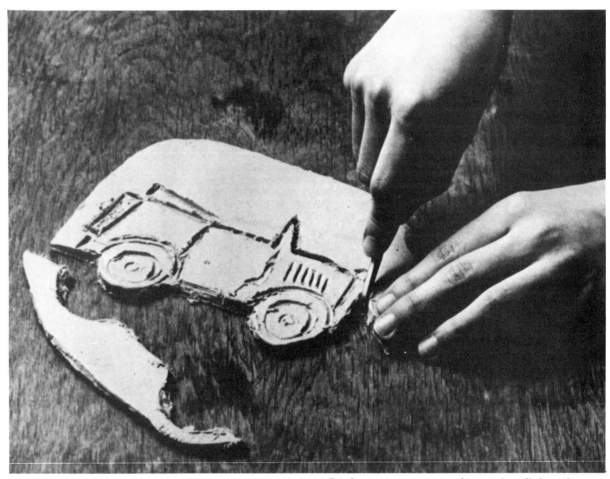

*Cutting out a motor car for use in relief work.
Pieces of clay can then be added and molded.*

was designed to permit children to bend the wire more easily in their hands and also to improve clay adhesion, but more interesting from many modelers' points of view is the fact that the wire can be left exposed to give quite an unusual look to the models.

Modeling in relief

Another aspect of this craft is modeling in relief, which differs from those procedures already described in that there is, or can be, a tremendous amount of technique involved. The methods of working in relief are fascinating and well worth your time, although in fact the result may be of only limited use, for anything bigger than a cameo can be difficult to place. Normally, one might use modeling in relief for the de-

velopment of a tiled area for exterior use, in which case the tile would have to be fired.

Consider for a moment the head of a coin and realize that although the nose is, in fact, on the same level as the ear, the modeler has persuaded you that this is not so. It is indeed a highly skilled mystery with no space to probe.

To begin your work in relief, sketch a rough outline of your intentions across the face of the surface to be treated. Dampen the area with a sponge and build out from the surface with small pellets of clay. Alternatively, draw on the surface of a very thin tile, cut away the excess clay, and then model the rest. This separate item can be welded, with others, to a clay backing using

Pots and a dish that have been treated to insure durability.

liquid clay, called slip, or, on drying, can be glued to a backboard. Very large relief panels can be built up in this way.

To increase durability

The procedure by which you work on an object to achieve durability will depend on the material that you use. Wherever weather or water are involved, firing or casting will be a necessity. But these methods are complicated and often costly, and for this reason manufacturers are producing useful alternatives. The different treatments as prescribed by the makers usually will be sufficient for indoor use. (It is a bit of a trick, but one means of containing water in a clay vase is to incorporate a plastic beaker or bottle into the construction!)

Decoration

Strangely, the finishing off of your work could pose the greatest problems. You would be well advised to try out the different effects on your early pieces so that your experience in modeling techniques matches your experience in finishing. The surface qualities of any material can always be enhanced.

Any water-based paint can be used on modeling materials, and these can be covered later with a vinyl gloss or satin finish. Add a little adhesive to the water used for painting to prevent smearing. All of these modeling materials are inert, so they can be expected to accept almost any medium. Oil paints if you wish, bronze powders in shellac, polyester resins with metal fillers, acrylics, cellulose all can be used — there are plenty to choose from and many clever techniques. But don't be hidebound by the conventional. Try a brick dust in weak glue or stone dusts. Glue parrot seed all over the surface. Tiles impressed with mixed seeds are a satisfying exercise for children. Weave a line of string over the surface of your modeled object, glue it in place, and then fill up the different areas with color and texture. Think up new ideas and try them out.

POTTERY

A definition of pottery is "fired clay"— clay that has been made red-hot in a kiln. But if we are to understand the full significance of the term, we must first know a little about what we mean by clay. Scientifically, clay is mostly aluminum silicate, but that fact need not concern you a great deal. More to the point is the fact that clay is at times a wet sticky substance and at others, a rather hard and brittle rock found in quantity in many gardens. But whatever the condition of this garden clay, it is unlikely to be of any use to the potter. Mostly, such clays are full of impurities and have a tendency to shrink badly and crack on drying. You can, if you wish, experiment with them, and you may learn much, but I do not recommend garden clays for anything requiring permanence. There are too many imponderables even under ideal conditions.

Clay is a plastic rock malleable in the hands, yet when subjected to heat it can be transformed into a substance that only the very hardest steels can scratch. These facts have made clay uniquely useful to man—

23

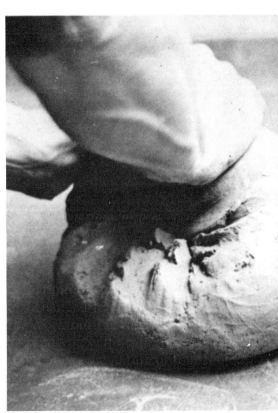

In wedging reverse the top half before banging it down on the lower.

Knead to remove air bubbles.

kind. The qualities of clay vary from place to place, and much time and money is spent on categorizing even the limited number of clays put at our disposal by the industry. You will do well to get yourself a few pounds of a prepared clay as opposed to a dug clay. It may cost you up to 25¢ per pound, but at this stage it will be worth it and will probably last quite a long time.

A prepared clay is one where the natural clay has been reduced to a liquid for the purposes of cleaning and for the addition of other ingredients calculated to provide the user with the properties required to fulfill particular needs. One of these additives will almost certainly be "grog," i.e., ground pottery or ground firebrick. This reduces shrinkage, opens up the pores, and also endows the clay with a gritty-ness—a texture considered by most to be highly desirable. After the mixing, the surplus water is filtered out and the residue packed for use. Even at this stage, the clay still contains about 20 percent water. Using this mixing method, the natural clay can be easily

modified with any of a dozen or so additives, which will insure, among other things, that it matures at a specific firing temperature. This may be anything from about 1500°F. up to 2400°F., or even higher—anything from earthenware to stoneware or porcelain. Here we shall concern ourselves almost entirely with earthenware fired at more than 1800°F.

The first thing to remember is to take care of your earthenware clay. Out-of-condition clay is a sad business; in condition it is a joy. The most suitable container is a plastic bin of some sort, plus an extra bucket or two for damping down the odds and ends that have been allowed to harden. To reclaim dry clay, break it into small pieces and sprinkle with water periodically. Just how much water will be required and how long it will take, you will have to find out from experience. The rate at which various clays absorb water differs, and so too does the amount of water they will hold, depending upon the size of the particles making up the clay structure. Anyway,

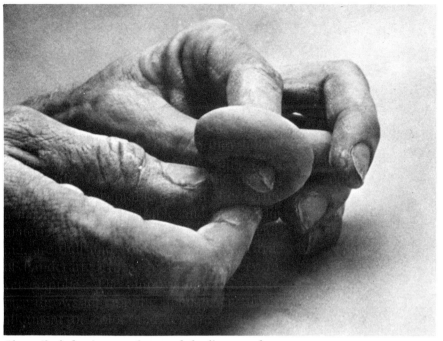

If a coil of clay is wound around the finger and does not crack, the clay is in good condition.

you are bound to be surprised by the quantity of water required, usually around 20 percent by weight.

Wedging

Clay that has been reclaimed needs to be worked into a smooth, even consistency, free of lumps and, if possible, free of air bubbles. The former is achieved by cutting through the block with a brass wire-like cheese cutter and then thumping the top piece hard down on to the lower. (This process is referred to as wedging.) Do this a few times and then, depending on the state of the clay, do it a few more times for good measure. It is a most satisfying performance, so you won't mind the extra effort.

Kneading

Air bubbles are removed from clay by kneading. Just how this is done almost defies description. Bernard Leach in his *A Potter's Book* does it well—but that is only one of many reasons why you should read

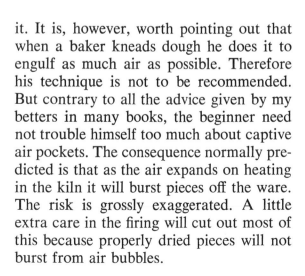

A group of interrelating geometric shapes.

it. It is, however, worth pointing out that when a baker kneads dough he does it to engulf as much air as possible. Therefore his technique is not to be recommended. But contrary to all the advice given by my betters in many books, the beginner need not trouble himself too much about captive air pockets. The consequence normally predicted is that as the air expands on heating in the kiln it will burst pieces off the ware. The risk is grossly exaggerated. A little extra care in the firing will cut out most of this because properly dried pieces will not burst from air bubbles.

25

A pinched bowl made from the ball of clay.

Shaping the clay

When the prepared clay arrives on your doorstep it usually is ready to use with a little kneading. Drag it into your workshop and open the plastic wrapping. There may be a certain amount of sweating over the surface of the clay due to humidity changes as it traveled. Pull the clay to pieces and drop it into your bin. Even that little exercise may have taught you something—clay is unexpectedly heavy for its size. There is, however, a great deal more than that to be learned about the clay you have chosen. Some factors could be described and categorized, others are just personal reactions—feelings not easily defined but aspects that add up to the personality of the clay. You like it or you don't like it. It suits your purpose or it does not. It will take time, but you will come to these conclusions eventually.

Pull off a piece of clay and smear it through your fingers. Any gritty-ness can be accounted for as sand or grog, introduced to add texture to the clay and reduce the

A sphere engraved with concentric circles and later treated with copper carbonate.

shrinkage (neither sand nor grog shrinks on firing). Roll a piece into a long, thin coil. Do this by rolling the piece backward and forward under your hands on a table. Now wind it around your finger. A good clay in good condition will show no signs of cracking. Now lay it out flat and make two

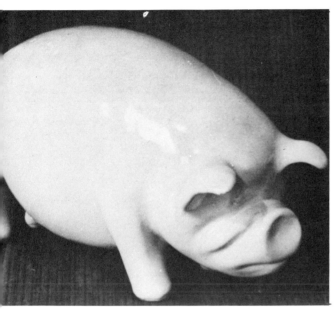

A pig created by a student from a clay "egg."

A group of "pebbles"; some are real, but others are modeled.

marks on it ten inches apart. Measure it again once it is dry and calculate the degree of shrinkage. A probable figure will be 8 to 10 percent or thereabout. If you don't think that is of much importance you are due for a surprise. One of the important parts of the whole pottery process is the attempt to come to terms with shrinkage.

Making a start. Start making some shapes. Pull off another piece of clay and roll it into a ball—a smooth round ball that is nice to hold. Put it down and make another shape to put alongside it—a tall cone or a long, thin cylinder, a half hoop, anything. Position it and then reposition it and consider the effect. Note that as the gap between them increases, the dominance of one shape over the other decreases. Bring in a third and fourth shape and play architect. Design your contribution to Expo 2000. If you teach children, give them this as an exercise: a group of shapes on a thin tile base. By now you will have noted that your inexpertness in forming these shapes causes you to be slow, and drying cracks form on the surface. Obviously a small sponge is called for to replace the moisture as you work.

A pinched dish. To return to the ball: make another, but don't fuss too much with it. Now push your thumb steadily but firmly into it, right into the middle of it, but not quite so far that you penetrate the other side. If you now turn the ball with your other hand and, at the same time, rhythmically pinch the clay that rests between your thumb and finger, you will steadily enlarge the hole. The trick is to turn the original solid sphere into a hollow hemisphere. This is not easy, but as a technique it is one that will serve you well and is worth acquiring.

This hemisphere, raised to a high state of perfection, can remain as a small bowl. Just what one means by perfection must be a personal matter, but in this context it must have something to do with accuracy. As the clay stiffens on drying, you can begin to beat it gently on the ouside with a flat slat of wood, supporting it on the inside with the fingers. With some care very delicate shapes are possible.

Developing a ball. You could make two pinched bowls and, while they are still in the rough state, join them edge to edge. The result is a hollow sphere that is relatively light for its size. Large, solid masses of clay are usually undesirable. Take care with the joint, insuring that the clay is welded together before smearing and smoothing.

27

A simple figure using clay coils.

Here again, time spent on the ball can result in an accurate shape that feels right and true in the hands; a shape that offers some scope for superficial development in terms of incised, overlaid, or colored decoration. A pinhole inserted before firing will allow the compressed air to escape from any enclosed shape—because the piece shrinks in firing, this is a very necessary precaution.

Developing a basic shape

By using a basic shape, you can develop a great range of models. Here a number of typical pieces will be selected, and the reader will work out the changes.

First there is the pebble. If you collect pebbles, pick out one that has the qualities you find interesting and then work out your own interpretation of it. Use your wooden slat to re-form the ball until it takes on the same type of pebble shape as your specimen: perhaps not quite the same, but rather a shape that gives you the same feeling; a shape that distinguishes between the weather-worn, the sea-rolled, the stratified, or the crystalline. Smooth it, roughen it, sculpt or dig holes in it, most anything goes; although, on the last point, it is worth mentioning that all the time that your shape contains trapped air, it will remain fairly firm. If you puncture it, most of the strength hisses out with the air. As the clay dries, the lost strength will steadily return.

A ball shape can be reformed into an egg, and from this egg, not surprisingly, a great range of birds and animals can be developed. This will require the addition of more clay pieces—heads, wings, feet, arms, etc. Care with the joining is important. Try not to trap air under these additions and, wherever possible, weld the clay together. A little water or slip (a liquid mixture of clay and water) daubed on the joint area will assist the bonding process.

As your skill increases so will your ability to make larger spheres. A diameter of four or five inches should not be too difficult. This is large enough to form the basis for modeling a head—not life-sized, but large enough to be able to develop the features. Having made a rough ball, beat it into an egg shape and then set it aside. Now press out a flat strip of clay that can be bent around into a neck, and then place the egg on top of this with the point of the egg downward and overhanging the neck a little to make a chin. Smear in some clay to make a joint and, when all feels firm, use your beating stick to improve the shape. A few structural guidelines sketched over the surface and the real modeling begins.

No comment or advice is offered on how to model but—just to repeat—you cannot expect soft clay to bond to hard clay. Do not allow the model to dry out; dampen it with water now and again if necessary, and when leaving a piece for any length of time, cover with a damp cloth and some plastic. Also, make sure that any addition of any size is bonded strongly.

The coil

The technique of rolling coils is so necessary and so much used by the studio potter that you can be pretty certain that after a

*The early stages of
coiling a pot.*

few years you will have added several yards to the many miles of coils fabricated throughout history. The method by which these coils are achieved is described in the section on modeling in this chapter. When you start you will rapidly conclude that a smooth, even coil is not within the bounds of possibility, but in no time you will find it almost as difficult to roll a bad coil. Probably the greatest yardage of coils is used in the building of pots: pots of all shapes and sizes, some too big to be thrown on the wheel, but mostly the more usual sizes, for which the potter prefers this method or the intended shape makes the wheel inappropriate.

Small coiled figures. Before actually trying to make a pot, play with a few short lengths to make some coiled models. With the minimum of fuss join a few bits and pieces neatly together to make little figures and animals.

A coiled pot. Now try your hand at a small coiled pot. There was a time when every student of pottery occupied much of his or her time in the production of coiled pots. I was never a great enthusiast, although I have seen some fine examples on occasions. Like them or not, I think that as an exercise, coiled pots are worthwhile.

Make the base for your pot by rolling a piece of clay into a ball and then pat it flat into a disc. Now roll a coil and form it into a ring around the top edge. Join it by smearing a little of the clay from the inside of the coil downward to the base. The outside of the coil remains exposed, unjointed, as it will all the way up to the top. This presents a real challenge to the coiler, for the shape of the pot must be accurately formed as the coiling progresses.

Proceed by placing ring upon ring, always smearing the inside of the coil down on to the one below. If, through your slowness or the warmth of the room, your coils get a little on the dry side, wipe them with a damp sponge. Let the moisture soak in before carrying on. Never attempt to join a soft coil to a dry or even a very firm pot. To make such a joint is not difficult, but it will crack away some time later as it shrinks. Store your unfinished work in a plastic bag to retain its condition. The shape is created as you go, with little chance of changing it appreciably at a later stage. There will inevitably be some stiffening of

A group of coiled pots shows the coils forming part of the surface decoration.

The coiled method of construction on this has been smeared over and developed further.

the body of the work as you progress, and this is desirable because the weight of the clay could cause some sagging if the body remained soft, particularly in a full-bellied pot. As you begin to finish your pot, there may be a need for some extra emphasis on the top rim: a thicker coil, a broad band, possibly tooling of some sort. It also could be desirable to break up the monotony of the coils with tool marks or finger marks.

A pot from coils. There is no logical reason why coiled pots should have a circular section, except that the fact of leaving the coils exposed seems to insist that this should be so. However, once you change from coiled pots to pots made with coils—for which the method of construction is obliterated by smearing the surface

both inside and out—you will then feel free to break with almost all convention, free to sculpt the shape as you wish.

It could be that this is the time to sit back with pencil and paper and do a little planning. You should by now begin to know a little of what is and what is not within your capacity. Think back to those early shapes—the little, solid forms we started with. See them now as larger shapes —large pots if you wish — sketch them, modify the form, and finish with a complete, fully designed drawing. The pot may not work out the way you've designed it (they seldom do in my experience); it could even be a massive failure—a "back to the drawing board" job — but this does not invalidate the argument for doing the design.

A much more robust approach is acceptable when you make pots from coils. You can build with thicker coils and, once the joint is well smeared over, reduce the thickness by pinching the rim to increase the height. Even before you have reached the top, begin to beat the pot into shape. Support the wall by using a hand on the inside while you're beating. This will enable you to strike more firmly, compacting and strengthening the walls. Having completed

A coiled pot developed into a reclining form.

the shape according to your own specifications, I think there is every excuse for modification, even reconstruction, if the result does not satisfy. To insist on sticking to the original idea could show a very unadventurous attitude.

Lugs and handles

Fresh clay can be tooled onto the surface of a pot to develop an area; lugs or handles can be fixed as a useful or decorative feature. Handles that are to be used as such are difficult to make and position, but it is possible to modify a coil to give a passable imitation of an expertly pulled job. Do not be restricted by the fact that you originally decided to call what you are making a pot. If necessary cut a few holes in the side and thereby render it useless for holding water and maybe the next one will be ideal for daffodils.

Slabs

It often happens that the shapes you so painstakingly coiled into a round form were eventually beaten into a square. It will then have become obvious to you that there is an alternative method of doing this, namely from slabs. Six slabs of clay joined together at the edges and you have a box. What could be easier? This is an ill-informed thought. This method is by no means easy, with such inherent difficulties that it has the experienced craftsman struggling at times.

Slab construction. It is worth trying slab construction, and there are some interesting exercises from which you can learn something. Just as earlier we used the coil for simple models, so the slab can be used for some basic constructions.

Roll out a few pieces of clay on cloth and allow them to stiffen. Now cut them into a variety of shapes — rather angular, mechanical pieces. You will need no special plan in mind. Pick up a few pieces and join them neatly together to form a structure. Add a flying buttress, a tower; add pieces that have no special point or meaning, except that you feel they look right. Treat the whole business very lightly if you wish but,

31

In slab construction roll out a few pieces of clay and allow them to stiffen.

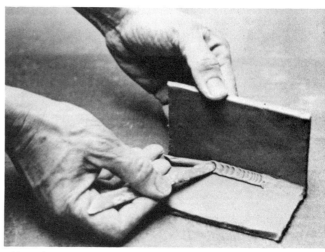

After the pieces are cut in slab construction, you might want to lute a joint to erect other structures.

if that goes against your nature, then treat it with the utmost seriousness. Structures developed in this way will help the understanding of mass space relationships, and that is what sculpture is all about.

It is not necessary or desirable to follow everything through to the firing stage. Make them and break them, but every now and again put your work to the test by completing the process. You might find that a little copper carbonate scrubbed on to the surface and fired at about 2000°F. will be all the decoration you need. The very permanence of the fired piece will cause you to assess your own standards more critically. It will also invite criticism.

Larger shapes. Once you get on to the making of larger objects, one unexpected difficulty will arise from the very speed with which the sections can be prepared. If you roll out a lump of clay on a cloth to about one-half-inch thickness, cut shapes (the whole process will take no more than ten minutes), and try to put them all together, you will get into all sorts of trouble. The clay *must* be allowed to stiffen appreciably before you are able to handle it sensibly, and yet it must still be sufficiently soft to enable a good joint to be made. Run a damp sponge along the edges and then press the joint firmly together. Follow this

by running a thin coil along the inside corner, tooling it in position to form a neat fillet. This process is called luting. The lute is vital to the joint. It must be realized— indeed you will find out soon enough if you are careless—that the strain imposed by uneven shrinkage on these slabs is very considerable and, since the outside of any container will always tend to dry more quickly than the inside, uneven shrinkage is inevitable. One of the most difficult shapes to make successfully is an open box. Even by taking the greatest care it is still next to impossible to finish with flat and not incurved sides — not to mention open seams. Teachers be warned: the box is a tempting little exercise but one fraught with troubles.

You might feel, as I do, that completely flat-sided objects are rather dull. So, before you close the top in, work the shape over with your wooden beater. Soften the corners maybe, dome the sides a little, slope the shoulders, and, incidentally, compact the clay. All these things increase the strength factor and also provide interest. Where some degree of accuracy is needed in the final piece it will be necessary to wait until the clay has reached an advanced state of drying and then use a broken hacksaw blade to scrape the surface. The body will

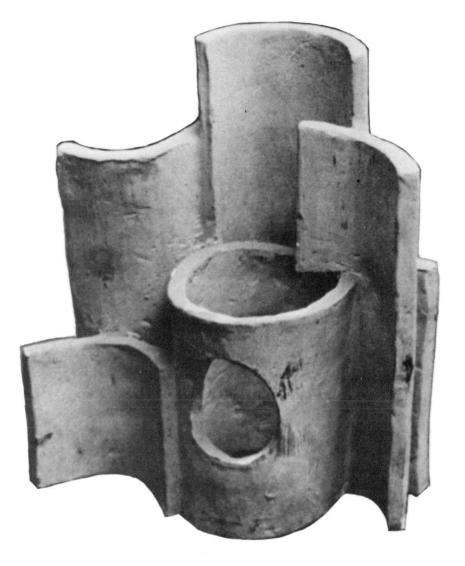

An abstract construction in slab work.

lose its soft clay look, but this may not be important.

The tile. For a very long time the tile was the only acceptable method of covering a flat area with a durable and impervious material. Commercial tiles, generally speaking, are dull and cold, but this is not true of handcrafted tiles. In fact, the very reverse applies. The bumpy, impractical surface throws up rippling lights, each tile an allotment of color and texture contained by neat black or white paths, keeping them apart yet pulling the whole thing together. I like crafted tiles, but they are so heavy. However, there has been some improvement concerning the weight problem in recent years (and this we will discuss later), but the means and method of production are much the same.

Make your tiles from one of these two ways:

1. Roll out a slab of clay, using side sticks to set the thickness, and then, once the clay has stiffened, cut around a cardboard template made for the job. With most clays something over 4⅜ inches square will be necessary to finish at 4 inches. (Your shrinkage calculations will tell you this more exactly.) This is a short, quick process, and you soon will have a set of tiles.

2. Slower in production but more accurate for making tiles is the tile frame. This can be made out of four sticks joined with halving joints to give a flat top and bottom surface. The frame is laid on a piece of cloth, and lumps of clay are rammed in to fill the well. A wooden or metal scraper will take off the surplus clay, and a drip or two of water will help smooth the finished surface. On drying it will shrink out of the frame.

Drying. Clay tiles always require careful drying if they are to remain flat. Normally, the thinner the tile the greater the tendency to warp. Good staking and slow—very slow —drying is the key to success. Build your

An assortment of tile cutters.

tiles into a pyramid but with an overlap of no more than a quarter of the length, thereby leaving holes through which the air can contact the clay: But no moving air, no draughts, just still, drying air.

I make no mention here of decoration and firing because they are described later. However, I will mention that although the first is not too difficult, the firing is always tricky. Use the same stacking method as you would for other pieces to be fired, and use the middle of the kiln if possible.

Tesserae. There is no lower limit to the size of a tile, but once you get down to the square half inch the purpose has normally changed and the pieces will most likely be intended for use as tesserae in the making of mosaics. The subject of mosaics can be quite exciting; it is also a very old art. Unfortunately, the discussion here must confine itself to the making of these little tiles.

Initially, in making tesserae, one must expect to work with a very limited palette, of, perhaps, half a dozen colors. The picture or pattern must be thought of in these terms. By this simplification, the quantity of tesserae can be limited to manageable proportions. However, when you make and color the small tiles, always make a little more than you estimate you will use. Then, you probably will not run out and have to

go through the whole process of making, coloring, and firing new tiles. Often it is hard to get the exact colors in a second or third firing.

Make the sketch for your mosaic in color and, from this estimate, the quantity of tessarae required for each color. Assuming that 100 square inches of pale blue tesserae are needed, pull off handfuls of clay and roll them out on a cloth using a wooden rule on each side as a thickness gauge. One-eighth inch is about the right thickness for tesserae. You will probably need three or four good-sized slabs to make 100 pieces of tesserae. Allow them to go leather-hard and then turn them over to score the backs to the greater part of the depth of the clay. Depending on your nature, you will do this freehand or use a set-square. The size of the pieces is optional —meticulous squares or random shapes. Take some care with the scoring, for it will determine how easy it is to break the pieces after firing. If you score the top side, the groove will fill with glaze and nothing will be gained.

The adhesion of tiles to a surface presents no problems these days. There are so many appropriate tile adhesives on the market that time would be wasted in describing the process. Buy any adhesive and

Tiles stacked for drying.

A slab of clay scored for tesserae.

read the directions; then grout (i.e., fill in the gaps between the tiles) with a plaster-sandpowder color—polyvinyl acetate emulsions mixture.

Plaster molds

When you use plaster of paris molds for your pottery, you do so at some risk. It is difficult to think of pottery without including plaster (the industry would fall apart if supplies dried up), but it does hold some danger for the careless or uninitiated. So, before going further, let us try to understand what we actually are dealing with in plaster of paris and how to use it.

Plaster is made from rock gypsum, and much of this originally came from the area surrounding Paris. Gypsum is a white crystalline rock, which the manufacturers reduce to a fine powder. It is then dehydrated by raising its temperature to about 580°F. By returning the moisture, the crystals are allowed to re-form and lock together, making a solid. This process can be speeded up by using warm water, but the crystals will be smaller and the material relatively weaker.

Mixing. To give some idea of the quantity required, 2/3 pint of water is needed to make 1 pint of mixed plaster. Break the

powder into the bowl of water by the handful until the peaks reach the surface. Stir gently, and it is ready for use.

Now for the dangers of using a plaster of paris mold. Number one is the little chips of plaster that can so easily stray into the clay. At some later date, a piece of your ware, fired and glazed, will shed a flake from its side—forced from the body as the plaster that was dehydrated in the kiln grows in size on taking moisture from the air. The second danger comes from the careless disposal of waste plaster down the sink. If you finish up a mixing session with a sink trapped solidly with plaster, you will not be the first. *Never pour waste plaster down the sink.* Throw it into a cardboard box and pick it out later when it has set; then get rid of it in the garbage can. If you absolutely must pour it down the sink, then have the tap going at full force to wash every bit away.

There are two distinct types of molds: those for press molding with firm clay and those for casting with slip. Now that you

35

The clay is shaped to receive the plaster.

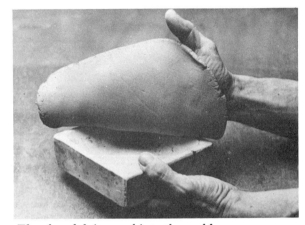

The clay slab is eased into the mold.

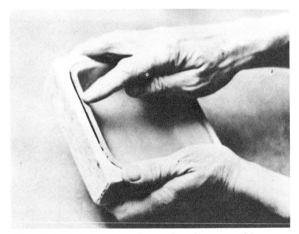

The dish shrinks away from the plaster mold.

The dish is extracted from the mold.

are aware of the dangers, let's look at the types of plaster of paris molds.

Press molding is a process by which the shape is accurately modeled and then covered with plaster. Later the original clay is removed and a succession of reproductions pressed out. This process can be fairly simple, as with a dish mold, or very complicated, as with a figurine. Let us talk about the simple one, the dish mold.

Take a piece of paper the size of this book and draw on it the outline of a dish viewed from above. Keep it simple: barrel-shaped, pear-shaped, a teardrop, but no incurves to begin with if you can help it. Now imagine your dish inverted on that shape, and model it in clay. Make the flat base about a quarter of the total area so that as the sides curve away from the base to the edge they will be almost the size of your original drawing. Care and precision are essential.

Surround the shape with a wall standing about 1 inch higher than the dish. Make it from clay, cardboard, roofing tile, or whatever, but do fill in all the little holes with clay, and then be ready with some more for the inevitable emergencies.

Now, assess how much plaster you will need to fill up the space around the clay, but be prepared to be wildly wrong. Too much and you will have to throw the rest away, but too little and you will have to mix more immediately before the rest hardens. If it does harden, however, score the surface of the first lot so that the second will bond strongly. Should you at any time not want plaster to stick to a surface, wash that surface with liquid clay.

A few hours after you've poured the

A Wedgwood teapot showing a traditional sprigged design.

mold, you should be able to pick it up and carefully remove the clay. However, it might be well to leave it for a couple of days to dry out before you attempt to make your first dish.

To use the mold, roll out some clay to a thickness of about ¼ inch and one inch or so greater in area than that of the dish. Pick up the slab and gently ease it into the hollow of the mold. Try not to mark the top surface, and use a wet thumb rather than a sponge, which can badly score the surface. Use a wooden tool to carve away the surplus clay from around the edge.

Methods of decoration will be discussed later in the chapter, but it should be pointed out here that if slip is to be applied to the surface, it should be used at this stage. Pour it in, swirl it around, and then pour it out. The water contained in this amount of slip would crack an unsupported dish, so this method of applying the slip is to be used only with supported pieces.

The combined effect of the absorbent plaster and the drying air will eventually cause the clay to shrink away from the mold, so that it will soon be ready to be tipped out.

There is no obvious alternative to this method of making dishes if you want them to have uniformity. Circular dishes can be thrown on the wheel, but this is even more difficult than you might imagine.

Sprigging. Nothing is ever easy in pottery, but the production of molded dishes can be classed among the more basic tasks. This is not true of the more complicated mold-making required to produce figures of humans and animals. There is, however, an associated exercise for molded dishes that is well worth trying. It is called sprigging.

Although, as a piece of pottery, Wedgwood jasperware leaves me unexcited, it is, nevertheless, a splendid example of sprigging. Generally, Wedgwood can be identified by its near-opaque white figures in Greek regality, with accompanying flora on a deep blue, unglazed ground surrounding a ware. Each section is exquisitely modeled by sensitive craftsmen and then welded to precision pottery.

Suppose that you have created your pot and wish to decorate it with sprigging of some sort—a spray of lots of identically-shaped leaves. On the surface of a glazed tile or a piece of glass, model just one of

37

the leaves. When it is finished, mix up half a cup of plaster and heap it over the shape. There is no need for a retaining wall because the amount of plaster is so small, but you might want to take the opportunity to practice modeling the plaster.

Once this mold is well set, ease it off the tile and pick out the original clay. Clean the mold carefully and let it dry for a day or so. Then, pull off a pellet of clay and press it into the mold; then scrape off the surplus with a wooden tool. Wait a few moments more and then, with another piece of clay, press it gently against your mold and pull it out. Look at it carefully and note that even a fingerprint has been faithfully recorded. As you make more sprigging, rest the leaves on a damp cloth until you have enough for your purposes. You can now apply all the leaves to your pot in one session. Use a little liquid clay slip as an adhesive.

Casting. Using liquid clay in a plaster mold to cast shapes is to my mind an unsatisfactory method for the studio potter. At an industrial level it is a highly specialized technique used to produce millions of inexpensive cups. You can recognize such a casting by noting that the inside shape exactly follows the outside. Where the foot of a cup shows no comparable depression on the inside then some other method was used. This would be the product of the jigger and jolly. Lovely names these, used to describe a mechanical method of producing circular shapes, where a lump of clay is dropped into a spinning mold and, under the pressure of a metal former, pressed against the sides to take up the shape of the mold. The clay dries a little and is then picked out to be put on a moving belt, where on its travels it meets a handle. The two are wedded with a dab of slip and pass on their way together.

But to return to the casting. The mold is made by covering the clay pattern with plaster to a thickness of about two inches. This extra thickness is needed to take up a great deal of water out of the slip. Once the mold is set and dry and the original clay removed, slip of a thick consistency is poured in, topped up when necessary, and then, after about 10 minutes, poured out again. A residue of firm clay will cling to the plaster walls and, once this has dried, come away as an exact reproduction of the original, except that it will be some 10 percent smaller. If this does not sound like much shrinkage, then you may be surprised. You will find that you need to take this shrinkage into account when size is important. A small coffee cup reduced by 10 percent would double as an egg cup.

Throwing

Most books on the craft of pottery include a section on throwing, and the notes are usually supported with copious action shots. However, this has always seemed to me to be like learning to ride a bike by pictures. Throwing can be learned only by doing it, and then only under instruction.

Perhaps learning to ride a bike is a poor analogy because by comparison, it is a lot easier than learning to throw successfully. The art of the thrower is a skill that is acquired over years, not minutes. It can be defined as the technique whereby a mass of clay is spun on a turntable wheelhead and formed into a round and hollow shape in the hands. The skill is ages old and is still considered by some to be the essence of the potter's craft. If this overrates it, it is nevertheless a highly satisfying process and one that readily allows the performer to demonstrate the depth of his understanding for the material he uses.

Decoration

It has been difficult but necessary as we went along to refrain from comment on the decorative aspects associated with the various types of modeling because most of the same techniques are used to decorate no matter what you make in clay or synthetic modeling materials. Let's look at most of

1. The ball of clay is placed on the wheel.

2. The clay is centered on the wheel. Note the position of the hands.

3. Hollow out the center.

4. Draw up the pot.

5. Form the rim.

6. Develop the shape.

7. Cut away the surplus clay.

8. Pick off the pot.

the general methods for decorating as applied to different modeling techniques.

Two methods that require nothing extra in the way of materials are incised and applied decoration, i.e., cutting back and building up. Texturing, of course, can be something of each of these.

Incised decoration. Incised work can be delicate—as in the case of the small depressions along the rim of a dish, which are later filled with glaze, finally showing as dimples—to massive holes cut through the side of a pot or both sides to give an added eclipse effect. Texturing can be achieved in various ways: for instance, by superficial scratching with the coarse teeth of a hacksaw blade or deep depressions hacked or beaten into the firm clay surface.

Applied decoration. The reverse of incised decoration is the delicate or heavy application of quantities of clay to the surface. More care is called for here as you will probably be adding soft clay to firm. The stress resulting from the shrinkage differential can be sufficient to lift the outer layer from the surface of the object. Roughen the surface of the firmer clay to permit a good bond; any slip or water used to assist adhesion should be applied to this roughened surface and then left for a short time to allow it to soak in a little. Clays vary so much in their rates of shrinkage that one cannot be dogmatic as to what is and what is not possible. You will learn from experience. This much is certain; it is unwise to join two different types of clay together, and it is difficult to persuade large masses of the same clay to adhere to a surface.

Color. Any addition of color to your ware will involve the use of metal oxides. These are, I believe, the only form of pigment that will withstand the heat of the kiln. Almost all clay has in it at least a trace of iron oxide, which causes the original white to fire cream or, as the percentage of iron increases, turn an increasingly deeper shade of red-brown. Iron and many

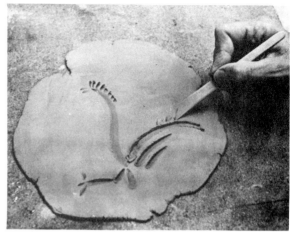

Practice making an incised motif.

A thin white glaze over copper oxide was used on this coffeepot and mug.

other metals can be purchased in their oxide form and as such can be painted (when mixed with a little water and some wood ash) directly onto the surface of the clay. For the beginner this form of coloring is confusing because the final result bears so little relationship to the original powder and the fact that the final color varies with the firing temperature and the atmosphere prevailing in the kiln. A solution to this problem is offered by the manu-

For this teapot oxides were brushed onto the raw clay to produce the design.

Practice brush strokes.

facturers who supply very predictable prepared colors called underglazes for use on the clay. Other colors, called on-glaze, are for use on the raw glaze. These do provide an answer, but one that I, for one, do not suggest as a good one, although such things are largely a matter of personal taste. If you want a palette of true-to-shade, obvious, rather flat, but very stable colors, then these underglazes and on-glazes are for you. If, on the other hand, the element of chance sounds more interesting, then take to the oxides—where copper oxide, for instance, starts as a black powder yet turns green in a glaze; but when applied too lightly might disap-

pear altogether; or when applied too heavily forms a black metallic skin over the surface.

Here is a list of the more common oxides and the colors (under what might be called normal conditions) that you might expect from them:

Iron oxide: yellows, browns, near blacks
Copper oxide: pale green, dark green, and metallic black
Cobalt oxide: blue
Manganese oxide: browns
Chrome oxide: green
Antimoniate of lead: yellows

You will notice that no reds are included. At this level reds are virtually nonexistent. The oxides will give varying colors depending on many factors. Copper, under very special conditions, will in fact provide red —the Chinese *sang de boeuf* (oxblood)— but I have never succeeded in achieving this color.

The underglaze and on-glaze colors are purchased from a long list of exotic titles. They too have a metal base but are often the result of very sophisticated processes including firing, sintering, and then grinding. All very clever and fairly expensive, but not used too much by the studio potter.

Applying the color. Color can be applied to the surface of a piece by any method you feel suitable. A potter brought up in the Leach tradition will tend to reach for his Chinese brush and with it demonstrate great dexterity and feeling for the value of the brush stroke. And what a joy the results can be.

However, we know better than to restrain ourselves to any one method of application. When you have made up some color into a paste, use a sponge to stipple it onto the surface. Now, overpaint that with a more fluid color using a one-inch wide brush. Finally, texture the color by scratching through the surface with a piece of stick.

This pot is an example of how the waxed areas have resisted the glaze.

Wax resist. For this method of coloring, melt a little candle wax in a dish, add some oxide and, while it is still runny, brush a few well-chosen strokes onto the clay surface. (Try this in the hollow of a dish.) Now brush over this with a watery wash of another oxide. The wax will resist the water, although a little may rest as globules on the top, and the colors will be separate from each other.

Slip. The same oxides that are used for wax resist (but *not* underglaze colors) may be added to liquid clay to provide colored slips. As mentioned earlier, slip can be poured over a surface, completely covering it, or confined to a limited area of color. A full round form can be dipped just a little on one side, which will result in a colored panel suitable for other decorative treatments such as *scraffito*. This is a process of scratching through the slip to expose the clay body underneath. Do it when the slip is still wet and a soft fluid line will result. If the slip is dry the line will be hard and sharp. Dust a little powdered oxide onto the wet slip, and brush it across the surface with bold sweeping strokes.

A very traditional form of decoration is the trailing of one liquid color over another. A rubber bulb or turkey baster full of slip is used to apply the color, the slip being allowed to flow out as lines or blobs. If you make a mess, shake the object a little and the liquids will run together to produce what is called marbling. With some control of the baster you can draw pictures. A past master in this art was Thomas Toft (mid-seventeenth century).

To prepare slip, reduce clay to a liquid by the addition of more water. It is necessary to pass the liquid through a sieve to get rid of the lumps, and the consistency should be that of cream. Oxides can be added in approximately the proportions given below, after which it should be sieved again. Both white and red clay are necessary to make slip.

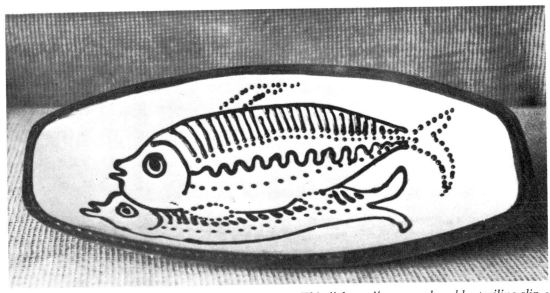

This fish motif was produced by trailing slip over the surface of the dish.

White: white clay
Green: white clay plus 5% chrome oxide
Blue: white clay plus 1% cobalt oxide
Brown: red clay
Black: red clay, 4% manganese oxide, 1% cobalt oxide
Yellow: best obtained by the addition of a yellow body stain

Glazing. Glaze is glass. When you glaze a pot you put a layer of glass over the surface usually with the object of sealing the pores. The cup that you drink from is coated with glass, sometimes clear like window glass, but it may be opaque.

In effect it is applied as a powder, white like snow, and, like snow, it can be melted by the application of heat. When the heat is withdrawn it freezes again into ice-like glass.

You could, if you so wished, demonstrate this point by crushing a piece of window glass in a mortar, mixing it in water, and then dipping a pot into it. You would fire the pot at around 1800°F. Of course, this process is bound to be hit and miss if you don't know what type of glass you are working with. Obviously, this is a clumsy and unsatisfactory way of glazing, for, among other things, different glazes should be used for different requirements.

A recipe. Glass is a fusion of silica, but silica has an extremely high melting point, at 3600°F. — higher than clay in fact. Added fluxes lower the melting point. The higher the proportion of flux the lower the melting point. Such fluxes are lead oxide, lime, potash in the form of feldspar, borax, and many others.

Glazes are made from recipes combining glass with varying amounts of fluxes. You can make glazes yourself. Here is a recipe for a clear glaze that will melt at around 1940°F. You will note that it has a lead content that makes it unsuitable for use in schools or for cooking and eating ware.

Earthenware pots and mugs.

The quantities are percentages by dry weight.

Clear glaze:

Flint (silica)	18%
Lead Carbonate	42%
Whiting (lime)	5%
Feldspar (potash)	29%
China clay (kaolin)	6%

Ready-made glazes. You can also buy glazes ready-made. Ready-made glazes never use raw lead oxide, and for this reason, as well as that of simplicity, I suggest that you opt for one of these.

The catalog. A pottery catalog can prove to be a very confusing document. Many different types of equipment are offered but be cautious.

When in doubt about which glaze to use write to the company from which you bought your clay and explain to them your requirements; e.g., an opaque white matt glaze for use on their brand X clay, and firing at about 1980°F. They probably will answer by offering you a choice of two or three glazes. If you don't know the difference, take the cheapest.

Adapting a glaze. Let us suppose that you have ordered 28 pounds of a clear glaze, which cost you about $5.00 plus shipping. This can be divided into four lots, each weighing about 7 pounds, with which you can experiment.

The first 7 pounds can be mixed with water to the consistency of thin cream, run through a 60-mesh screen, and then be ready to use as your clear glaze.

The second 7 pounds can be made into an opaque white glaze by the addition of a glaze opacifier—usually between 5 to 10 percent. Tin oxide is the best of these for bringing out the color of your oxide painting, but it is also the most expensive. There are other opacifiers, such as zircon, which are more reasonably priced than tin oxide. The difference between the expensive oxides and the inexpensive opacifiers is in the quality of white. The difference will be in the quality of the white — like soap powders.

The third and fourth lots of clay can be colored, opaque, or clear, whichever you wish. Six percent manganese oxide will give you a deep brown; 1 percent copper oxide will give a hard green; add 1 percent of iron oxide to it and the green will be softened. A quarter of 1 percent of cobalt oxide gives a blue, and so on. After some initial experiment settle on a few basics and then try to improve on your handling and methods of application rather than switching from one color to another.

Application. In earthenware, glaze is normally applied to the bisque-fired ware. The method used depends to some extent on the area to be covered. For the inside of a pot, pour the glaze in, swirl it around, and pour it out again. For the outside, you can dip a pot into the glaze, but it is usually better to pour the glaze over it from a jug, with one steady, continuous action. Glaze can be sprayed on, but this is not a method to be recommended except for small items. Brush it on if you like; sponge it on; put it on and rub it all off again, leaving small traces in crevices to indicate its presence, to fill the pores, and to get rid of the dryness.

Broken glass. As an interesting experiment with future implications, make a tile with a number of depressions in the surface. Fill each of these with a different glaze, a mixture of glazes, glazes with added oxides, and so on, and in other depressions place pieces of broken colored glass. Fire the tile and see the effect. The implications are for

Stoneware bowl and pots.

you to decide, but it might be a good idea to make notes for later reference.

Glazing, as with every other part of the pottery process, must be thought of as a part of the whole. It will take time to develop a feeling for it, but start before you even begin to think in terms of the finished piece. A pot or model that is made for glazing should be different in many ways from one that is to remain unglazed. The very clay that you use will have a tremendous influence on the type of work that is possible. You are entitled, indeed expected, to change your mind as you go along, but that is different from just muddling through.

The kiln. The beginning potter should have a small electric kiln. It is possible (and the occasional book will suggest that it is the correct approach) to start with your own homemade kiln in the back yard. It is possible, but the results will have little to do with the type of pottery described here.

45

A kiln partly packed for glaze firing.

Fascinating as this primitive approach may be, it would be misleading to suggest that it is easy to follow or even much cheaper. It could well be the reverse. You can get an oil-fired or gas-fired kiln, but here again the difficulties are very much greater than with electricity.

The electric kiln. An electric kiln is really just a well-insulated electric oven. The wire of its elements is thicker to withstand the higher temperatures, and, of course, the walls are thicker (about six inches) and are made from a light insulating firebrick held tightly together by a metal frame. The heating element is made up from a series of springs that rest in slotted firebrick. The ends pass through the back wall of the kiln to join up with one another. Usually these connections group the elements into two banks so that when the kiln is switched on low heat these two groups are connected in series. On medium just one of the banks is on full; on high both banks are on full, etc.

The beginner should look for a kiln new or secondhand with a firing chamber of 1 cub. ft., or thereabout, using a current of 15 amp. or 3 kw. at 230 v. This will permit the kiln to be worked off the normal household current. One or two shelves will be needed with a few fireclay supports to hold them up. The possession of a pyrometer, from which you can read the temperature, is a nice luxury, but, if you do not have one, you will have to use temperature cones that can be seen to collapse at the specified temperature viewed through the hole in the kiln door. All these items can be seen in the catalogs.

Firing. By raising the temperature of clay to something above red-heat it is changed into pottery. The process is irrevocable. Clay can be turned into brick but not brick into clay. Any heat over 1100°F. will alter the chemical composition of the clay. One of the effects of this temperature is that more water vapor is driven off. This is just one of the facts that must be taken

46

into account when a kiln full of pottery is fired.

Normally, the top temperature with which you will be concerned is something over 1800°F. Indeed, I have a fairly specific temperature in mind when writing this. All these notes apply to the making of earthenware at about 1940°F. There are lower temperature earthenwares, and there are higher temperature stonewares that you can make, but with these there may be greater problems.

Moisture and shrinkage. The two crucial considerations in the firing of earthenware are: (1) moisture (for obvious reasons, it is driven off at 180°F. and more still at around 1800°F.) and (2) shrinkage. By going through a firing cycle we can see how these points are taken into account.

Before placing any work into the kiln it must be as dry as anything can be that is left out in the air. Any damage that occurs in the nature of a blowout will almost certainly be due to moisture still in the clay. Occasionally, a blowout will be due to air in the clay. Drying out will exercise your patience, but any attempt to rush it will increase the chances of failure.

Biscuit firing. The first 180°F. then must be taken slowly to allow the remaining moisture a chance to escape from the pot. In terms of an electric kiln this means "low" with the door open a few inches. After a couple of hours close the door; an hour after that switch to "medium." This setting should increase the temperature up to 1260°–1440°F. in about six hours—just red-hot. Toward the end of that period, the chemically combined water will have gone. Now proceed on "full" to the temperature that you require. This may take only an hour or so but, having reached the temperature, try to hold it there for at least half an hour. This is necessary because small kilns are notoriously bad for producing big temperature differences throughout the chamber. An extra half hour soak will help the temperature to stabilize. You must

realize that a large pot in a small kiln can force a temperature variation of as much as 180°F. difference from top to bottom. This, of course, can be crucial when you are getting close to the vitrification point of the clay, because some shrinkage will be taking place and unless it is even, cracking will result.

The whole process of firing takes about twelve hours, and the kiln requires another twenty-four hours to cool down after it has been shut off. Don't rush the cooling, or you may be in trouble. Once the contents of the kiln have been removed, it is good policy to get on with the glazing as soon afterward as possible. If a pot is handled frequently after it has been fired, a layer of dust will stick to the surface and hinder the adhesion of the glaze.

Glaze firing. When the glazed pot is returned to the kiln a great deal more care will be required with its positioning. Little pointed stilts are available on which the pot may be stood. Alternatively, wipe the powdered glaze from the bottom of the pot, or it will weld itself to the shelf. Glazed pieces must not touch one another for the same reason.

Start firing slowly to dissipate the accumulated moisture, but between 360° and 1440°F. the increase can be much more rapid. The glaze will begin to melt at these temperatures. The powder will solidify and then eventually liquify like taffy, but not always without some convulsions. Many things happen within the glaze, and it is not uncommon to see bubbles form. Allowed to heat soak for a while, the glaze will usually settle down again. Soaking is as important for glaze as it is for clay. Without it you may hear that all-too-familiar "ping" of cracking glaze as you take the cool pots from the kiln.

Eugenie Alexander

collage

COLLAGE, which is the name given to the method of making pictures or decorative panels by pasting materials onto a background, has become one of the most popular media of the twentieth century. There are three main types: fabric collage, paper collage, and three-dimensional collage. It is possible to combine all three methods in one picture as long as the whole composition does not become overcrowded, and a firm enough background is chosen.

FABRIC COLLAGE

A firm background such as canvas board, masonite, or stretched canvas should be used for fabric collage. For beginners and preliminary studies, clipboard and poster board may be used. Anything thinner tends to buckle from the moisture of the glue. Only heaviest boards should be used for relief work. Other materials include:

Plenty of scraps—lace, net, dress samples, burlap, cheesecloth, or cotton printed fabric. Very heavy materials are not easy to glue on to the backing.
Elmer's Glue-All, polymer emulsion, or Sobo are three adhesives frequently used.

Paintings, advertisements, and postcard reproductions can serve as a stimulus for designs. Sometimes, for instance, a piece of figured drapery fabric will spark off an idea —a tiger in a jungle, a maskfaced fish. The design should be drawn first and traced on to the material before cutting out. Alternatively, paper patterns can be cut from newspaper. The design may also be cut out and pasted directly on the canvas or working board. Remember that too many colors can cause confusion and often lead to a lack of color impact in the final work. A few colors in varying tones give a better unity.

Materials can be folded over, frayed, and treated in various ways. Embroidery stitches can be added for extra richness in fabric collage: for example, blanket stitch for rooftops or feather stitch for a bird's tail. Machine-stitching with various colors, dif-

Fabric collage using felt and net on a textured background. The stitches used are simple. Various effects are achieved by using different kinds of thread and wool.

ferent lengths of stitch, or the automatic embroidery stitches incorporated in some sewing machines, can also be used.

When rayon or thin material is used as a background, a white cardboard mount one inch smaller than the allowed border is required. The picture is then stretched by using stout linen threads laced up and down and side to side across the board at the back to prepare it for final framing.

PAPER COLLAGE

White or colored mounting board, plus a selection of cellophane, various colored tissue papers, wallpapers, gummed glossy papers, newspaper, colored reproductions

A tissue paper insect collage.

from magazines and gardening catalogs can be used. The same glues used for fabrics can also be used for paper.

The illustration "Jungle" shows that magazine reproductions make a splendid starting-off point for a composition. Photographs of one's family or friends, pets, houses, etc. can be combined to make an interesting and intimate picture.

RELIEF WORK COLLAGE

Hardboard, nails, glass, plaster of paris, wire, wood scraps, shells, lentils, pasta, string, whalebone, safety pins, broken crockery, and milk bottle tops are only a few of the many things that can be used

"Jungle," by Janet Thorndike.

Margaret Martin's "Cat and Bird" collage incorporates imaginative uses of plaster and string.

for relief work collage. Sobo or Liquitex emulsion glues or one of the wood-sticking glues are best for this type of work.

Heavy board should be used as the background for this type of work, which can become practically sculptural. Usually the designs, by nature of the materials employed, take on a more abstract flavor, though a semirealistic sea scene fits nicely into this category. Exhibitions of collage may be advertised in the daily newspapers. Examples can be seen locally in art schools, at colleges of education, or may be displayed by women's organizations or other community groups.

Elizabeth Carpreau

copper enameling

THE ANCIENT CRAFT OF ENAMELING has recently undergone a revival. On a large scale, artists are using enamel on steel to decorate the outside of buildings. Enameling is equally ideal as a home craft because the basic techniques are simple, and, when executed on a small scale, it is not expensive. Students often find that their very first experiments can be used to make simple items of jewelry. Later, more advanced techniques can be tried and the results combined with other media.

Enamel is clear glass combined with metal oxides for color. This combination is ground to a fine powder and used dry or mixed with a liquid and used as paste or slush. Enamel lumps, shot, chips, and strands may be used in addition to the powder for more interesting effects. Enamel may be transparent, opaque, or opalescent. It also varies in hardness.

Copper, silver, brass, gilding metal, aluminum, and steel are all used for enameling. Of these, copper is the most suitable for the beginner as it is relatively inexpensive when used on a small scale, and it is easy to handle.

MATERIALS

It is possible to buy enameling kits, which include a small kiln, vials of ground enamel, copper shapes, jewelry attachments, and tools. In addition, it would be useful to have 20-gauge copper sheet, copper wire, copper foil, snips, tweezers, small pliers, lump and strand enamel, gum arabic, paint brush, asbestos sheets, and a solution of vinegar and salt.

METHOD

When using prepared copper blanks the only preparation needed is cleaning. Sheet metal must be cut to shape and then the edges filed. If the surface of the copper is very smooth, it may be given a little bite by using emery paper, abrasive pads, or even Ajax or Comet. It is essential that the copper be absolutely clean before applying the

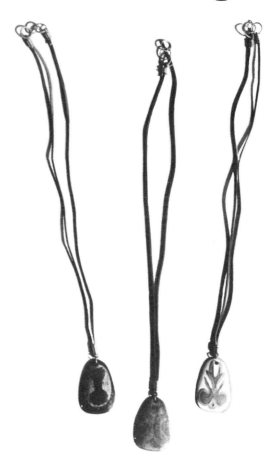

Copper enameled pendants were made using the stencil, or masking, method. Note the interesting method for fastening and attaching the pendants to the leather thongs.

enamel. A solution of vinegar and salt will do this. The copper should be removed from the vinegar after a few minutes, rinsed in clean water, and dried with a tissue. Lay the copper blank on a piece of clean paper. Do not touch it with the fingers. Apply a thin coat of gum arabic over the surface of the copper, and the piece is ready to receive the enamel. Shake the enamel evenly onto the copper working from the edges inward. When the piece has dried completely, it is ready to be placed in the preheated kiln,

51

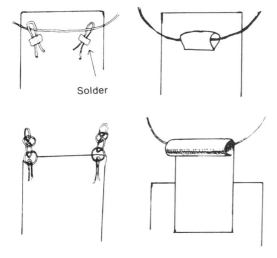

Findings are sweat soldered onto the back of a work, using sheet copper and copper wire. Paper clip (left) is used to hold solder and wire in place while applying heat.

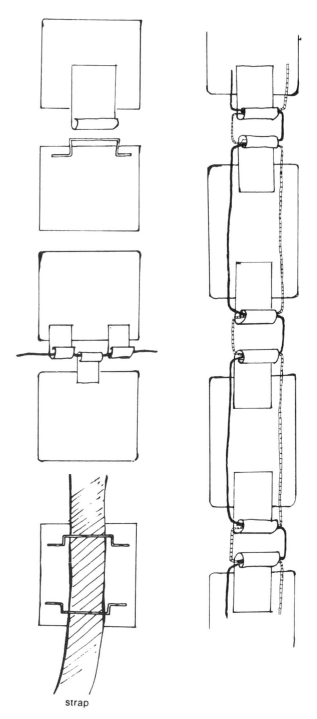

strap

using a spatula or a broad knife. After a few minutes the copper will glow red and the enamel will appear shiny. Remove from the kiln and place on a sheet of asbestos until it has cooled. It is possible to fire small pieces of enamel by holding them with tongs and firing from below, using the flame of a domestic cooker. A plumber's propane gas torch will fire small pieces very efficiently, while larger pieces can be fired using more than one burner at a time.

When the copper has received a base coat of enamel, it may be enriched in many ways. The following methods may be used singly or in combination:

1. Lines or shapes may be formed by pouring the enamel out of the shaker vial freely.

2. Pieces of paper can be cut and used like stencils to mask certain areas when the color is applied.

3. Lines or shapes may be drawn in gum. Enamel is shaken on and the surplus gently tapped off.

4. Copper wire that has been pre-shaped and cleaned can be placed on the prefired base coat and pressed in when the base is hot. This wire may be left as a linear design or may serve as an outline to be filled in with various colors.

5. Copper foil can be used in a similar manner to copper wire by forming flat shapes, which can serve as a base for a transparent enamel or can be left plain.

6. Interesting results can be achieved by firing two soft coats of enamel with a hard layer in between. This causes a bubbling

Enameling kiln, tools, tubes of enamels, copper shapes, and jewelry attachments.

Open firing technique using a propane gas burner. A group of enamels, tools, and copper blanks are shown in the foreground.

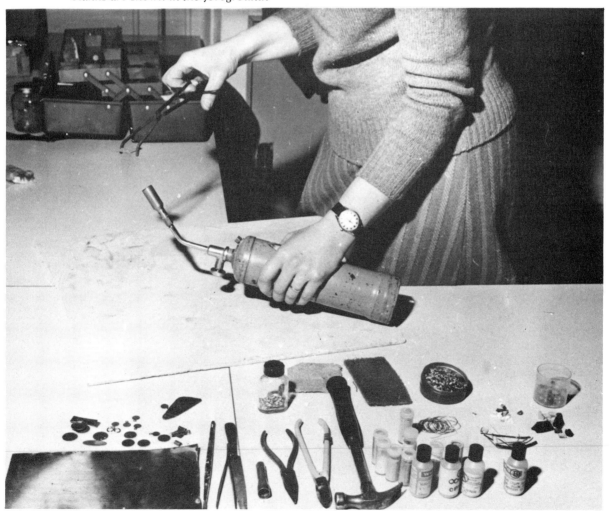

Various examples of copper enameled bowls. Wet paper stencils were used to mask areas of the design.

effect. White, then transparent brown, followed by black produce this effect. Strands or lumps of enamel can be placed on the base coat and when the lumps are soft, swirled or drawn across the work.

7. A layer of unfired enamel sprinkled on the fired base coat may be scratched with a pen for decoration.

The back of the copper will have become blackened with fire scale. This copper oxide can be removed with Ajax and a scouring pad. Alternatively, a suede self-adhesive contact can be used to cover the back of jewelry. The edges should be gently filed, working with strokes away from the finished surface. Emery paper will give a final smooth finish to the edges.

Jewelry findings are easy to solder to the reverse side of the work provided the surface of the copper is absolutely clean. Cut a small length of soft solder (wire) and flatten it. Rub a little flux paste onto the back

of the copper. Place solder and finding in position. Place the piece on the cover of the kiln until the solder melts. Simple fittings are made from strips of copper and copper wire and soldered in place.

Small enameled pieces make unusual, decorative clock faces, box and table tops. Combined with other materials in a mosaic, enamel can give brilliance and add to the variety of the surface.

Fire scale formed by heating copper is sometimes used to advantage by leaving it under clear and opaque enamels. If the flame of the torch is played over the piece, reduction causes the fire scale to turn pink. If the flame touches the molten enamel a luster will result.

It is possible to melt pieces of glass from bottles or jars onto the enameled surface. Not all glass will combine with enamel, but the smaller the pieces the greater the possibility of success. One method of breaking

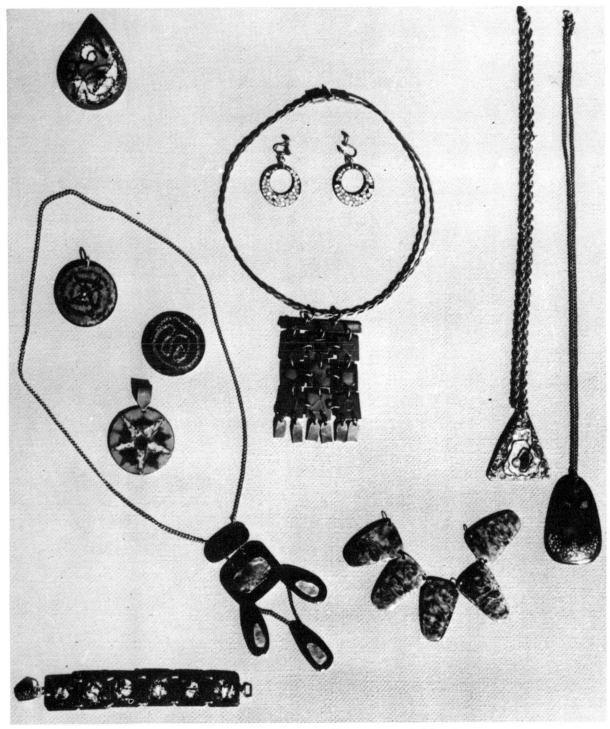

Copper enameled jewelry.

up the glass is to heat it in a flame and then drop it into cold water.

Simple enameling can serve as an introduction to the major arts of enameling and jewelry-making. On the other hand, many enameling students have gone on to develop an interest in metalwork, ceramic glazes, glass, and modern methods of mosaic, as a result of these simple beginnings.

Mary Oliver

fabric printing

HAND PRINTING FROM BLOCKS produces a quality that cannot be easily reproduced by other hand methods. A very slight unevenness of cover gives an all-over softness and variety to the print. The method of block cutting dictates the style of design, and this should be carefully considered at the outset.

Blocks can be made from a variety of materials:

1. Potatoes, turnips, and carrots.

2. Thin cardboard or heavy cartridge paper, mounted on tagboard and waterproofed with varnish.

3. Linoleum of good quality, at least ⅛ inch thick, preferably brown cork lino containing no coloring matter.

4. Wood, end or side grain, cut or printed on the grain.

5. Nails or other small objects capable of creating a slightly raised surface.

6. Strips of metal knocked into a block of wood.

7. Expanded polystyrene or foam rubber, cut or chipped.

8. Corrugated cardboard, mounted on plywood and waterproofed with varnish.

9. Woven rush or cane, embossed or molded materials, natural objects such as heavily veined leaves or tree bark.

Lino cuts

The best tools are V- or U-shaped blades about 3½ inches long capable of being sharpened on a stone and fitted into graver handles. These are preferable to the inexpensixe nib tools found in most art shops. When cutting the lino block the tool should be held with the handle in the palm of the hand and the index finger along the blade. The block should be held firmly with the other hand, and the cutting action made away from the body or other hand. An exercise in free lino block cutting that exploits the material and at the same time achieves a variety of effects is as follows:

Take 1-inch square piece of lino and freely cut into it areas of tone, half-tone, and white. Print, using finger pressure in

A group of printed patterns from a single block.

different ways but maintaining in each individual printing sheet the same arrangement. Through this procedure try to achieve numerous, all-over, repeating patterns that vary according to the direction in which the block has been placed. This same

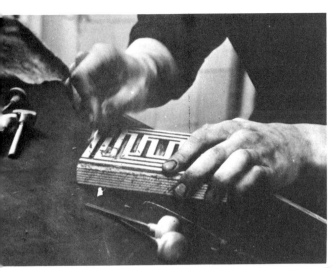

In this linocut the lino has been mounted on a block to facilitate printing.

Block printing can be done with a special hand-held mallet.

overall pattern design also can be achieved with larger blocks. Avoid pencil drawing on the block to outline your design. Only the tool should be used.

Printing on cloth. The lino block, no matter what material, is backed with plywood to give it stability, using water- and turpentine-proof adhesives.

Fabric printing inks. The oil-bound fabric inks are mixed to the required shade in a container and a small quantity rolled on to a palette with a rubber roller; then the color is transferred onto the block and subsequently onto the cloth, which is stuck or pinned firmly to the printing surface. A special mallet or foot pressure can be used for printing larger blocks requiring greater pressure to print evenly.

Pattern registration is achieved by drawing a line at right angles to the selvage across the cloth. Register the block against this line and the selvage and print across the cloth.

If a second color is required in printing, take a block identical in size to the first, carve the second color pattern, ink it, register it similarly to the first line on the cloth, and print. When you are finished, hang the cloth to dry and clean your utensils and

block with turpentine substitute immediately.

Pigment or direct dyes. The block should be flocked for pigment dyeing. The flocking adhesive is rolled out on to a palette and then onto the block; it is then covered lightly and generously with flocking powder and left to dry for 24 hours. If necessary a second coat is applied after brushing off all excess powder. The dye pad, made from sponge rubber covered firmly with a layer of absorbent cloth on a wooden base, is evenly coated with color using a 2-inch brush. The block is then pressed onto it at random until the surface is fully charged with dye. Print as before. Overloading with color fills the interstices of the block, which should be cut deeply.

Potato cuts. The potato can be cut with a knife or lino tool. The block is pressed onto the color from a palette or pad, and the printing follows the same procedure as for lino cuts.

SCREEN PRINTING

This technique is commonly used in commercial production and derives from sten-

A block is covered in flocking powder after being coated with flocking mordant, using a roller.

The block is pressed into the dye pad after it has been coated with color.

Organdy is stretch and stapled to a wooden screen to be used for a silk screen printing process.

cils imported from China at the beginning of this century. The highly delicate Chinese motifs were held together with human hairs. This work inspired a new approach to printing, at first very flat and simple but developing rapidly into a highly sophisticated technique capable of producing a wide variety of effects.

The frame

This can be made from 2 inch by 2 inch flat pine strips with firm corners. The size should be at least 12 inches by 16 inches on the inside. If large printing areas are required, a screen covering 6 inches over the cloth width at each selvage and containing more than one repeat is advisable.

Silk, cotton organdy, or polyester is stretched along one side of the frame, on the straight of the weave, and stapled at ¾ inch intervals. The opposite side is similarly treated, pulling firmly against the first side and subsequently the remaining sides, ensuring a drum-like surface. Sheer polyester curtaining available where you purchase draperies is also suitable for this purpose.

Placement design on screen

The motif should be placed on the screen in such a way as to allow 2 inches on either side and 5 inches at the top and bottom. After the design has been applied by one of the following methods, the screen should be masked with adhesive tape to prevent unwanted escape of color.

Simple gelatin method. The outside of the screen is painted with three coats of gelatin (¾ ounces to 1 pint of water, dissolved in a double boiler). Allow each coat to dry thoroughly before applying the

After plugging up pinholes in the screen with varnish, clean the printing areas of the varnish with a clean rag.

next. Then, the area to be printed is painted in thick lacquer on top of the gelatin, dried, painted with potassium bichromate solution (10 percent in water), and exposed to strong light until the gelatin hardens. Wash off the hardened gelatin from the inside of the screen with warm water. This dissolves the gelatin beneath the lacquer, allowing the latter to peel off. Previously designed patterns can be traced on the inside of the screen and lacquered on the outside.

Gelatin-potassium method. In this method the screen is coated with the following mixture.

1. In a double boiler dissolve 10½ ounces of gelatin in 35 ounces of water (A).

2. Dissolve ½ ounce of potassium bichromate in 4 ounces of water (B).

Then mix (hot) 3 parts A to 1 part B in a dark room. Coat the screen with mixture while it is still hot; do not work mixture into screen. Leave screen in dark room to dry. A positive of the design has previously been prepared on tracing film using a photo-

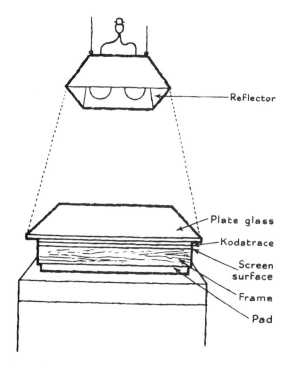

A good setup for the gelatin-potassium method.

opaque paint. The screen is placed, with the surface up, on a flat resilient pad; the tracing — paint side against the emulsion — is placed on top of the screen, and the paper and screen are covered with a piece of plate glass, weighted to insure perfect contact on all surfaces. The paper and screen are exposed to light, a 150-watt bulb or daylight, until the emulsion hardens. Then wash the screen off in a bath of warm running water and gently agitate it or hose it lightly until the mesh that the emulsion has been protected by is cleaned away. To strengthen the screen and to fill pinholes, coat the screen completely with varnish on the inside. The printing areas should be rubbed clear from the outside with a clean rag.

The gelatin-potassium mixture can be used for producing open textural effects by painting the areas required to be white directly onto the screen. The mixture should be kept warm in a double boiler, and all excess should be thrown away.

With polyester mesh, hardened emulsion can be removed after use in a bath of weak caustic soda. Shellac, varnish, or any waterproof substance can be used to block out the screen.

To achieve texture on a gelatined screen, press a sheet of coarse sandpaper to the inside of the screen and rub the outside surface with a black wax chalk, making a resist to the potassium mixture.

Stencils. Paper stencils can be used on a screen to print short runs. Masking tape can be used for stripes; scatter patterns can be obtained by arranging torn paper on the printing surface. On one sweep of the squeegee, paper will stick to the screen and form a stencil.

Profilm stencils. Profilm is a resin-coated paper. The shapes you are going to use in your design are cut out of the resin layer and removed without cutting the paper that holds the remaining shapes in place. The outside of the screen is placed on to the profilm, resin side uppermost, and ironed with a hot iron from the inside, which dissolves the resin into the screen mesh. The paper is peeled off and the design is imbedded in the screen.

Printing

The table to be used for printing should be 6 inches wider than the cloth to be printed, and a convenient length. The top is layered evenly with newspaper or felt and covered with oilcloth. These are all firmly fixed to give a perfect surface, mounted on a stable base. The cloth to be printed, previously coated with a thin layer of gum arabic or tragacanth, is ironed onto the table. If the cloth is fine, it should be pinned on to a back-cloth, the selvage parallel to the table edge.

Registration. A metal registration bar is placed along one side of the table. The screen is positioned to fall correctly on the cloth, and screws fitting firmly against the registration bar are fixed in the side of the screen at each corner. An angle is fixed on the screen to register against the repeat stop on the bar, the stops being previously

The labels in the diagram:
Reflector
Plate glass
Kodatrace
Screen surface
Frame
Pad

Registering the screen.

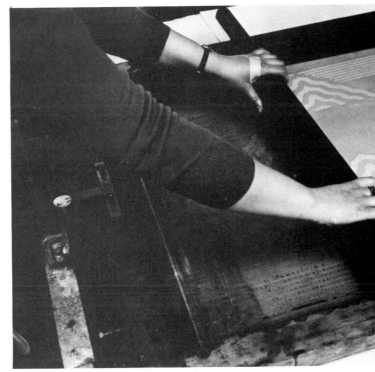

Use the squeegee to sweep the color evenly over the screen.

fixed at the required intervals. A small screen containing one repeat is registered against lines marked accurately and faintly on the cloth and the screen frame.

In printing, the dye is put in the end of the screen nearest the operator, the squeegee placed behind it to sweep the color firmly to the opposite end and repeated sufficient times to charge the cloth with color. The color should not be exhausted during printing.

OTHER PATTERN TECHNIQUES

Some other techniques for fabric printing can be achieved:

1. Spray painting can be done over a firm stencil using a hand spray or pressurized gun containing thin color in gum.

2. Hand painting can be done with dye or pigment color mixed as you would for printing.

3. Cylinders of varying diameter can be placed firmly on the cloth, filled with dye, and dragged across the cloth to make trail patterns.

COLOR

Pigments, of which there are a number of good brands, are easy to use for fabric printing.

Block printing with helizarin pigments

60 parts helizarin color
890 parts helizarin binder FD
30 parts methyl cellulose DKL (7% solution)
20 parts Condensol A (1–1 in water)

Methyl cellulose solution

Dissolve ¼ ounce of methyl cellulose DKL in 3½ ounces of water. Allow to thicken for 24 hours, until a gel is obtained. Print and fix as described previously.

Screen printing with helizarin pigments

10–80 parts helizarin color
350 parts helizarin binder D
580 parts helizarin reduction binder
20 parts urea
20 parts Condensol A (1–1 with water)
Print, dry, bake, or iron with hot iron
During baking, these colors give off toxic fumes. In most cases ironing is sufficient and recommended to fix the color.

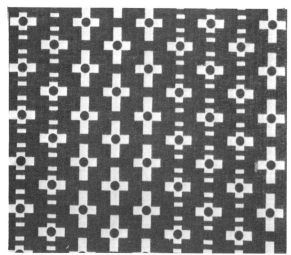

Fabrics designed by the author are: "Jericho,"   "Palmyra,"

"Jerusalem,"   *and "Sidon."*

Aniline dye for block or screen

Direct dyestuffs are suitable for cotton or viscose rayon.

⅓–⅔ ounces of dyestuff

1¾ ounces grams urea

¾ of a pint of hot water

Mix all together and boil to insure solution. Add to 1½ gal. thickening; when cool, add ½ ounces of disodium hydrogen phosphate.

Print fabric, dry, steam 30–45 minutes, and wash out in cold running water.

All utensils, blocks, screens, etc. should be washed in cold water immediately after use with pigment or aniline dyes.

CLEANING THE SCREEN

To clean the screen remove the excess pigment. Rub the screen with a rag soaked in Colasyl A50, with a dry rag on the reverse side to absorb pigment. Repeat procedure on the other side of the screen; finally wash off with water.

THICKENING

Gum tragacanth is best for thickening. To make it mix ½ ounce gum tragacanth flakes or powder with 1 quart of cold water and allow the mixture to stand for 2–3 days. Stir occasionally. Boil in double boiler for 8–12 hours. If too thick add water. A few drops of oil of cloves or phe-

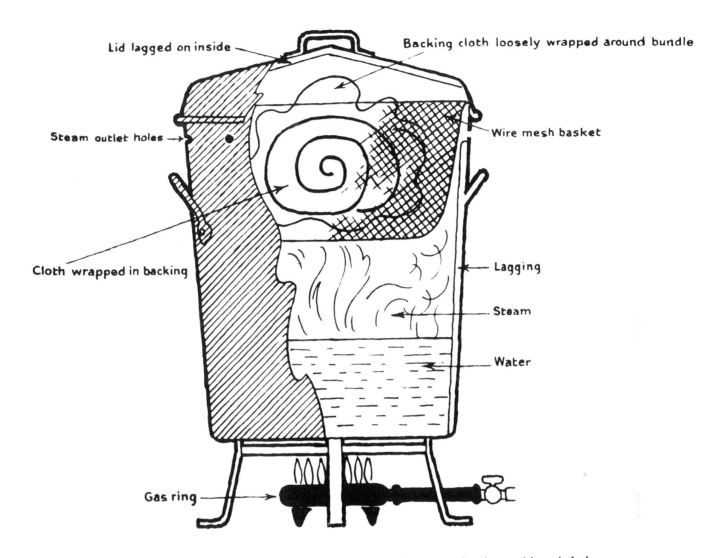

Lid lagged on inside

Backing cloth loosely wrapped around bundle

Steam outlet holes →

Wire mesh basket

Cloth wrapped in backing

Lagging

Steam

Water

Gas ring →

Section of steamer showing position of cloth.

nol keeps the thickening for 2–3 weeks.

STEAMER

A fabric steamer can be made from a metal garbage can or boiler. A metal basket is fitted into the top half of the boiler, the outside of which is lagged to prevent condensation. The lid is also lagged inside and fits well. The bottom quarter of the container is filled with water and brought to a boil. The cloth is folded into a clean cloth, rolled into a package, and placed in the basket, lightly covered with a cloth to prevent dampness from condensation. Cover the cloth and steam for required time, keeping water boiling; open package immediately on removal from steamer.

63

courtesy Gemrocks Ltd.

gem cutting and polishing

THROUGH THE AGES man has been fascinated by the countless beautiful rocks and minerals found on earth. Ancient civilizations, the Chinese, Egyptians, and Aztecs, learned to cut and polish many of the harder stones, using them to make jewelry and ornaments. In the following centuries, better tools and improvements upon the old and rather crude methods of cutting were gradually developed. Now modern engineering has made it possible for even the amateur to buy reasonably inexpensive machines and cut stones, even those with complicated shapes.

Stones vary in many respects, but the one factor affecting virtually all forms of cutting is the relative hardness of the material chosen. Stones to be cut must be hard enough to take a durable polish, and the tools used must be made of, or faced with, harder material or abrasive. The one exception to this latter rule is, of course, the diamond, which is the hardest material known to man. As the amateur is unlikely to be able to obtain rough diamonds of a quality suitable for cutting, this chapter can be confined to the softer stones, such as the quartz family — amethysts, agates, jaspers, opals, citrines, etc., which are easily obtainable.

The one essential common to all forms of cutting is the need for absolute cleanliness during all stages of the work. Machines, stones, and hands should be kept free of grit and particles as progress is made from one stage to another. Coarse grit left on at the polishing stage can ruin otherwise perfect work with scratches.

METHOD

Other than the simple sawing or grinding a flat surface on a slab and subsequently polishing it, there are basically three forms of lapidary work:

Tumbling, or barreling

The pebbles on shingle beaches are tumbled by the action of the tides, but machines can speed this process of tumbling a stone

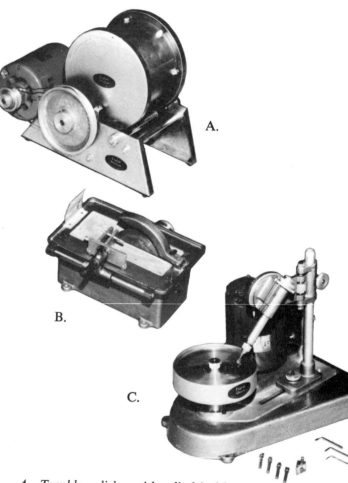

A. *Tumble polisher with cylindrical barrel.*
B. *Trim saw.*
C. *Faceting machine.*

to a high degree of polish in 20 to 30 days instead of the centuries taken by nature. Tumble polishing machines provide the easiest form of cutting, that is, grinding with the help of abrasive grits or powders. The machine is basically a drum or barrel that is made to rotate quite slowly. The supporting chassis, rollers, and electric mo-

An assortment of cut and uncut stones:
(a) snowflake uncut, (b) quartz uncut, (c) citrine
uncut and cut, (d) agate cabochons, and (e) tiger's
eye cabochon and uncut stones.

tor are necessary only to support and rotate the drum. A drum speed of 35 rpm is quite sufficient.

Into the drum should be mixed fragments of stone of equal hardness but preferably differing sizes, up to about 1 inch across. Water is added to cover and give a load of about 60 percent of the volume of the drum. The work is divided into three or four stages, commencing with the addition of coarse silicon carbide grit, going on to a medium grit, and then a final grit of a very fine grade. The last stage is carried out with one of many polishing powders. Each stage takes from four to six days (and nights) of continuous rotation of the drum. The re-

65

sultant beautifully polished stones of unusual shapes are very suitable for use in modern and inexpensive items of jewelry.

Combination or cabochon units

These units are small grinding and polishing machines used to fashion dome-shaped stones—known as cabochons. The machine can be fitted with a diamond-impregnated saw blade for initial shaping, and one or more silicon carbide grinding wheels in differing grades for reducing the stone to its final shape. Lastly, a hard felt or leather wheel is used to polish the stone. These processes all require a water drip feed and fairly high speeds, varying from 500 to 3,000 rpm, obtained through multi-speed pulleys with a small electric motor. The stone is fixed to a small dop, or stick, to facilitate working it on the various wheels. Cabochon stones are used for rings, earrings, and all forms of jewelry.

Faceting machines

The third and most sophisticated method of cutting is faceting. The faceters available for the amateur are precision machines designed to produce varying shapes of stones (such as rounds, squares, oblongs, pear shapes, and other forms) that are totally covered by small facets, or flat surfaces, cut on at regular angles. These facets refract and reflect light inside and out of the stones, giving them sparkle.

Basically the faceting machine consists of two parts plus an electric motor. A horizontally rotating table (known as the lap), dressed with diamond powder or some form of abrasive or polish, is made to revolve at a medium speed. The stone to be cut is mounted on a small stick or rod (the dop stick), which is fixed into a movable arm. The arm can be moved to varying angles and can also be rotated to set positions. The former adjustment produces the angles of the facets, and the latter gives the stone its outline shape. Modern machines have fairly simple instructions, and after a little

Combination unit.

practice it is possible to cut a stone in a matter of three or four hours.

Generally, stones that are used for faceting are of a higher quality than those used for the other two methods of cutting; the finished stones are therefore more suitable for use in better types of jewelry.

Apart from their use in jewelry-making, stones can, of course, be cut for the pure joy or interest of the pastime and in the formation of a comprehensive collection. There are several good books available, and some adult education evening classes teach gem cutting and polishing. There are also quite a number of lapidary clubs throughout the country that welcome new members. These clubs often have machines available for their members' use.

Peter Tysoe

glass

GLASS IS A HARD, noncrystalline substance that is created by fusing silica sand with solvents or fluxes. There are different types of glass depending on whether lead, soda ash, lime, or boric acid is used with the sand to produce the metal (glass material). Each of these fluxes will produce a material with varying characteristics. Oxides of cobalt, copper, gold, iron or selenium, etc. are used for coloring glass. Cobalt, selenium, and manganese are decolorizers used in small quantities to eliminate the green color in glass, which results as a by-product of impure silica, or silica high in iron content. In the molten state glass can be blown, rolled, pressed, threaded, and twisted.

Glassmaking is thought to have started at least 4,000 years ago—probably by the accidental fusing of sand and minerals onto ceramics by Egyptian or Mesopotamian potters. Its use was developed to make beads and then it was formed (by a process referred to as sand core) around a core of clay or sand to make jars or other vessels. When the glass had cooled, the core was removed. Blown glass was not fully developed until the Roman era, when it spread with the trade routes throughout North Africa and into Europe. Following the decay of the Roman Empire, Venice developed as an important center of glassmaking after 1200 A.D., and the eventual spread of Italian craftsmen into other countries led to a revival and the further development of glassmaking as far away as Britain.

TYPES OF GLASS

Blown glassware is the traditional method of making glassware by taking a hollow iron tube, four or five feet long, dipping it into the molten glass, and gathering a blob of glass on the end, which can then be blown and formed into a free shape or into a mold. Since 1962 there has been a revitalization, which started in America, in the exploration of free-form blown glass by artists and craftsmen working in the me-

Glassblowing.

dium. In the commercial field hand blowing has had a revival with certain specialty glass companies. Automatic blowing is used for large-scale production of bottles and other glass containers by large companies.

Pressed glass is made by pressing a molten lump of glass into a mold. A slab of molten glass can have simple shades pressed into it to form decorative slabs. The production of glass bricks, ashtrays, etc. is carried out on a large scale using automatic presses.

Flat glass is now mainly mass-produced

67

A coat of arm by David Peace was engraved in situ by a rotary carborundum tool in a hand-chuck. Details are added with a dental drill or, as in the picture, a diamond point.

by drawing out and rolling a continuous ribbon of glass from large tank furnaces. Sheet and "figured" (decorated) glasses are made in this way. Plate glass is polished to achieve a flat surface, and there is the new invention of "float glass," requiring no costly polishing procedures, for which a continuous sheet is drawn over a bath of molten tin. Some flat glasses are obtainable in gray and bronze tints and in color.

Antique glass is the handmade sheet glass made by hand blowing a large cylinder and cutting it lengthwise to allow it to fall flat into a sheet. It is irregular in pattern and thickness and can be very beautiful. Its main use has been in the making of stained glass windows, and it is obtainable in clear colored tints and in rich colors. A color may also be flashed onto the surface by dipping the glass blob on the end of the blowing tool into a glass of a different color. When blown, the surface has a thin surface layer of the color.

Slab glass is cast in a mold and is approximately 1 inch in thickness and 12 inches long by 8 inches wide. Slab glass is also available in white and colored tints and full color.

CUTTING

Flat and slab glass is cut by drawing a diamond or a wheel glass cutter across the flatter surface with a firm stroke where the break is intended. Then, holding the glass in the left hand, flat glass is tapped firmly under the cut line with the "heel" of the cutter. The waste piece will either break off with the tapping under the score line, or it can be broken off with a firm breaking motion with the two hands, holding the glass at its edge on either side of the line. A straight cut may be broken by pressing on the edge of the bench. Deep curves can be nipped out with glazier's pliers. Edges can be scraped against another piece of glass to remove sharpness.

Slabs are also scored with the wheel cutter and are usually divided by striking

This window, by Keith New, combines two contrasting techniques, leaded glass, and glass mosaic, juxtaposed in clearly defined areas. This arrangement forms the main image, which is sandwiched between plate glass on the inside and figured glass on the outside. This doubling up of layers achieves a density of color plus great brilliance.

downward over a sharp steel edge, well secured and pointed upward. The slab should be held firmly with one hand on each side of the cut line. Slabs may also be chipped away or cut with a tungsten-edged hammer or with diamond chip impregnated saw blades lubricated with water.

DECORATING

Engraving. Diamond point is executed by hand using either a small diamond set in a holder or a pencil-like, tungsten, carbide-tipped steel tool. The surface of the glass is scratched in dots or short delicate lines, which appear light against the darker background of the untouched glass.

Wheel engraving is carried out using a series of copper or stone wheels mounted on

69

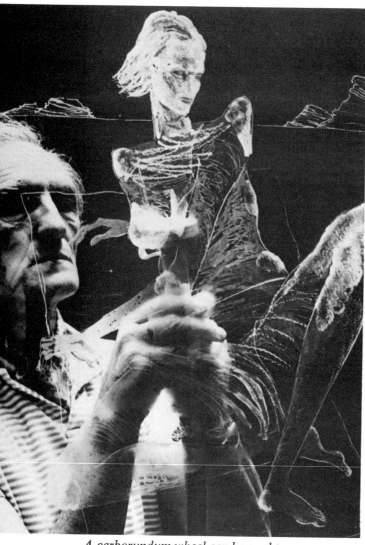

A carborundum wheel can be used to engrave a glass panel.

steel spindles in a lathe. The glass has to be moved to bring it into contact with the wheel. Designs can be engraved in low or high relief. John Hutton, who produced the engraved panels for the Great West Screen of Coventry Cathedral in England, has developed his own method of using grinding wheels that are driven by a flexible drive shaft on an electric motor. Using this method, the artist can work freely over fixed glass panels.

Etching. Glass is attacked by hydrofluoric acid, which can be used to achieve an etched design if a resist wax or varnish is painted all over the surfaces to be immersed in the tank of acid. The design is cut through the protective surface to allow the acid to eat into the required glass areas. Various depths can be obtained, and both a clear and a white etch are possible.

Sandblasting is a process by which unprotected areas of a glass are exposed in a special cabin in which an abrasive powder is blown at it under pressure from a compressor. Various depths of sandblasting are obtainable by covering previous areas that have been blasted. Subsequent exposure of areas already exposed will result in their being a deeper level. Glass can be lightly peppered or deeply engraved using this sandblasting technique.

Enameling. Colors for enameling are available from ceramic manufacturers. These colors will fire at a variety of temperatures on various types of glass. Enamels can be hand painted or screen printed onto the surface of the glass and fused in a furnace. Transfers holding enamel pigment can be made or bought ready for applying and firing on the glass.

Stained glass. The traditional use of leaded colored glass in windows is known as stained glass. This type of glass developed and came to full flower in the Middle Ages in Northern Europe, an excellent example being the windows of Chartres Cathedral in France. Since the rather dead work of the Victorian era, stained glass has been revitalized by work done by individual artists and craftsmen. The term stained glass should be applied to leaded antique glasses, usually with designs painted on with an iron oxide mixture, which fires onto the surface of the glass, giving a brown-black color. Stippled and scratched as well as brush painted, lined effects are obtained with this iron oxide pigment. Silver stain can also be fired on to give a pale yellow or a deep orange color. Flashed antique glasses can be etched to give light patterns against color. After firing, the separate pieces of glass are fixed together with leads, ready

Detail of an architectural panel by the author in 1-inch thick slab glass set in clear resin with aluminum tubes.

for framing into a window or screen panel. Designs for stained glass are drawn up into full size cartoons, over which the glass pieces are placed while they are being cut to shape.

Glass appliqué. This technique is carried out by bonding glasses — mostly antique colored glasses—to a base panel of clear plate glass. The adhesive most generally used for glass appliqué is an epoxy, which has good bonding properties if both surfaces are absolutely clean and free from grease. Any number of variations can be achieved in glass appliqué, using the adhesives now available. Intermediate spaces left between the cut pieces of colored glass can be filled with a dark color to give added definition, if needed. Colored glass decorations can also be sandwiched in between two layers of plate glass in order to give complete protection. Both polyester and epoxy resin can be used on their own, without filler, to bond colored glass, which is completely clear or translucent, into panels.

Colored glass. This technique, an extension of stained glass, uses 1-inch thick slabs cut to shape and set into concrete panels for decorative walls. A further development of this has been to use the new plastic resins—for example, polyester and epoxy, which have been developed since the war—to produce thinner, lighter panels than can generally be obtained with concrete by mixing them with sand or other filler powder. The resin, like concrete, is poured around the glass pieces, which are placed in a casting frame. Many recently built churches, cathedrals, and secular buildings have colored glasswork of this type built into them, giving structural character as illuminated walls rather than glass windows.

GLASS CONSTRUCTIONS

By using the new resin-based adhesives and resins, some contemporary sculptors and craftsmen have executed some exciting two- and three-dimensional work by bonding glass both to the resin and to other materials such as metal using the resin adhesives. These resins, together with additional fixings available by using mechanical methods, allows for the development of complex three-dimensional forms. In architectural work, this new-found freedom has resulted in a complete break away from the idea of stained glass as such, and the term stained glass should not be used to describe glass-construction sculpture or colored glass panels.

Resin-based adhesives and resin are of great advantage for the craftsman and teacher because they offer a cold cast technique, and any heat that may be required for helping resins to set can be provided by electric radiant or fan heaters. Expensive kilns or furnaces are not required. The main cost will be in the glass and resins themselves, together with the materials needed to make wooden formers (tray-like frames) to hold the glass pieces while the resin is poured around or over them. Sheet polyethylene or cellophane make good releasing agents in order to stop the panel from sticking to the wooden frame. Both

71

A fused silica/quartz panel.

antique and slab glass can be used in these constructions with any other type of glass that is desired. Fiber glass matte can be used to give additional strength to panels, which can be made of practically any thickness, and metal strengthening bars can be incorporated into the laminates as part of the design.

FUSED GLASS

In their molten state pieces of glass can be fused together. There are difficulties, however, when glasses of varying composition are fused because their coefficients of expansion may vary, leading to cracking. When glasses of the same type have various oxides added as coloring, there is also the same problem of cracking.

An interesting technique using fused silica sand and quartz is being carried out by some companies. From pure silica, absolutely clear quartz-like decorative panels are produced in furnaces working with temperatures up to 3600°F. Opaque colored

work is also made from silica sand with oxide added. This material is thermally stable; that is, it can be heated and cooled at will without danger of cracking. This technique of fused silica sand and quartz is highly sophisticated and requires elaborate technology to handle the high temperatures.

A pottery kiln can be useful for experiments in fusing plate glass to make small constructions and panels. (Reading should be done on annealing before undertaking this work.)

Unfortunately, it is not possible in a limited space to deal in detail with the great variety of techniques mentioned above. Further reading is essential to cover full technical details, but it is possible to start working in glass, with simple equipment and materials, in the school or smaller workshop.

72

Dorothy Wright

glove-making

MAKING GLOVES is a lovely craft for the needleworker. It requires no tools or space and can be done at home. Although making leather gloves is not inexpensive, the saving in making them over buying them is sizable. Also there are the advantages of more exact sizing and fit and a choice of styles, together with the fact that hand-made gloves are always more elegant than machine-made ones.

It used to be said that all beginning glovemakers should start with natural chamois. However, it is much easier to learn on a firm-grained leather, such as imitation peccary, which will make an everyday glove that does not demand the finest stitching. From this the glovemaker can advance to dress gloves made of suede and grain gloving, chamois, doeskin, and pigskin.

Other leathers and their uses are:

1. Cape and extra heavy chamois, for men's gloves.

2. Wool lamb and sheepskin, for winter gloves and mittens.

3. Coney skins, for fur-backed gloves and linings (silk and fleece linings may be bought by the yard). There are also crochet-backed gloves with leather palms and nylon fabric gloving, which is sometimes sold in kits.

PATTERNS

The patterns most commonly used come in normal length, in quarter sizes from 6 to 7½ women's and from 7½ to 9 men's. They are cut for long hands and tend to be slightly larger than commercial sized gloves.

Adapting the pattern

After some experience, patterns can be adapted for the shorter and broader hand. The size of a pattern is the measurement in inches of the hand around the knuckles. A sizing tape measure can be bought and is a good rough guide. Where a short, broad hand differs from a long, narrow one is in

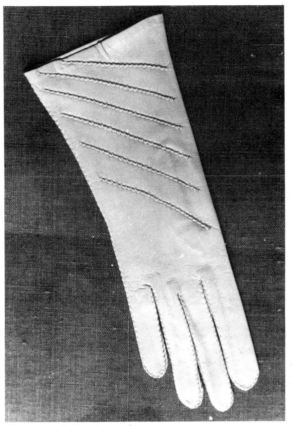

Glove made by the author.

the finger length and in the distance between the base of the thumb and the base of the first finger. This can be gauged by slipping the pattern over the thumb. If the distance is too long, the thumb hole should be moved up when marking out the pattern on the skin. If the fingers are too long, they may be cut and reshaped after being cut out.

Never attempt to alter the width of the fingers of the pattern. For thinner or thicker fingers narrow or widen the forchettes. The width and length of the top of the thumb may be altered. The choice of pattern size also depends on the skin you are using. A thin and stretchy one calls for a smaller pattern size.

73

A glove pattern is easily lengthened at the hem, but the maximum width of the new edge should not be more than 9 inches. The sides should be slanted off in a straight line away from the thumb hole.

EQUIPMENT

Sharp cutting-out scissors.

Small scissors (optional).

Needles. No. 7 sharps or betweens. (Three-edged glover's needles are rarely used and only on the toughest leather.)

Threads. Buttonhole twist for most skins. D.M.C. No. 12 can be used for some sport gloves. Thicker D.M.C. for men's gloves.

Tape measure, glover's (optional).

Paper clips.

CUTTING-OUT

Most gloving skins are sold to make two pairs, the area being about 5 square feet. The skin is best divided across and not down. Unless otherwise indicated by the makers, the main stretch of the skin is from side to side; therefore all pieces of the pattern are laid pointing up and down the skin since the stretch goes round the hand. The best-looking area of the skin should be at the back, although there may be a rather hard passage at the very center, which should be avoided. In general, forchettes should be cut from the flanks, which are thinner and more stretchy. Areas B in the diagram of the skin may have the stretch going slightly sideways; in this case, the forchettes should be slightly tilted to follow the stretch.

The skin is laid top-side-up on the table, and the pattern pieces are carefully traced around either with the thumbnail or with a pencil; never use a pen. The pattern pieces are reversed for right and left hand. Great care should be taken with marking and cutting. Wool lamb should be cut with a razor blade, holding the skin off the table so that the wool is not cut but only parted.

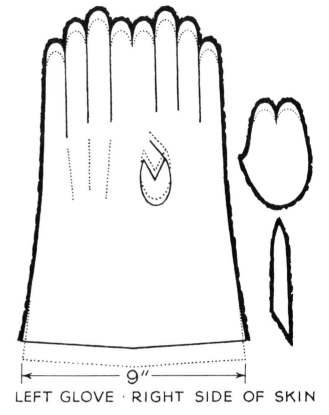

LEFT GLOVE · RIGHT SIDE OF SKIN

The dotted line indicates the original pattern; the black line indicates the adaptation.

ASSEMBLY

Pins and tacking are never used in assembly to secure the leather because of the permanent holes they may leave. Wire paper clips should be used instead. The usual order of assembly is:

1. Hems
2. Points, if used
3. Side seams
4. Thumbs
5. Forchettes joined in pairs
6. Forchettes sewn to the backs of the fingers
7. Forchettes sewn to the front of the fingers

Stitching. Use a short thread and begin and end with a knot.

Prix, or stab, stitch should not be too small and should be pulled fairly tight.

Single oversew may be done with contrasting thread.

Double oversew is the best seam for

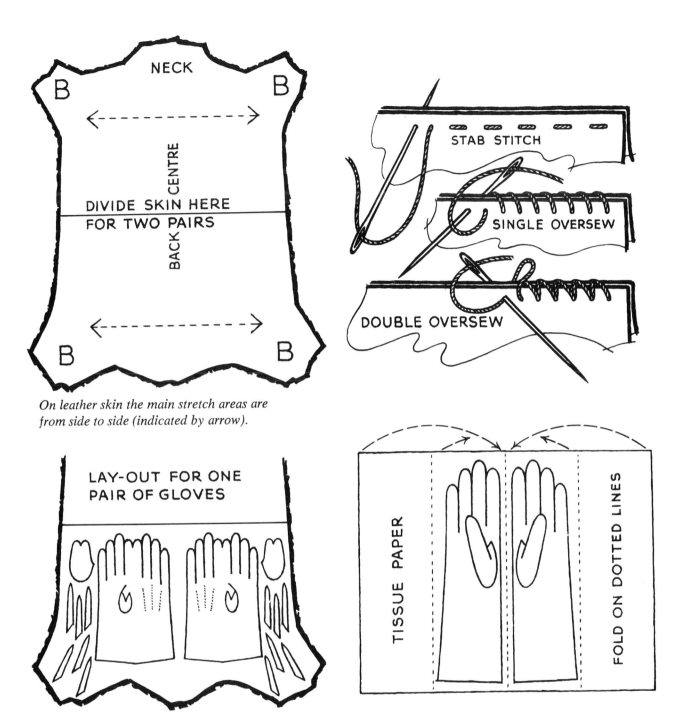

On leather skin the main stretch areas are from side to side (indicated by arrow).

One pair of gloves can be laid out on half of a skin.

dress gloves. It should be as near to the edge as possible.

Decoration may be done with points, hems, vents, and buttons. The wear of most gloves is improved by some treatment of the hems. The turned-up hem should be sewn very tight.

Facings may be done on the inside or outside of the glove. The narrow inside facing should be cut across the leather, damp-ened, and stretched fully before sewing.

Bindings should also be well stretched.

Pressing. The finished gloves should be carefully arranged in tissue paper as shown in the accompanying diagram, then folded together and put between the pages of a stiff magazine. Then sit on the magazine for a few hours, if possible. Nothing presses gloves better than this!

Mabs Tyler

improvising dolls

OF ALL THE THOUSANDS OF TOYS invented and manufactured over the years, dolls (which are among the earliest ones) have retained the interest and affection of children above all others. Many families can still produce a battered, well-beloved doll or teddy bear, passed down from mother to child, and sometimes handmade. Children, particularly, will contrive to make just the doll they need for their immediate purpose from all kinds of apparently useless, highly improbable materials. The wise teacher or parent will exploit this imaginative, exploratory, inventive young thought by providing the kinds of materials that will enable the child to try out his ideas. Sometimes, indeed, the material itself will suggest an idea. Nothing bought or manufactured can provide the satisfaction of something developed and made successfully from an original idea.

Quite obviously, the young child's rough-and-ready first efforts at doll- and toy-making can be related to the early dolls of bone, wood, or clay, carved and fashioned with primitive tools. And like them, children's dolls bear no likeness to the sophisticated manufactured products of recent times. For the child its own efforts have great value in that they give tremendous scope and opportunity to his ingenuity and imagination.

In many homes and most primary schools the junk box has for many years served its purpose for the enthusiastic child, who suggests, selects, tries, discards, and finally produces something that satisfies him with the junk. This "something" that the child creates easily can be changed or adapted as the idea grows and develops. It is something that to an adult—particularly one with a passion for neatness, tidiness, and good finish—still remains junk! In all free, doll-making activities the most important item is a scrap box of bottomless depth and infinite variety, which child or adult can sort through and experiment with every possible kind of fabric and trimming: velvet, silk, cotton, wool, tweeds, burlap, fur

and fur fabric, ribbons, lace, braid, cord, sequins, beads, feathers, and so on. It helps if the different kinds of materials are sorted into bags.

The young child needs quick results—something for immediate use—so that early efforts are often sketchy, imagination playing a greater part in "using" rather than in "making." As experience grows, "making" becomes of greater interest; each finished doll becomes a stepping-off place or practicing of skill for the next undertaking. So that at each stage signs of increasing skill in all the techniques used are seen. Older children and grown-ups will make use of more advanced materials, which their improved dexterity allows them to handle. More advanced dolls, particularly regional or period dolls, will necessitate research from books, libraries, and museums if costumes are to be authentic and true to the period or the country they represent.

Different in style and concept from the period dolls are the simple, soft, cuddly dolls made for pleasure from cotton, socks, felt, rags, and knitting. These are easy for the beginner and also can be developed into more elaborate dolls. Other soft toys, such as balls and animals, can be made from these materials.

As the beginner progresses in doll-making, he will need other skills. He will need to calculate and measure, to deal with shapes, to use fractions, to incorporate other craft materials, and to use new tools that involve him in new skills and new techniques, leading to wider fields of experiment and a broadening of his interests.

PAPER-BAG DOLL

To begin, you will need a plain paper bag, stuffing or newspaper, ribbon, string, and wool. The youngest children will enjoy making this from a plain paper bag; even adults might enjoy it. A colored pattern can be painted or crayoned all around the open end (skirt), and features can be marked on the closed end of the bag. A ball of stuffing or newspaper tied tightly around the neck with a ribbon forms the head. Wool hair can be sewn or stuck on. The doll will stand by itself if the paper bag is a thick one, or it can be used as a puppet if a hole is pushed in the head to attach the string.

PLASTIC BOTTLE DOLL

To start, have on hand a plastic bottle, dowel rod or stick slightly longer than the bottle, a piece of soft wire or three pipe cleaners twisted together to measure 16

Paper-bag doll.

inches, stuffing, an old nylon stocking, wool, and string.

Pad one end of the dowel rod with wadding, cover it with a light-colored nylon stocking, and tie tight. Before the rod is inserted, the bottle can be weighted with sand or clay. Insert the rod into the neck of the bottle, wedge firmly around the neck, and Scotch tape it in position. Cover the head and the entire bottle with the nylon stocking so that the toe fits over the head. Pull the stocking tightly and twist under the bottle; sew securely, keeping seam as flat as possible so that the bottle will stand. Starting at the middle, twist the piece of wire around the neck of the bottle. Bring the two ends back to neck and twist firmly into two loops of wire to form arms, leaving small loops for hands. Bind the wire with nylon; paint or embroider features on the nylon, sew or stick on wool for hair, and dress as required.

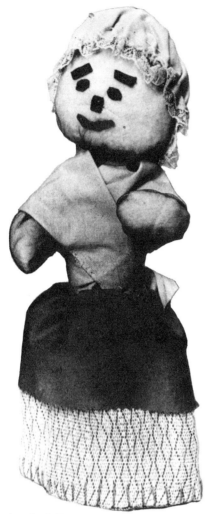

Plastic bottle doll.

CARTON OR SMALL BOTTLE DOLL

To make this doll, you will need various cartons and bottles, a piece of thin wire about 20 inches long, stuffing or newspaper, old nylon stocking or any stretch material, and wool. Families of dolls can be made by using different sizes of cartons or bottles. The open end of the carton becomes the base of the doll. Make a hole in the bottom of the carton. Fold the wire at the center, insert finger in loop, and twist around two or three times to make loop for head. For arms, bend ends back about 3 inches from neck and twist together about ½ inch from the neck. Bring the two re-

maining ends together in a triangle shape and twist them leaving two ends. Push these ends through the hole in the carton and twist and knot firmly inside. If the carton is a deep one, then make two holes opposite each other in the carton, thread the wire through each hole, and knot separately. Wedge the neck tightly and Scotch tape it firmly. Pad the head loop with a ball of stuffing or newspaper and cover smoothly with a nylon stocking or any other stretch material. Bandage arms and hands with similar material. Paint or sew on features, stick or sew on wool for hair, and then dress.'

WIRE DOLL

To make a wire doll, you will need a piece of wire about 30 inches long to make a figure about 6 inches high. You also will need stuffing or newspaper, nylon stocking or stretch material, and wool. Make head and arms as for a carton doll. Twist the wires together from the arms to make a waist, forming a triangle with the shoulders. Make legs in the same way but slightly longer according to size; for example, about the waist. Finish in the same way as the carton doll. For animals, the wire should be longer according to size; for example, about 72 inches is needed for a giraffe. Make an animal in the same way as the doll, lengthening the neck or body as required. Bend the head back and the legs forward; the end of the wire should be used to form the tail.

WIRED NEWSPAPER DOLL

You will need three pieces of wire 12 inches long, newspaper, and padding.

Wired newspaper dolls do not need so much padding when they are formed. Wrap each of the three pieces of wire in a rectangle of paper and Scotch tape each firmly. Tie these three pieces together in the middle. Fold over the top of the middle piece of folded newspaper for the head and the bottom of it for the body; the four remaining pieces form the arms and legs. This makes

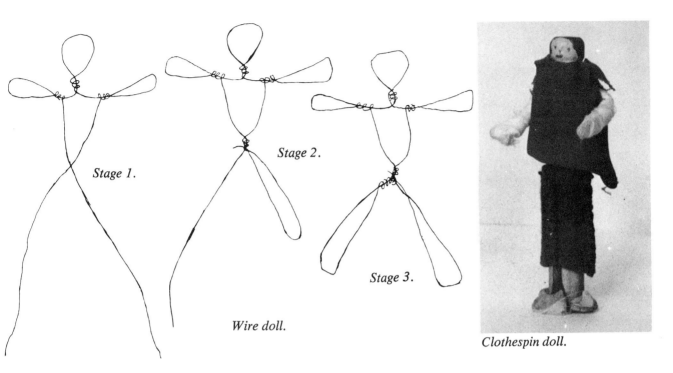

Stage 1.

Stage 2.

Stage 3.

Wire doll.

Clothespin doll.

a flexible doll that can "run," sit, and hold positions. A little padding is needed for the head and body.

The wire-newspaper form can also be used for a variety of animals. For example, for a giraffe, tie the wires in two places using the middle wire. One of the ends of tied-off wire will be used for the head, the other end for the tail. For a crocodile the wire for the head, body, and tail should be twice as long as the other two pieces. Again tie the middle wire in two places. Pad and paint or embroider the features.

CLOTHESPIN DOLL

To make a clothespin doll you will need wooden or plastic clothespins, stuffing, nylon stockings or stretch material, pipe cleaners, and wool. Small dolls such as these can be made quickly. The head can be padded with stuffing and covered with nylon or stretch material; pipe cleaners twisted around the neck make arms; painted features; wool for hair. Push "feet" into a balsa or plastic block to stand it up.

CARDBOARD DOLL

To make a cardboard doll, you will need stiff paper or cardboard, glue, paper clips, staples, and wool. Cardboard dolls are pantins with movable limbs fastened at the shoulders and hips with paper clips. The features are painted on and wool stuck on for the hair. When made by young children, cardboard dolls usually are very simply dressed.

The clothes usually are stuck on from the front with staples or glue of some sort. All ages of children can use these cardboard dolls to illustrate stories—rhymes for the younger ones perhaps; literature, history, or geography for the older ones. More elaborate dolls should have more elaborate costumes with greater attention to detail and finish. Paper clothing patterns can be made by tracing around the cardboard doll, allowing a little more paper at the corners where the clothes will be folded around the doll. Hats can be fitted on by cutting a slit along the brim and putting the doll's head through the slit.

CHICKEN WIRE DOLL

You will need a piece of soft 1 inch mesh chicken wire 18 inches by 15 inches (15 inches being the height and the firm edge

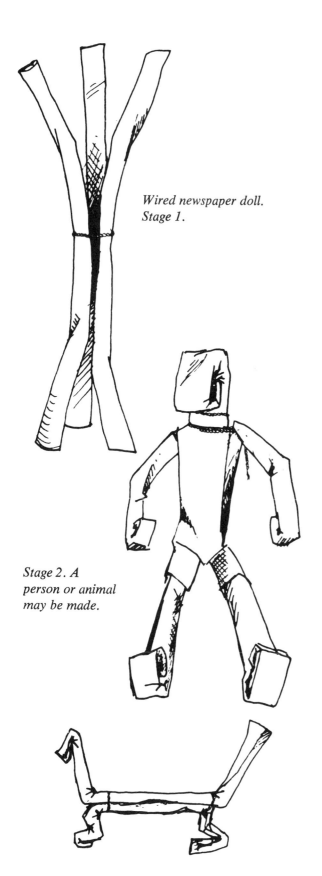

Wired newspaper doll.
Stage 1.

Stage 2. A
person or animal
may be made.

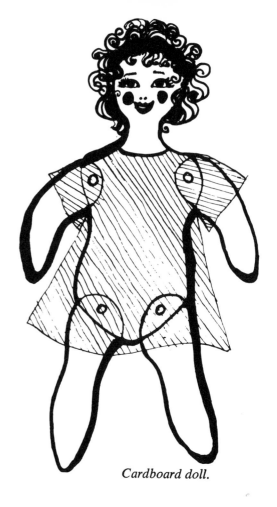

Cardboard doll.

being the base of the doll); a length of
single strand wire, or pipe cleaners; stuffing;
pale pink stretch material, such as nylon,
wool, or silk. Molded chicken wire forms a
firm-standing, durable base for costume
dolls. Much greater skill is needed in the
use of stitches, fabric, style, and planning
when making costume dolls. You also will
need to do some research for details of costumes.

Form the chicken wire into a cylinder,
turning in the cut wires. Mold the head and
body, taking care to keep the head small to
allow for the padding. Squeeze the neck
and waist in tight, using pliers if necessary, to give an elegant figure. Form the
arms by doubling and twisting the wire,
leaving a loop for the hands. (Twisted pipe
cleaners also can be twisted for hands and
attached to the end of the arm wires.) Then,
pad and cover the arms and twist into the
chicken wire at the shoulders. Pad the head
and body with thin layers of stuffing, keeping the face (and shoulders if they will be
exposed) smooth and free from wrinkles.
Cover the entire doll with pale pink stretch

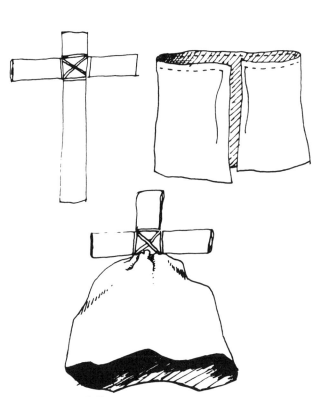

Newspaper doll.

material, such as nylon. Paint or embroider the features and make hair from wool or silk.

If a man or boy doll is required, before molding, cut the wire up the middle about 5 inches from the base (about one third of the height) for the legs. Form the legs into cylinders and mold to shape. Then proceed to completion.

CYLINDER DOLL

To make a cylinder doll, you will need a cardboard cylinder (for example, a toilet roll base); four pieces of string 12-14 inches long; four newspaper squares 3 inches square; four newspaper pieces 1½ inches by ¾ inches; padding; nylon stocking or stretch material; and wool.

At both ends of the cylinder that you have selected pierce holes opposite each other. Wind one 3 inch square paper around one piece of string and Scotch tape it for the arm. Tightly roll up one of the smaller pieces of paper and tie it at the end of the string for the hand. Thread the other end of the string through both holes at one end

Sock doll.

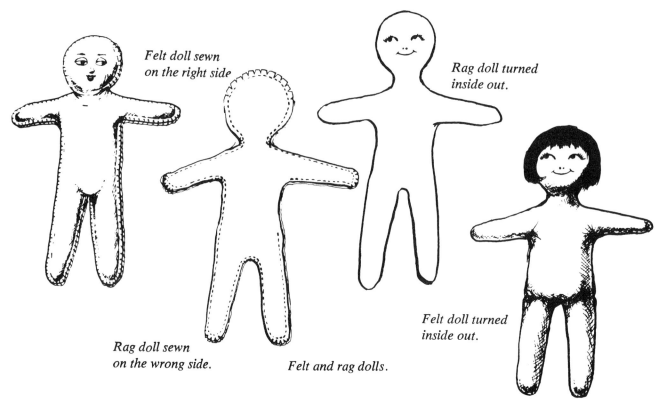

Felt doll sewn on the right side

Rag doll turned inside out.

Rag doll sewn on the wrong side.

Felt and rag dolls.

Felt doll turned inside out.

of the roll. Make another arm and hand at the end of this string. Repeat with the other piece of string to make legs. Pad the clothespin for the head and cover the padding with nylon, pulling it tight. Embroider the facial features and sew on wool hair. Slide the legs of the peg over the taut string stretching across the end of the cylinder and wedge in.

NEWSPAPER DOLL

You will need a double sheet of large newspaper and wool or string. Fold half the newspaper sheet four times to make a neat strip for the head and body. Make similar smaller strip for the arms. Fold the body strip in half and put the arms through the fold and tie the body tight above and below the arms. Fold the piece to be used for the skirt once each way and join the piece at the back with Scotch tape. Bind the lower edge of the skirt with Scotch tape to make it stand firmly. Fold remaining quarter sheet of paper six times and stuff it between the head folds. Pad the head, paint the features, and sew on the hair.

SOCK DOLL

To make a sock doll, you will need a white or pale pink sock, stuffing, wool or floss silk. Use a sock with no holes or darns in the back, because the heel will be used to form the face. Cut off the toe at the instep and cut in two lengthwise to form arms. Fold sock in half at the back of the heel and cut up the middle of the ribbing for legs. Backstitch the legs inside out, turn right-side-out and stuff. Stitch across the tops of the legs to make a joint. Stuff the body, tie tightly around the neck, stuff the head very firmly, and draw the cut edges together at the back of the head. Sew and stuff the arm pieces and sew them on across the top of the shoulders. Embroider or paint the features, and make the hair of wool or floss silk.

RAG DOLL

To make the still very popular rag doll, you will need pale pink or unbleached muslin, stuffing, and wool. Trace the shape of the doll from a pattern onto muslin. Sew together both halves of the pattern with a

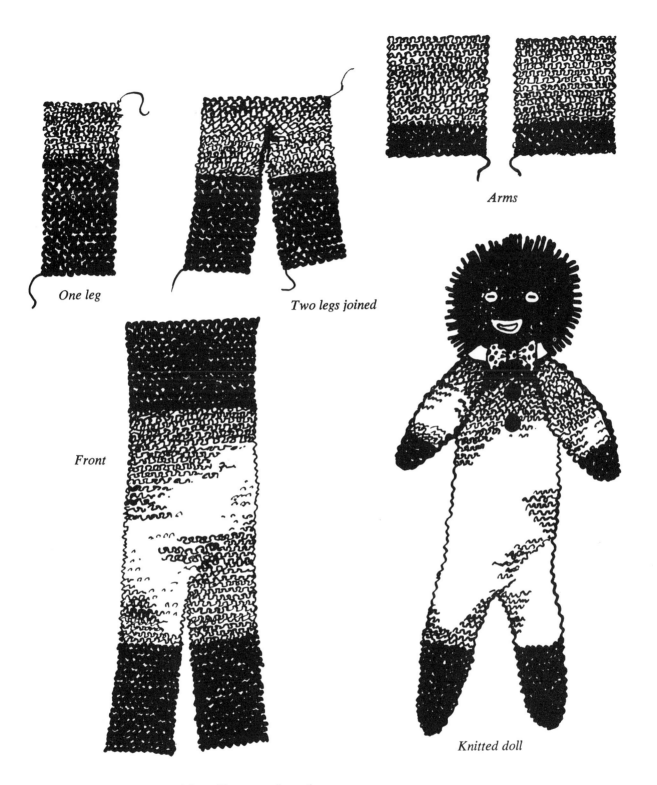

One leg

Two legs joined

Arms

Front

Knitted doll

backstitch or by machine. Be sure that the side you want to show in the end is turned inside out leaving one side open for stuffing. Cut small Vs out of all curved edges and snip the corners close to the stitching to allow the seams to lie flat when the work is turned right-side-out. Again, paint or embroider the features and sew on wool for the hair.

FELT DOLL

Just a few materials are needed for the felt doll: natural felt, stuffing, and wool.

Using the felt, cut out the shape from a pattern as you would for a rag doll. It is not advisable to pencil the outline as marks on the felt are not easily erased. Joining is done on the right side either by overcasting

83

or stab stitch (see chapter on Glovemaking). Finish as rag doll.

KNITTED DOLL

All you need for a knitted doll is 4-ply or double knitting wool and stuffing. As with the cardboard dolls, knitted dolls can be made by very young children as well as older ones and adults. Starting with a straightforward teddy bear for the beginner and proceeding to the more elaborate pierrot, Puss 'n' Boots, and costume doll for older children and adults, in each case the same basic strip of plain knitting is used, which can be varied in size by adjusting the number of stitches. Knit two legs and put both groups of stitches onto one needle. Now knit twice the length required for the body and head, divide the stitches, and knit the back part of the legs. Fold the knitted strip in half and overcast firmly around the outside edges of the doll, being careful to match up knitted lines and leaving an opening for stuffing. Stuff and finish the doll as you like.

Children can be encouraged to make their own patterns and adaptations; for example, the cardboard doll pattern makes an easy glove puppet if the legs are omitted and the sides cut straight and wide to form a skirt. Patterns can also be traced from toys and animals—ducks, dogs, cats, balls, and bricks, among others. Children will contrive and experiment to make successful dolls from a variety of materials other than those suggested here—pipe cleaners, string and rope, raffia, hanks of wool, wooden spoons; in fact, the more varied the materials made available for children to use, the more satisfying and surprising are the results.

Knitted dressed doll.

Dorothy Wright

leather

MANY BEAUTIFUL AND USEFUL THINGS may be made from leather, and the better the leather the better the work. Nevertheless, good work may be done with inexpensive leather provided it is suitable in type and weight. Accuracy in measurement and good finish are essential, and both old and young will find satisfaction in learning the skills that come with a little practice.

There are four ways to join leather: stitching, sticking, thonging, and riveting. The first two are the ones most used today. Well-done handstitching is a decoration as well as part of the construction, and until the invention of the sewing machine, all leather was sewn by hand by the same methods that leather craftsmen use today.

LEATHER FOR CRAFTS

Hides from cattle are treated by the tanner in many different ways and are used for making luggage and car upholstery, among other things. Skins are very large, but it is possible to buy kip sides, which are smaller and suitable for heavier articles. Natural hide and calf are used for embossing or tooling, staining, and polishing. Skins run in sizes from 20–30 square feet, but leather may be bought in smaller sections.

Morocco is goatskin. The hard-grained skin comes in lovely colors in sizes between 3½ and 12 square feet. Every sort of small article may be made from this firm, fine-grained leather. There are two weights, wallet and bag weight. The soft-grain type is used for bookbinding (see chapter on Bookbinding).

Sheepskin is cheaper than morocco leather. In tanning, the surface is often embossed in imitation of the grain or surface of another leather. Roan, basil, and Persian are all sheepskins. Natural sheep is sold in some craft shops. It is cheaper than hide and can be tooled lightly.

Pigskin is a fine leather for the more advanced worker. Weight, that is, thickness, varies, and the buyer should state his purpose. Skins are about 15 square feet and

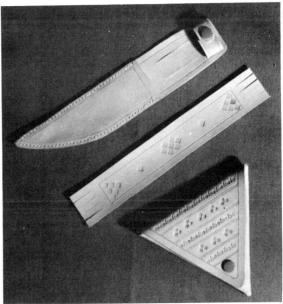

Knife sheath, book mark, and purse — all in natural tooling calf and tooled with homemade and commercial punches.

Snake-covered belts.

come in golden and tan colors with a distinctive marking of small holes, varying in pattern. (A pig-grained sheep will have an even pattern.)

Suede is not a separate leather but a velvety finish given to certain hides. It is used mostly for clothing or for the linings of bags.

Skiver is very thin leather from a skin split horizontally. It is used for linings or for something having a firm backing. All sorts of fancy surfaces are put on skiver,

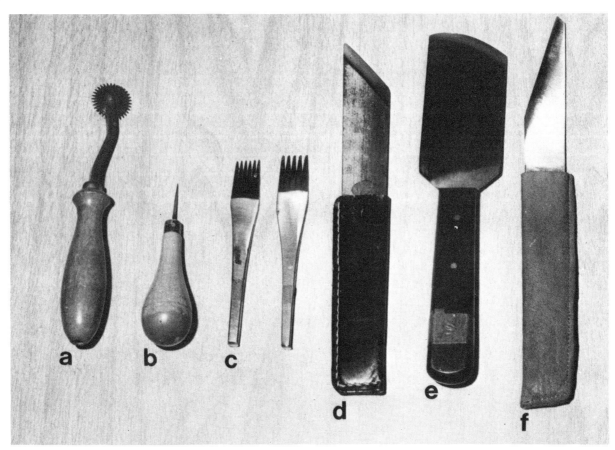

Essential tools are: (a) spacing wheel, (b) awl, (c) handsome stitch markers, (d) English skiving knife, (e) French skive, and (f) cutting knife.

but it has no tensile strength and without reinforcement will tear like paper.

Watersnakes are long narrow skins in jewel colors. They are paper-thin but quite strong, and with reinforcement, many things may be made from them.

Off-cuts. Mixed pieces of leather are sometimes sold by the pound. You must be very careful about your selection because the heavy, coarse-grained pieces and scraps of furniture hide are virtually useless. You should go to a good supplier for off-cuts.

Care of leather. Skins and pieces must be kept flat or rolled, never folded. It is almost impossible to get creases out of grained leather. The wrapping paper used to cover the leather should be fastened with Scotch tape or soft tape, never string or elastic bands.

ESSENTIAL TOOLS

For cutting-out:
1. Knives, one for cutting, one for skiving
2. Oilstone
3. Stropping board or razor strop
4. Shears
5. Metal square
6. Metal ruler

For stitching:
1. Stitch markers or thonging chisels
2. Stitch-spacing wheel
3. Awl, diamond-shaped point
4. Wooden mallet
5. Harness needles Nos. 5 and 6 (these have no points)
6. Linen or button threads

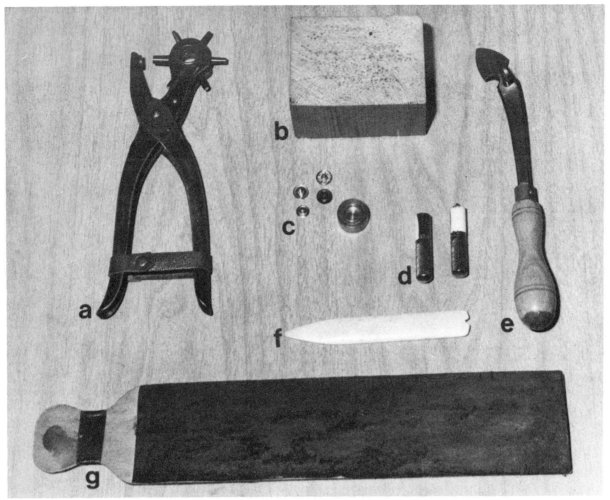

*Other tools include: (a) circular punch, (b) end-grain softwood block,
(c) four parts of snap fastener, (d) tool to set press fastener,
(e) screw creaser, (f) bone folder, and (g) stropping board.*

7. Beeswax
8. A block of end-grain wood
9. Improvised clamp

Finishing:
1. Concentrated leather stains
2. Creaser
3. Press stud tool

General:
1. Bone folder
2. Six-hole pliers punch
3. Iron hammer (household)

The experienced worker may add other tools to his kit. In a leather class most tools can be used jointly. A knife, ruler, awl, and, if possible, the stitch marker should be personal tools. A satisfactory knife with blades that can be used for cutting and skiv-ing is the Stanley Slimknife 5900. Blade 5901 is suitable for skiving, but the knife is not strong enough for heavy use by a number of people.

The stropping board for sharpening heavier knives should be made at home, using an emery cloth from a hardware store. Knives should be kept sharp by using a grinding wheel, taking care to hold the blade at the angle of the original level. Nothing is more essential to the craft than sharp knives, and they will need constant attention.

In times past, saddle makers used a wooden clamp, now unobtainable, to hold the pieces of leather together so that both hands were free for sewing. However, you can improvise a leather clamp by getting two pieces of hardboard, about 12 inches

Fastenings include: (a) three parts of a purse fastener, (b) button molds, (c) tubular rivets, and (d) tool for setting tubular rivets.

by 5 inches, and attaching them with two spring clothespins. This will hold small articles while sewing. Larger things may be held between the knees or on the table. Stitching ponies are available from leathercraft suppliers.

Fittings. Various fittings may be bought and need only simple tools and the knife, hammer, and six-hole punch to put onto the leather. Some of these include:

Snap fasteners
Eyelets
Heavy zip fasteners (dress ones will not do)
Rivets
Buckles
Purse fasteners
Button molds

Bag-making requires domes, rings, and turnlocks, which may be found at special suppliers.

ADHESIVES

The leatherworker should approach the variety of new adhesives with caution. Those he will use constantly are:

Rubber cements such as Sanford's, which is a spirit solution. These are flexible and should be applied lightly to both surfaces and allowed to become tacky before joining. Household white emulsion glues, such as Elmer's and Weldwood, are satisfactory for some leatherwork, but these are not waterproof and not as lasting as contact cements. Always check the labels of a product for its suitability before using on leather.

Contact cements. These include Barge's, Master's, Craftsmen, and Weldwood and are permanent, waterproof, and flexible. They are applied to both surfaces of the leather to be glued. The surfaces of the leather are scraped and scratched to assist adhesion. Place the contact cement on both surfaces and allow to dry for 15 minutes. Then, press both sides together. Once they are adhered, the pieces cannot be moved or readjusted. Epoxy glues also may be

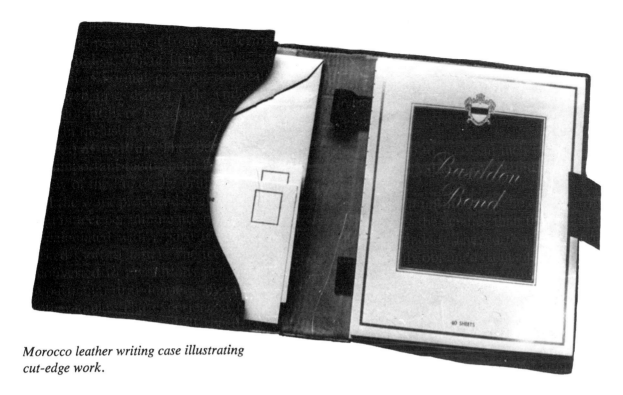

Morocco leather writing case illustrating cut-edge work.

used, but these are not as convenient as contact cements because they require mixing.

Reinforcements and padding. Some small leather goods are reinforced with cardboard and flexible white tagboard, bought at any art supply store. Thin foam-rubber makes useful padding between leather and lining or as reinforcement and gives a rich look and feel. Thin leathers such as fancy or ecrase skivers may be backed with nonwoven interfacing (used by dressmakers) to strengthen them. Rubberized linen is sold by the yard for belt and bag-making and can be ironed on.

LEATHERWORK

Cut-edge work is the simplest type of leatherwork. Morocco, pigskin, sheep, and fine hide are excellent for cut-edge work that can be used for wallets, purses, writing and key cases, photograph frames, portfolios, and many other things.

Turned-over edge work requires good skiving and assembly, sometimes with reinforcing and padding. Leathers used for this type of work are the same used for cut-edge work, in addition to soft goat and sheep for flexible articles.

Sewing kit made from soft-grained leather lined with suede and illustrating turned-over edge work.

Leather watch straps.

89

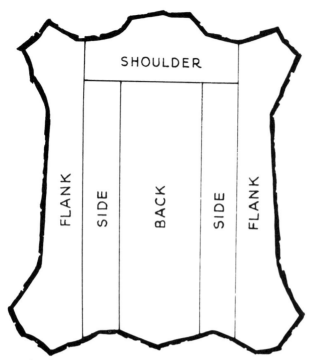

Fig. 1.

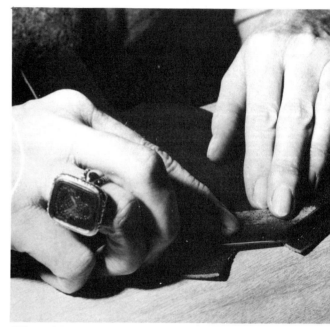

When skiving or shaving with an English knife, use your free hand to control the action.

Tooled or embossed work is suitable for blotters, bookmarkers, and small purses in simple shapes.

Built-up work. Leather is mounted over a rigid foundation such as cardboard to make folders or boxes. Sticking is used more than stitching, and grained skivers may be used to good effect.

Dress accessories. Covered belts, buttons, and hair slides are made from watersnakes and skivers, belts from hide, and contemporary watch straps from off-cuts. Suede is suitable for sectional berets, soft bags, and belts. Here stitching is done on the sewing machine and the work turned. Hems may be bonded with rubber cement.

TECHNIQUES

Cutting-out. Lay out pattern on morocco, pig, or sheepskin (Fig. 1). The back is the firmest and finest grain. Main pieces and those that show most should come from here. Sides and flanks are looser and often thinner, so these should be used for pockets and gussets. As a rule, pieces for one article should run either up and down or from side to side of the skin. Leather is expensive,

and economy and care are needed in cutting-out, but the pieces can be laid right against each other so there need be little waste. Scraps saved will often be useful for small articles.

Patterns. Always cut a really accurate cardboard pattern first. (Professionals use sheet zinc.) The time and trouble expended in doing this is well worthwhile. Such patterns are valuable tools with which to learn accuracy in cutting squares and curves and by saving them, you can always repeat the article without trouble. A pattern with a tricky shape should be cut in paper first, folding at the center so that both sides are alike. Then it is transposed to cardboard. Cereal boxes can be used for pattern-cutting.

Mark the right side of the leather from the pattern and cut all straight lines with a straight edge and knife; cut curves with shears or scissors. Hardboard makes a good cutting surface.

Skiving. When more than two surfaces are to be joined, the edges may have to be thinned by what is called skiving or paring. The edge of the leather is held at

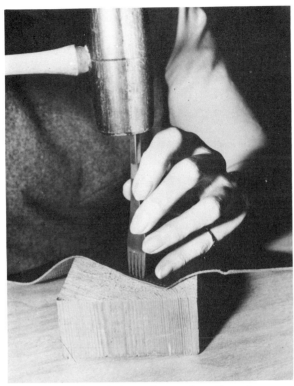

When using the stitch marker and mallet, place the leather on the end-grain block.

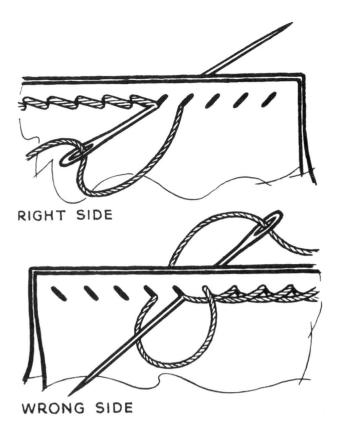

RIGHT SIDE

WRONG SIDE

Fig. 2. Stitching with one needle.

the edge of the table and is beveled for about ⅜ of an inch. The knife is held almost flat and must be very sharp. Paring requires practice and is an essential part of turned-over edge work.

Stitching. The most important operation in stitching is the marking of the holes. First, use the creaser or ruler and bone folder, mark a line the width of a stitch from the edge. Holes may be made in two ways:

1. With the stitch marker or thonging chisel and the mallet. The leather is placed on a piece of end-grain wood and the chisel held with the left hand vertically on the marked line. It is tapped lightly and smartly, not bashed hard. Then the first prong is placed in the last hole made, the other prongs on the line, and so on. The operation is completed by going through the holes with the diamond-pointed awl, holding it vertically and at the same slant to meet the holes. Some workers use the awl as they sew.

2. With the stitch-spacing wheel, which runs along the marked line making dots, which are afterward awled through. Pro-

vided that the diamond awl is used and held in such a way as to make the holes on a 45° angle to the marked line, this is quite a good method.

Sewing. When both sides of the work are visible, sewing is done with two needles, one at either end of a long length of waxed thread. The work is held with the edges just showing in the improvised clamp, the marked side facing the right hand. Starting with the hole farthest away, put the right-hand needle through and center the thread by holding the needles together above the work. Then put the right-hand needle through the next hole coming toward you and the left one in front of it in the same hole. Pull both through and repeat this procedure until the entire side is sewn. If you are left handed, reverse the procedure. The threads should drop below the work, well out of the way.

When only one side of the stitch line is visible, one needle is used in a backstitch. The thread at the back of the work must be held forward so that the needle is always behind it; this looks like stemstitch on the back. The ends at start and finish are fin-

91

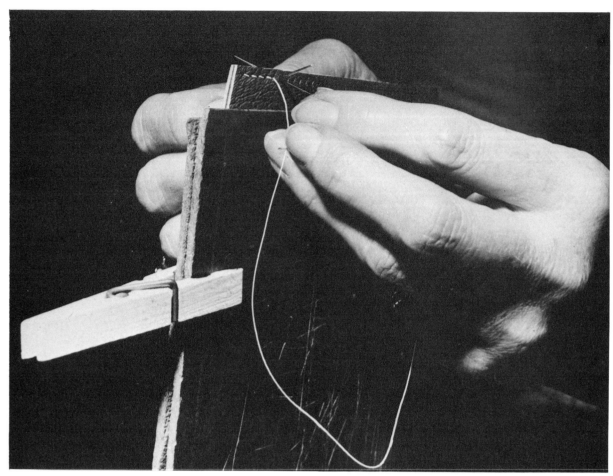

Closeup of sewing with two needles showing the stitches, the holes, and the position of the hands. Note the improvised clamp holding the work.

The embossing tools held by the leatherworker are four punches made from brass screws and nails filed into patterns and set in dowels. On the table are two commercial punches.

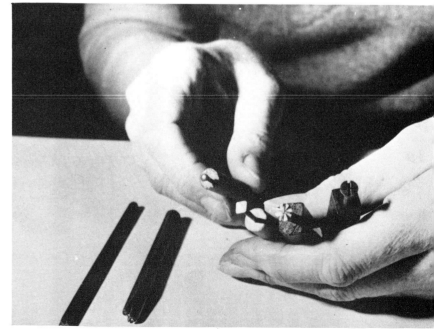

ished off on the back of the piece (Fig. 2).

Finishing. The edges of morocco, pig, and sheepskin articles should be finished with a color stain, thinned with water, and polished while damp with a soft rag. This improves the appearance of the piece and seals the edges. The polishing is done with a pinching action, using the finger and thumb. The final finish is to crease a line with an edge creaser on damp leather. The creaser should leave a clean polished line. These finishes are done to the edges of necklines and armholes before a piece is assembled.

Tooling or embossing. Natural hide, calf, and sheep may be decorated with lines and patterns stamped into the damp surface of the leather. Lines are made with a tracing tool, and patterned punches can be bought or made from filed brass screwheads set in short lengths of dowel. The simplest method for tooling is to draw a design on thin paper first and then lightly mark through the paper design to the leather before hammering the punches with the mallet. Hide may be left plain or stained with spirit stains and polished.

L. A. G. Howard

metalwork

THE CRAFT OF THE METALWORKER has a long history. The importance of the craft in shaping the destiny of mankind can be readily assessed by the student. If one accepts the term in the broadest sense, metalwork is a craft that can be practiced at home with the simplest of tools yet can range to the complex industrial processes of mass production. What follows is a simple account of some aspects of metalwork. It is hoped that the reader will be induced to practice and study in greater depth this fascinating and rewarding subject.

BENCHWORK

Benchwork forms the basis of most of the metalworker's activities.

The metalworker's bench should be of sound and rigid construction. Ideally, the bench top should be of hardwood at least 1½ inch thickness. The edges need protection, and this is given by angle iron housed flush with the top and screwed in position. The bench height is a matter of personal choice; 30–32 inches appears to be the norm.

The engineer's parallel vise. Being solid and strong with a positive parallel action, this vise is most suitable for general benchwork. Removable jaws are fitted as standard and have either serrated or smooth faces. The body of the vise is made of cast iron, and the vise jaw is made of hardened steel. The body is of a brittle nature and should never be struck heavily with a hammer.

Vise clamps are protective pieces of soft sheet metal fitted over the vise jaws. They prevent the gripped metal from being marked. They are simple to make, the most suitable metals being lead, copper, brass, or zinc. Clip-on vise clamps with fiber faces can be obtained ready made.

Hand vises. These are small portable vises for holding small work. They also provide the craftsman with a "steel hand" to hold sheet metal in position for machine drilling.

Gas welded figure showing how textures can be built up in blobs and ridges by painting with the welding flame and texturing with a brush.

The toolmaker's clamp. This clamp is used to hold pieces of metal together in a firm, precise manner. Marking out, drilling and cutting are some of the techniques carried out on metal held with a toolmaker's clamp. Heavy treatment of the clamp must be avoided because once it is bent, the screws will render the clamp useless.

The hacksaw is a frame saw that uses replaceable blades. A wing nut and screw enable the correct tension to be given to the blade. The shape of the handle may be D-

94

shaped or pistol-shaped or cast in aluminum alloy or simply a wooden file-type handle. The frame is normally adjustable to allow blades of various lengths to be fitted. The depth of cut is limited to the depth of the frame. Provision is made to overcome this by allowing the blade to turn at right angles to the frame. Depth of cut is thus made unlimited; only the position of the cut from the end of the work is restricted by the frame.

Cutting technique. The hacksaw cuts only in straight lines. Slight errors can be corrected by twisting the handle in the opposite direction of the error. The cutting action is continued until back on course, and then the slight twisting action is released.

Junior hacksaws are small hacksaws that hold their blades by springiness in the frame. The frame and handle form an outline shape in one piece of metal. The blades have fine teeth for small work.

Hacksaw blades are made from high speed steel and are either "all hard" or "flexible."

The flexible type, as the name suggests, will take more misuse without breakage than the former. The teeth of the blade are set to give clearance to the thickness of the blade (0.055 inch), and when fitted the teeth point away from the handle. The number of teeth per inch (TPI) are obtainable at 14, 18, 24, and 32.

The following table will enable the reader to select the correct blade for the job in hand.

TPI
14 Soft metals of thick sections
18 Harder metals of thick sections
24 Hard metals of small sections
32 Thin walled tubes, hard metals of thin sections

Tension files are held in the standard hacksaw by special clips. Being round in section, the cutting file can move in any direction with ease. Correct tension in these files is important to avoid breakage.

Piercing saws are used by decorative metal workers. The pierced work produced is the counterpart of the woodworker's fretwork. The frames are adjustable to enable broken blades of reasonable length to be used.

Slotting blades are hacksaw blades that cut slots of special widths, for example, a screwdriver slot on the head of a screw.

Sheet saw uses the standard hacksaw blade and has no frame, allowing unlimited positioning and depth of cut. The hacksaw blade is attached to the bottom edge of the sheet saw blade, which in appearance is similar to the carpenter's hand saw.

Files are of great importance to the metalworker. The function of the file is to remove waste metal and in the final process to impart a surface finish. Filing by hand tends to be an arduous process, and, therefore, the amount left after cutting should be minimal. About 1/16 inch to be removed by hand filing would be an acceptable margin.

Files are designated by length, cut, and section. They are made in a variety of types and sizes. The following are in common use.

1. Flat—tapers in width and thickness from the middle to the tip. The file teeth are cut on both faces and edges. The flat is used for general work.
2. Hand—tapers in thickness only, the width is parallel. Normally, one edge is smooth (safe edge) to enable accurate corners to be filed.
3. Half round — segmental shape used for filing flat and concave surfaces. It is also most useful for filing sharp corners.
4. Round — used for concave surfaces and the enlarging of circular holes.
5. Three square—used for forming accurate corners. Sometimes called triangular.
6. Square — used for filing slots and holes that are rectangular or square.

Cuts. The teeth of the file can be formed by either single or double cuts. Single cuts are parallel and at an angle of 55°–60° across the blade. The double cuts crisscross to form a surface of diamond-shaped sections. Single cut files are used on softer metals, such as aluminum, because the teeth do not clog easily. Double cut files are suitable for iron and steel.

Grades. For general use the following grades are used—rough, middle, bastard, second cut, smooth, and dead smooth. For heavy work the first three grades are used. The most useful file for general work is the second cut. The smooth file is used for general finishing, and the dead smooth grade is for finishing on hard metal.

Lengths. Files in general use are made in lengths from 4–14 inches. The blades are made from hardened and tempered cast steel, the tang being left soft to avoid breakage and perhaps injury to the user.

File handles. A file must never be used without a properly fitted handle. The handle may be of wood or plastic, and some of the latest types have excellent methods of securing the handle to the file tang.

Filing technique. Filing is a difficult art to master. The student will need practice and guidance in the workshop situation. The correct stance is important. The feet are positioned in a natural splay; the body remains stationary. The action comes from the shoulder, the file blade moving parallel with the floor. The movement and stance are comfortable and natural. A speed of 60 strokes per minute will produce maximum results with the minimum of fatigue.

Drawfiling. This is a finishing process, imparting to the metal an accurate surface with the sheen that is characteristic of good work. In drawfiling the file is moved over the work at right angles to its path of motion. Both hands are used to hold the file, the index fingers meeting on the top of the file immediately above the work. A smooth or dead smooth file is the grade used, with

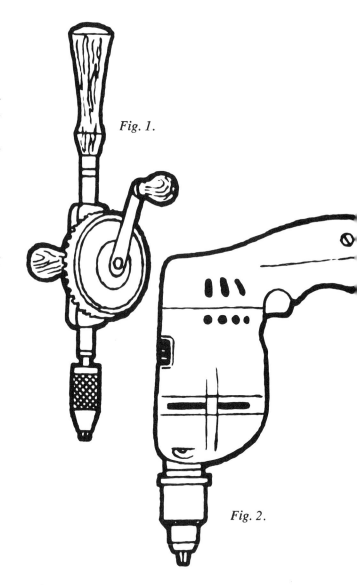

Fig. 1.

Fig. 2.

the unworn part of the blade near the handle area of the file chosen.

Pinning. During the action of filing, small pieces are apt to get lodged in the file teeth. Thus held, they travel with the file stroke causing deep unwanted scratches on the surface of the metal. Chalked files have less chance of picking up pieces. The pieces once lodged can be removed with a pointed piece of soft metal such as brass or mild steel. Wire brushes or file cards are used to clean files to prevent pinning, but overuse blunts the teeth and shortens the effective life of the file.

DRILLS AND DRILLING

Flat drills. These are simple to make and, in exceptional circumstances, are most useful, for example, when a special size hole is required and a twist drill is not available.

Twist drills. These are highly efficient when ground at the correct angle. The tip ends in an edge called a web; a spiral groove called a flute allows the swarf (waste metal) to escape. Modern drills are made from high speed steel.

Center punch. This is a hardened and tempered punch made from tool steel and ground to a conical point. The body of the punch is knurled (diamond-shaped segments cut by a knurling tool) to make for better gripping. The purpose of the punch is to make a conical-shaped indentation on the surface of metal in the precise position of the center of the intended hole. The center punch hole locates the tip of the drill (web) and prevents it from wandering.

Pilot holes. Where larger holes are required, it is normal practice to locate the larger web in a drilled hole (pilot hole). The pilot drill is positioned by a center punch in the usual way.

Speed of drilling. The speed of the drill is an important factor both from the point of view of the life of the drill and the quality of the work produced. Tables giving the speed in feet per minute are obtainable and are calculated with regard to the material worked (soft to hard). The feet per minute is converted to revolutions per minute for the particular drill diameter by reference to another table. The experienced craftsman can select the correct drill speed by what appears to be sheer instinct.

As a very rough rule-of-thumb guide, it can be said that the smaller the drill the more rpm; the softer the material the greater the rpm. Therefore a small drill in soft material will be set at a high speed; conversely a large drill and soft material will produce the need for very slow rpm.

Drill designation. Drills are generally designated in four size systems: (1) fractions of an inch, (2) numbers, (3) letters, and (4) metric.

Hand drills are used for work of a light nature on the bench or in the vise. (Fig. 1.)

Electric pistol drills are used for drill-

Candelabrum made by the author has a steel frame, brass holders, and copper spikes.

ing holes up to $\frac{5}{16}$ of an inch in situ. They are of great value to the maintenance fitter. (Fig. 2.)

Taps and tapping. The hole to be drilled must always be smaller than the size of the thread intended. The correct size tapping drill is easily obtained from a table.

Tap. A tap is a screw made from hardened steel. Flutes are cut along its length to provide cutting edges and to allow the swarf to escape. Taps are made in sets of three:

1. Taper—for entering and centralizing (starting the thread)
2. Second—suitable for finishing a through hole
3. Plug—used to cut a full thread to the bottom of a blind hole.

Dies are used with die holders to produce external threads by hand. The external thread (die thread) is always the last to be cut of a pair (nut and bolt) because of the adjustment in diameter size that is possible.

The popular die is circular and split at

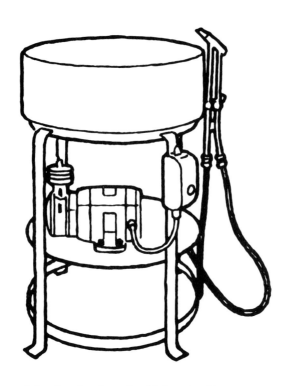

A revolving brazing hearth with brazing blowpipe.

A gas brazing torch used at the brazing hearth.

one radius. A tapered mouth allows the thread to be started. The split die can be adjusted by screws in the die holder, to close the split or allow the split to be fully open. This allows a small control over the exact size of the thread produced.

The die holder is used with the circular rebate uppermost. The work should be slightly chamfered to ease the start. Care should be given to start off square, or a drunken thread will result.

BRAZING,
HARD AND SOFT SOLDERING

Brazing is a method of joining metal by the fusion of brass (spelter). The metal must be clean where it is to be joined. The cleaning is best done with a file or emery cloth, and in some instances a small chamfered edge where the spelter is to run is an advantage.

Flux is Borax or a brand equivalent. This is supplied in powder form and is mixed with water to form a smooth paste the consistency of cream. The purpose of the flux is to aid the running of the spelter and to prevent oxidation during the brazing operation.

Technique. The job to be brazed is positioned on the brazing hearth with fire bricks placed in such a manner as to trap the heat from the torch around the job. The job is cleaned, fluxed, and the joint in position. The torch flame heats the job to cherry red, and the stick of brazing rod is touched on the joint line. If conditions are correct the brass melts on contact and floods the joint, forming a small fillet on either side. A clean job, the right flux, a good joint, and the correct heat will result in success every time.

Silver soldering. Much less heat is required for silver soldering than for brass brazing, but otherwise they have much in common. Borax or a brand equivalent is again the flux used. The solder is an alloy of silver, copper, and zinc. For general use in the workshop, the solder is obtainable in three grades: easy, hard, and enameling—in ascending order of their fusion point.

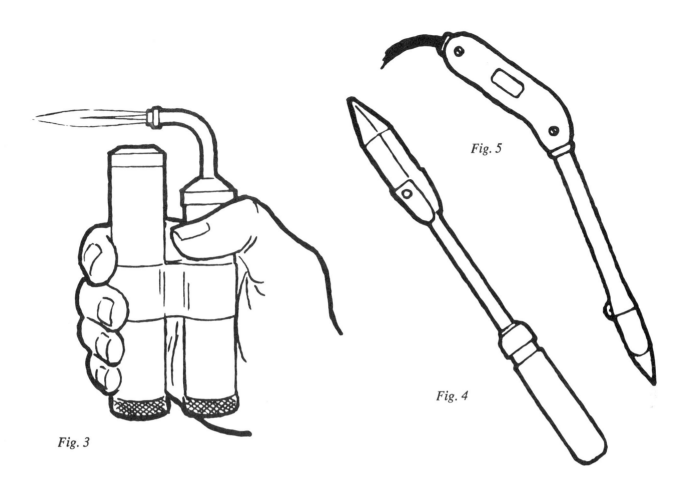

Fig. 3

Fig. 5

Fig. 4

Since they have distinct melting points it is possible to make joints close to each other without melting the previous joints.

Silver soldering is easily practiced at home; the equipment necessary is simple and inexpensive. A small square of asbestos, a gas or spirit blow torch (Fig. 3), and a few fire bricks are all that is required. For soldering silver only the best grade solder is used. This consists of four parts silver to one part copper and zinc.

Soft soldering is the term given to the method of joining metals together with an alloy of lead and tin. The solder is carried to the job by means of a soldering iron.

Soldering iron (tinman's) consists of a copper bit fixed to a steel rod, which in turn is fixed to the handle. The bit may be straight or hatchet-shaped and can be obtained in a variety of sizes. (Fig. 4)

Electric soldering iron is convenient to use, reaches the correct heat, and remains constant at that heat. (Fig. 5)

The techniques of soft soldering. The following notes outline the technique in-

volved for the tinman's iron heated by gas in the tinman's stove. Exclude the references to green flames and reheating when using an electric iron.

1. The point of the iron is first coated with solder (tinned). This is done by filing the copper bit bright and clean, taking care to remove a minimal amount of copper. The iron is now heated until the gas flame turns green (correct heat) and is then dipped into the flux and then into solder, twisting the bit to insure coating on all sides.

2. Once tinned, the iron is reheated, dipped again into the flux, and rubbed against a stick of solder.

3. Having thus picked up a liberal coating of solder, the bit is placed in position on the joint. Heat is transferred to the jcb. The solder flows into the joining gap. This continues as the bit is moved slowly along, the solder flooding the joint as it goes. When this ceases to happen, the process outlined in step 2 is repeated.

It is essential that the joint is clean (free from grease or oxides)—a finger mark will ruin the preparation.

Fluxes. These are either "active" or "passive" or, to put it in another sense, acid or nonacid. The nonacid types are usually resin-based and can be obtained in powder, paste, or grease form. Solder is used in a wire form with a core of this type of flux. Because the flux is nonacid, the residue left on the joint has no corrosive effect. All electrical work is soldered with this type of flux.

The acid fluxes are usually in a liquid form. Zinc chloride is the commonest flux and is used for tinplate, brass, and copper.

FORGE WORK

Of all the traditional crafts, none hold the magic of the past so convincingly as forge work. There are four main types of equipment:

1. The forge—for metal heating using blacksmith's breeze (small coke)
2. The anvil—for supporting the metal during forging
3. The tools—hammers, fullers, swages, etc.
4. The tongs—to hold hot metal

The forge consists basically of a brick-lined hearth, a hood to extract the coke fumes, and an air pipe to carry a blast of air to the forge fire (tuyere). The air blast can come from hand bellows, but it is more common today to use a mechanical blower. A water tank is fixed to the back of the forge for the purpose of cooling the tuyere. (Fig. 6)

The anvil is of the well-known traditional shape and may weigh up to three hundred pounds. The body is made of wrought iron, and a hardened steel face is welded to the top. The curved tusk is used for curving metal (beak). A small ledge close to the face is the cutting table. The hardened steel face is used to support the metal and should not itself be hammered. At the opposite end to the beak are two holes, one square

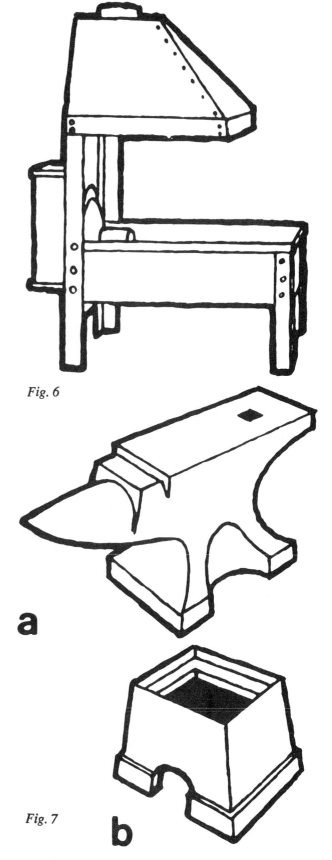

Fig. 6

a

Fig. 7   **b**

for holding various tools and the other (round) used as a punch hole. (Fig. 7a)

The anvil is supported at working height on a cast stand (Fig. 7b) or, in the manner of old, on a section of tree trunk.

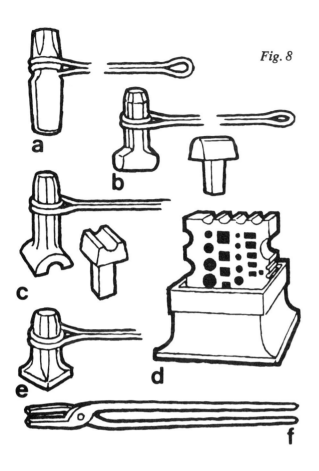

Fig. 8

Tools

Hammers. The larger weights of the engineers' hammers are often used in metalwork. There is, however, a special forging hammer with a slightly convex striking face.

For heavy work a sledge hammer is used. Two workers are needed for this, the smith and the striker. The smith holds the work and indicates to the striker with a small hammer where the blows are to be struck. The signal for the striker to stop is given by the smith ringing the anvil with his small hammer.

Chisels. These may be designed for cutting hot metal or cold metal. The hot chisel is never hardened and tempered and has a cutting edge of 30°. The cold chisel is hardened and tempered and has a cutting edge of 60°. Chisels are used in pairs, the bottom chisel's square shank fitting in the hardie hole. The top chisel is held by a long metal handle that is fitted at right angles to the

chisel and struck by a hammer held in the smith's other hand. (Fig. 8a)

Fullers are used for necking the work (a shoulder with a curved corner). The shoulder formed is often used as a start to a continuous reduction. (Fig. 8b)

Swages are forming irons and are used to produce work of hexagonal or round section. Fullers and swages are used similarly to the chisels. (Fig. 8c)

Swage block is made of cast iron with a series of grooves of various sized hexagon and round half sections around the edge (Fig. 8d). In the center of the block are an assortment of holes of useful size and shape. The blocks are usually 20 inches square with a depth of 7 inches. The block is used for a similar purpose to that of the swage and does away with the need for a huge collection of swages.

Flatters. These are used for finishing off a flat surface. Only one is used, the work being supported on the anvil. (Fig. 8e)

Tongs. The blacksmith uses a variety of shapes in the mouths of his tongs. Shapes in common use are the open mouth, close mouth, hollow bit, vise mouth, square mouth, and pick up tongs. (Fig. 8f)

Techniques of forging

Drawing down. The length of the metal is increased and the cross sectional area deceased on width and thickness.

Upsetting. This is the opposite of drawing down; the cross sectional area is increased at the expense of the length.

Setting down. Thinning down a local area.

Bending. Sharp bends are made in the blacksmith's leg vise. Softer bends are formed by forging on the anvil's beak.

Welding. This technique applies only to wrought iron and mild steel. The metal is heated to white heat, dipped in flux and hammered together. The joints used are the butt joint, scarf joint, and the V joint. The flux for wrought iron is sand, and for mild steel it is calcinated Borax.

101

An aluminum casting being removed from the sand mold.

Bending features. These are mechanical aids to bending and are most useful when a number of uniform curves are required. A lever causes a roller to bend the metal around a central disc.

Punching. The hot metal is held over the punch hole, and the metal is punched from both sides.

Drifting is a final stage in metalwork. The tapered drift opens up the punch hole to a particular shape or size.

Dies. When a die hole is used, punching is a straight through operation—the hole in the die block being the exact diameter of the punch.

Heat treatment of ferrous metals

Steel is a compound of iron and carbon (alloy). The iron and carbon change at 1620°F., and when the metal is quenched (rapidly cooled), the steel is hardened.

High carbon steel (HCS) is known as tool steel. The carbon content of HCS is from 0.60% to 1.50%, cutting tools such as taps and dies having 0.90% to 1.00% carbon.

Hardening. HCS is heated to cherry red and quenched.

Annealing. HCS is softened by heating to cherry red and cooling very slowly. Hot ashes or the hot bricks on the brazing hearth can be used for this.

Tempering. First, the metal goes through the hardening process. A section of metal is cleaned of oxide to a bright metal finish. The metal is reheated, and the color of the bright section will change to the following:

Tempering Color	Temperature °F.
Pale yellow	378
Straw	405
Golden yellow	432
Brown	450
Purple	486
Bright blue	495
Full blue	504
Dark blue	540

The temperature or color at which the metal is quenched determines the amount of tempering given. Where precise results in tempering are necessary, a muffle furnace is used and the element of human error is reduced, the exact temperature being recorded on a dial. Tempering is given to steel to impart a degree of toughness to the metal, because hardened steel is too brittle for most purposes.

Case hardening. An outer skin of HCS is formed on the surface of mild steel or wrought iron. The result is a tough core with a hard antiwear skin. The metal is heated to a bright red and plunged into a powdered carbon compound. The metal picks up the carbon on its surface. The metal is reheated, and the carbon is absorbed into the surface and produces a hard skin when quenched.

Heat treatment of nonferrous metals.

Aluminum, brass, and copper tend to become hard and brittle with cold working and they need annealing (softening) from time to time during the working processes.

Aluminum is annealed by heating to 720°F. and cooling. A piece of soap rubbed on the surface will turn black at this temperature. Cooling can be rapid or slow; the

A fired crucible furnace.

result is the same. Copper is annealed by heating to a dull red and quenching in water. The scale is removed from the copper afterward by pickling in diluted sulfuric acid. Brass is annealed by heating to a dull red and cooling slowly.

FOUNDRY WORK

Casting is a process whereby molten metal is poured or forced into a specially prepared mold. The basic equipment required for a sand mold is as follows:

1. A pattern
2. The casting boxes and sand
3. A means of melting the metal
4. A method and means of transporting the metal to the mold

The pattern is used to create a cavity in the sand. The casting boxes are open-ended frames, used in pairs, one above the other, and located in position by sockets and pins. The sand used by the molder must satisfy certain demands: it must (1) withstand the heat involved; (2) remain porous when compressed; and (3) be able to hold a shape when damp and compressed.

The sand when dampened with water is called green sand. Careful preparation is needed to make it. The molder tests the sand by gripping a handful and then opening his hand. The shape-holding qualities are checked—the wad of sand holding the imprint of the fingers. Experience and skill are of great importance at this stage. Then, the metal is melted in a cupola (small blast furnace) for ferrous metals, and in a crucible furnace for nonferrous metals. Because of the danger involved and the need for expensive equipment, ferrous metal casting is best left to the expert.

For nonferrous casting of a small nature, a steel ladle is used to transport the melt to the mold. But for normal casting, the metal is poured from the lip of the crucible, the crucible being lifted from the furnace by special tongs. Lifted straight from the furnace, the crucible is placed in the ring of a two-handled lifting device. This carrier is so designed that only one of the two operators can control the pour. All pouring operators must wear leather aprons, safety goggles, and asbestos gloves. Molten metal must always be treated with respect. Any left over from the cast is carefully poured into preheated troughs.

If the sand mold were to be inspected before the molten metal was poured, it would be in this condition:

A mass of damp sand carefully packed in molding boxes. In the center would be a cavity the shape and size of the pattern. Holes would lead from the surface of the sand to the cavity. One would allow entry of the melt (gate); another would allow the displaced air to escape and give visual indication that the mold is full (riser). A basin would be cut in the sand at the top of the gate to allow the dross to float to the top during the pour, and vent holes would be made through the sand with a long ½ inch diameter pin to within ½ inch of the cavity to help the sand disperse the locked gases.

The gates and risers are made by packing in tapered cylindrical pieces of wood with sand and carefully extracting later. The

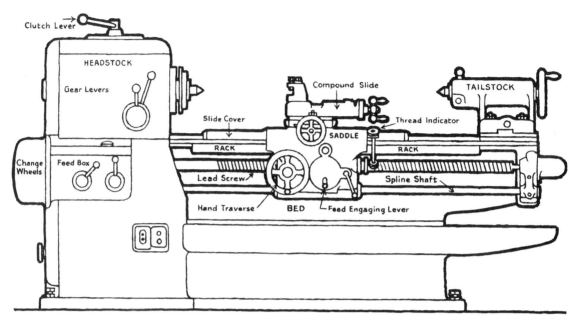

Center lathe

sand basin is made with one of the many trowels used by the molder. Powdered chalk is used to enable the pattern to be extracted without unduly disturbing the sand. Facing sand near the pattern gives the cavity smooth faces when the pattern is removed. The patterns themselves can be split, solid, flat, or cored (with holes).

CENTER LATHE WORK

The lathe is one of man's earliest machines. All lathes are similar in basic principle. The work is revolved against a fixed cutter. The cutter is fixed in the vertical plane but movable by the operator in the horizontal plane. The movement can be manual through a system of screws or automatic from the machine's own power. The basic turning operations of the lathe can be simplified to the following:

1. Straight turning (traversing). The movement of the cutter is parallel to the axis of the rotating work. The surface produced is cylindrical.
2. Facing. The cutter moves at 90° to the rotating axis of the work. The surface produced is flat and situated at the end of the work exposed by the lathe chuck.
3. Taper turning. A combination of the two preceding directions will produce a conical surface. In practice, only one control at a time is used—the compound slide for short tapers. For long tapers it is necessary to turn between centers, with the axis of the work offset by moving the tailstock to one side of the center line. The cutter moves along the correct path, the work's axis is offset.

Lathe parts

The four main parts of the lathe are as follows: the bed, the headstock, tailstock, and the saddle.

The bed is the foundation of the whole machine; it is machined and scraped to a high finish. The standard of accuracy must be exceptionally high because the tailstock and saddle will move along the bed. The bed usually is made from cast iron in one of two standard sections—the flat bed and the inverted V type bed (Fig. 9a).

The headstock. In the headstock are the gears, spindles, and shafts, which give power movement to the machine. The main spindle that rotates the work is bored to receive a center and externally threaded to receive a chuck. The spindle is hollow to allow work to pass through and on some machines can revolve clockwise and counterclockwise (Fig. 9c).

The tailstock is a unit that slides along the bed and can be clamped in any position. A hollow cylinder, bored to receive a center or shank of a drill chuck, is movable longitudinally in the stock. Both the stock and cylinder have independent clamping devices.

The purposes of the tailstock are as follows:

1. To support a nonmoving center (dead) in an accurate, solid position.
2. To enable drilling to take place by holding a drill chuck in the nonrevolving position (dead).
3. To provide a means to offset the axis of long work held between centers for the purpose of taper turning.

Saddle. This unit fits over the lathe bed and moves along the bed by a rack and pinion arrangement. The front of the saddle that is fitted with the controls is the apron. On top of the apron, fitted to a dovetail slide, is the cross slide, which, by its cross movement, enables facing to take place (Fig. 9b).

Mounted on top of the cross slide is fitted a swivel slide called the compound slide. This slide is movable to enable short tapers to be machined. On top of the compound slide, the tool post is fitted in a rigid nonmoving position. Tool posts clamp the lathe tools (cutters) in position and hold from one to four tools.

Screw-cutting. By a train of gears in the headstock, the leadscrew is rotated. The heavy long screw runs the working length of the bed. When a half nut device is pressed in position by a lever in the apron, movement parallel to the axis of the work is given to the cutter. The relationship

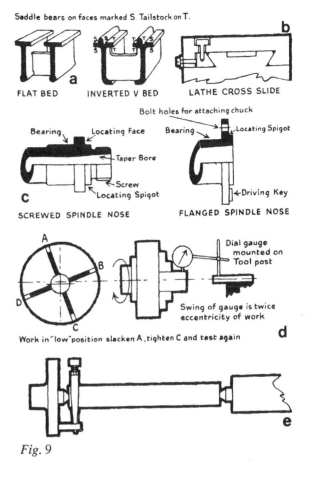

Fig. 9

between the movement of the tool (cutter) and the rotary movement of the work is precise and constant. Thus it is possible to arrange the train of gears in the headstock in such a way that the tool will cut a spiral groove, which is known as a thread.

Chucks. Three-jaw self-center chucks hold round section metal for turning. They are quick and easy in use. Four-jaw chucks have independently operated jaws. Square and odd shaped sections can be held accurately. Some skill is needed for precise setting up, which is usually a trial and error method of centering with an accurate instrument known as a dial test indicator (Fig. 9d).

Magnetic chucks hold ferrous metals that have large contact areas, the best type being a permanent magnet device (the electromagnet being dangerous in the event of a power failure).

105

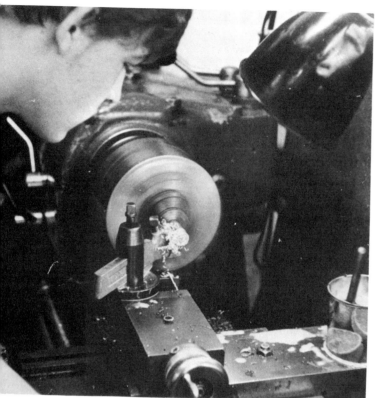

Center lathe turning.

Face plate is a large flat disc that is fitted to the headstock spindle. Irregular work is clamped to the plate by bolts passing through slots. Positioned on the face of the plate, the work can be machined.

Turning between centers. Long work is drilled centrally at each end by a Slocombe drill to receive the points of the centers. The work is positioned between the points with the minimum of pressure and the centers lubricated with tallow or grease. The rotary movement is given to work via a driving plate and striker contacting to a lathe carrier clamped to the work (Fig. 9e).

Automatic feed. Movement of the tool for traversing or facing comes from a feed shaft. This shaft runs underneath the lead screw on most lathes. Once set in motion the machining is completely automatic, although the operator's full attention is required to turn off at the required moment and to check the quality of the work produced.

Sculptured cast form.

Elizabeth Holder

mobiles

IT MAY BE SAID that the history of the mobile began in 1678, the date of the earliest known chandelier. Movement, it is true, was limited, but the basic idea was there. The mid-Victorian bead curtains and hanging lusters were developments of this idea. It was not, however, until the 1930s that the mobile as a moving sculpture became an art form, thanks to the inspiration of Alexander Calder. The purpose of a mobile is to give visual pleasure. It is purely decorative, but if it is to give restful and interesting enjoyment to the beholder it must be well designed on aesthetic principles. The mobile can be a specialized form of craftwork in its own right, but it can also be used as a means of displaying other techniques, for example, embroidery or weaving.

It is important that a mobile should hang freely, so that it can move easily in small currents of air. As it turns it displays constantly changing designs in form and color. The stringing and hanging of a mobile should be in character with its fundamental idea. For example, a mobile embodying the idea of flying birds or kites requires an airy effect and should therefore be strung lightly with invisible nylon thread. In contrast, a heavier droplet design, if it is to be aesthetically pleasing, needs to be balanced by horizontal wires and thicker, more showy supporting thread. A mobile constructed of interesting units, carefully designed and pleasantly colored, can have a most soothing and enjoyable effect on a person watching its continuous, slow movement.

The simple and easily available materials required for this craft make it one eminently suitable for the school or home.

MATERIALS

Scissors; pliers; wire-cutters; Elmer's glue; needles; threads of various types, including invisible nylon thread; paper; card; foil; balsa wood scraps; string; scraps of fabric, felt, and ribbon; beads; sequins; feathers; leaves; twigs; shells; and a variety of other things that you can think of.

Natural objects such as shells can furnish ideas for mobiles as well as provide materials from which they can be made. In addition, the home or classroom scrap bag and other odds and ends offer numerous possibilities. Simple mobiles can be made from paper. Children will enjoy making one composed of a Christmas ring from which the single letters, cut from various colored paper, HAPPY CHRISTMAS could be suspended.

107

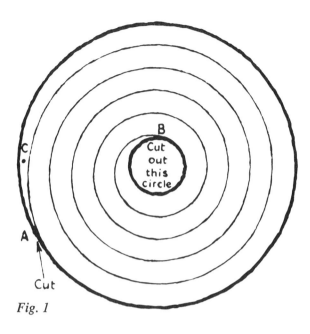

Fig. 1

A more interesting example is the spiral, which is made of paper or tagboard and, as it turns, gives the impression of a climbing motion. The method of construction is shown in Fig. 1. This circle, 7 inches in diameter, should be cut out from brightly-colored tagboard. Starting at A and cutting continuously until B is reached and the center drops out, a spiral is formed. The tagboard spiral may be hung on invisible thread through point C and will make an interesting, simple mobile.

A further development of this spiral theme is the "shower of leaves" mobile. Colorful leaves of decorative shapes are pressed, and then each leaf is made into a unit by mounting it between a piece of lightweight plastic film and an adhesive backed plastic. The adhesive backing on the plastic holds the leaf between the two sheets, and thus a protective film is formed on each side of it (Fig. 2).

Proceeding in this way, make eight units and suspend them individually from a spiral of copper wire of the thicker quality, which you can buy at any craft supply store.

Suspend twisted copper wire at S, Fig. 3, by an invisible nylon thread. In the center of the large spiral hang a smaller spiral to simulate a vine tendril. Wrap the wire of

the second spiral with florist's green para-film, though green tissue paper would be equally suitable, in order to give the idea of a grape vine with its leaves.

The various components of the shower of leaves mobile are comparatively simple to make, but advanced craft techniques can be employed in the construction of more complicated examples. It should be remembered, however, that a mobile is a three-dimensional object intended to be viewed with equal effect from any and all directions.

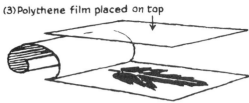

(3) Polythene film placed on top

(2) Leaf placed on sticky surface (1) Clear Fablon with protective cover removed

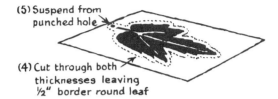

(5) Suspend from punched hole

(4) Cut through both thicknesses leaving ½" border round leaf

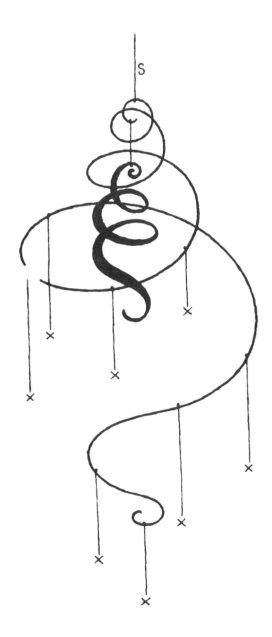

The completed "shower of leaves" mobile.

109

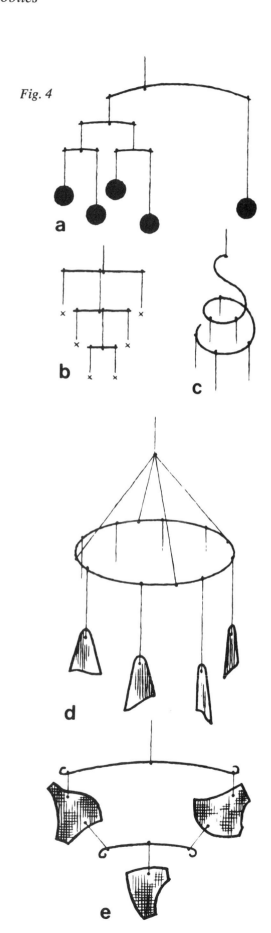

Fig. 4

a

b

c

d

e

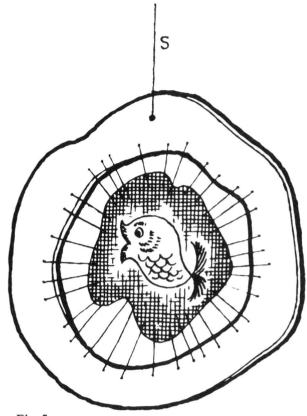

Fig. 5

The stringing of a mobile is a factor that is as important as the design and color of the individual units. Fig. 4 shows various ways of doing this, but very often the theme of the mobile and the design of the units will suggest a method of stringing.

The struts to which the strings are attached can be wire as in (a), in which case coppered welding wire of an appropriate thickness is suitable. Struts can also be made of thin wooden dowel, as in (b). The coil shown in (c) can be made from the springy toy-making wire mentioned previously. Sometimes the springing movement helps the play of the mobile. In (d) a large lampshade ring has been used as the main support of the units. In (e) you see a restricted form of stringing by which the units are linked and the movement of one unit causes the others to move.

Machine embroidery is a craft appropriate for use in the making of more complicated mobiles. Because the stitch is alike on both sides of the material, the piece can be mounted to show both sides, and beads, sequins, or hand decoration can be added on each face. The embroidery can be mounted

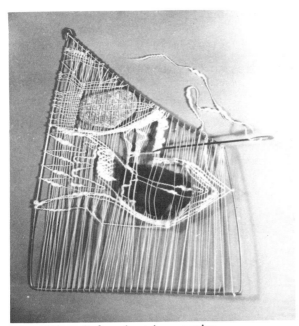

A mobile unit done in string weaving.

String can be used to support a glass drop to form one mobile unit.

between two thicknesses of tagboard, plywood, or plastic sheeting, or stitched to holes in the framework as in Fig. 5. The completed units of embroidery in mounts are then strung in an attractive way. To mount a machine embroidered panel, the material is stitched to the tile with white embroidery cotton. The whole unit is suspended on invisible thread (S, Fig. 5).

String weaving, with each unit made of string and supported on a framework of wire, also can make an interesting mobile. Aluminum wire found in the garage was used in the example shown in the photograph. The weaving can be made more interesting by the incorporating of pebbles or strange shaped twigs or sticks. These are placed in the warp and woven into the weft. Aluminum wire is formed into a frame on which a warp of string is wrapped. The weft of the string weaving is threaded in with a large-eyed needle.

A mobile with a banner motif can be made from woven material, without any wire framework, and can be suspended from one end. Ideas for decorating each side of the banner are infinitely variable.

Since the making of mobiles is a comparatively new craft, it affords considerable scope for individual choice and for experimentation, both in color and design. The making of a mobile by the simple processes of cutting and gluing can give great satisfaction. Furthermore, the introduction of mobility to a traditional craft or technique is a means of opening up new fields of interest and possibility for the beginner to explore.

G. Roland Smith

model making

PEOPLE HAVE MADE MODELS of various things and for various reasons since practically the beginning of history. The ancient Egyptians, over four thousand years ago, made delightful toy-like models from painted clay or wood, showing little figures busy using everyday objects. These miniatures were buried with the dead in the belief that they would somehow be of use in an afterlife.

Models have nearly always been made for some specific purpose. Unlike sculpture, they are seldom ends in themselves but generally convey, three-dimensionally, certain more or less precise information. They are not, strictly speaking, a medium for free expression but are an applied art, not a purely creative one. Models undoubtedly have aesthetic appeal. For example, some model-making techniques are related to paper sculpture, in which the expressive quality of the material itself can be exploited to imaginative effect. This section, however, refers to the practical applications of model making simply as a means of handling factual matter constructively.

A model affords the opportunity of reviewing the elements of some large project in advance. Town planners use models in this way, moving component buildings experimentally from place to place. A model stage set enables the theatrical designer to put himself dramatically in the position of the audience while there is still time to make changes. In industry, model ships and aircraft can be tested in tanks or wind tunnels before the elaborate costs of doing the real thing are invested only to find a mistake that could have been eliminated at the model stage. Engineering problems may be solved with the help of mathematical models representing the stresses involved in construction, as in bridge building, for example. Scientific ideas can often be best expressed by tangible models of crystal and cell structures, plant forms, and anatomical systems. Models are not necessarily miniatures; some are magnified versions of mi-

Roman merchant ship. While the model itself is not old, it resembles the sort of vessel once used for carrying corn.

croscopic things. Making factual models from observation can further the study of basic design. Working models are used to demonstrate mechanical principles. Historical and geographical models reveal perhaps the military strategy behind some famous battle, or the geological formation of a land mass. Relief maps and topographical models can be photographed at close quarters and have been used convincingly in filmmaking. In all these examples, accurate research and precision of scale are important. Museums make use of models. Apart from their instructional uses, such models appeal to the collector with limited space for preserving tangible records of historical objects—steam engines, veteran cars, furniture, etc. There is, moreover, the sheer fascination of making things small, as with the Lilliputian dolls' house, with the Victorian fort or cut-out theater, with ships in

This small-scale balsa wood model of a vintage motor car is approximately 5 in. long.

A composite model of a castle built by a group of children as part of a project on fortification. It measures about 5 ft. 6 in. across and is made primarily of wood and cardboard.

A small-scale balsa wood model of a ship, about 5 in. in length.

bottles, and with the toytown world of childhood.

Educationally, model making provides an incentive to research. Before children can make factual models, they must gather some facts. In schools, insistence upon perfect scale and craftsmanship is usually more trouble than it is worth. Children delight in making things well by their own standards. Professional techniques must be modified, and precise blueprints are out of place. They can be dangerous if they inhibit the spirit of practical inquiry that characterizes genuine project work. Models bring the environment into the classroom; they enable children to adopt a bird's eye view and to take in at a glance things that might normally be encountered singly. As a technical pursuit, simple model making uses applied mathematics in an attractive form. There is no better way of learning geometry. Children working in groups (on a dockyard, a village, or a castle, perhaps) develop social skills and recognize one another's talents. Farms or markets make excellent centers of interest to which various models can be effectively related. There is scope for the personal model also, possibly embodying some original design for a machine or a space ship. The experimental use of materials plays a vital part. Some school models are made strongly so that the finished article may be repeatedly used as a teaching aid. Temporary models take shape more quickly; their value lies in the activity rather than the end product.

A model of an Egyptian ship made about 2000 B.C., found in a tomb.

MATERIALS

The following materials are used commonly for measured model making (distinct from free modeling or sculpture): wood; hardboard; balsa wood; plywood; light metals: aluminum, tin, zinc; clay: synthetic and natural; self-hardening clay; plaster; wire mesh; fiber glass; expanded polystyrene, papier mâché; plexiglas adhesive surfacing materials; dowel rods; cane; cork: lumps and tiles; masking tape; paper; paints; poster color, powder color; varnish; cardboard (probably the best general-purpose material—heavy cardboard for sturdy construction; tagboard for structures requiring a good painting surface; post-cards; bending board or bristol board for detailed structures). Odds and ends may be useful, including: boxes, sponge, foam rubber, plastic, beads, sandpaper, wallpaper, cloth, corks, thread spools, cocktail stirrers, pipe cleaners, lollipops, leather, acetate sheeting, canvas, pins, felt, Scotch tape, raffia, wire, straws, and veneers.

For children, the following tools will probably be adequate: small hacksaws, scissors, pencils, crayons, rulers, paint brushes, paper clips, stencil cutting templates. The teacher or professional craftsman may also require a guillotine paper

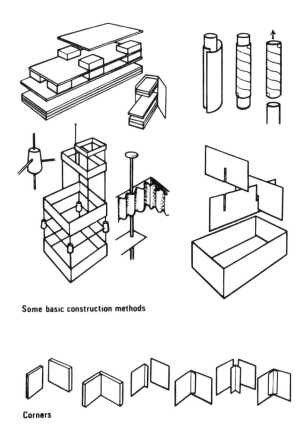

Some basic construction methods

Corners

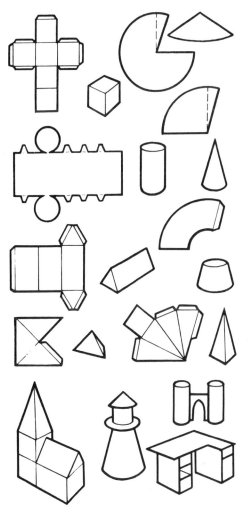

Simple geometrical forms

cutter, bookbinder's shears, knives, pliers, stapler, tweezers, steel ruler, file, and drawing instruments.

Adhesives include: vegetable glue for general school use, impact glue for strong fixtures, and cellulose paste for paper coverings. The following basic techniques relate to cardboard model making: blocks and platforms are made by sandwiching layers together or by introducing matchboxes or wood blocks in between. Corrugated cardboard also is helpful.

Hollow shapes are made by wrapping thin cardboard around a shaper, such as a broomhandle, jam jar, or some similar shape, binding with gumstrip, and removing the shaper when the cardboard has set. Skeletal shapes and open frames are built with knitting needles, dowels, lengths of cane or wire pushed into corks or inserted into punched or corrugated cardboard. Box-like shapes may be strengthened by insert-

ing internal partitions and carefully slotting together wall sections. Corners are formed by butt jointing (with thick materials, by overlapping tabs or using a sealing strip, such as gumstrip). Experience with uncomplicated mathematical solids (cubes, cones, cylinders, pyramids, etc.) opens up unlimited possibilities.

There are usually four stages in model making: (1) measuring and drawing, (2) folding and cutting, (3) assembling and fixing, and (4) decorating and finishing.

Lavinia Everard

modern embroidery

UNTIL QUITE RECENTLY embroidery was regarded as the Cinderella of the crafts and not taken seriously. It has been looked down upon by artistic highbrows as merely a pastime for ladies with too much time on their hands or as a nerve-soother. It is, of course, a valuable subject for occupational therapy, but in this, it is the simple repetitive performance of stitching that gives it its therapeutic value and not the creation of an embroidery design.

During the Middle Ages, particularly in the fifteenth and sixteenth centuries, English embroidery was famed throughout Europe and was, as a matter of interest, one of England's most important exports. Naturally, this embroidery found its way to America and was adapted. In England, the designs were mostly of religious subjects, and kings, noblemen, churches, and monasteries all paid large sums for examples, which were so prized that they have been preserved to this present day. Lovely work was lavished on the clothes of both men and women as well as on articles for the great houses—bed draperies and coverlets, hangings, table carpets, and curtains.

The slow decline in quality that came with the Stuart and Georgian periods was unfortunately accelerated by another factor—the Industrial Revolution. Fabrics could now be patterned so quickly and cheaply by machinery and, alas, so tastelessly, that quality both in design and workmanship deteriorated, and the demand for decoration by embroidery passed. Nevertheless women still embroidered as they had done through the ages, satisfying in some way a natural urge to create.

Ancient embroideries have been found in Egypt, and it is touching to think how, throughout history, women have stitched away their sorrows, found solace when waiting, and celebrated their happiness in weddings and christenings with embroidery. During the Crusades, the ladies of the castles embroidered heraldic emblems,

Jacobean embroidery

whiling away the long years while their husbands were away in the Holy Land. A quaint and spirited piece of embroidery still exists that was stitched by the delicate hands of Mary, Queen of Scots, who thus found solace while waiting in her grim castle prison for execution.

By the beginning of the present century the standard of embroidery had reached its lowest level and was generally spoken of as "fancy work," but in the thirties a minor revolt, led by Rebecca Crompton, reacted against the prevailing boring and lifeless designs. It is true that there were strongholds of good technique in England and America in the form of guilds, colleges, and schools, but good technique was rarely allied with original or lively design. The standard of commercially-produced transfer designs of this period degenerated into a dainty deadness; some of these are still stocked in the shops and look as if they were designed before the First World War.

Now the outlook concerning needlework is completely changed, and embroidery is, once more, a fashionable subject. There is, in fact, so great an interest in creative embroidery as a means of expression that, in the forms of panels or hangings, it is accepted at the highest levels as a new art form—in fact it needs a new name. This revival is encouraged and helped by the ever-widening variety of inspiring new materials and threads, unconventional textures, and effects now available. Materials are available in smooth, rough, dull, shiny, knobby, metallic, fluffy, and shot finishes. They come in beautiful colors, bright, rich, intense, subtle and somber. Much of this new material is a result of man-made fibers.

Better teaching has made people realize that embroidery is not merely the embellishment of an article; it must be thought of, and thoughtfully planned, as part of the thing. An exciting piece of embroidery can exist in its own right. The finest examples of embroidery have been for the enrichment of religious and ceremonial articles, but here are a number of everyday articles you could embroider today: chair backs and seats (try a stool for your dressing table) —rugs—cushions (how about a personal one for a special person?) — bedspreads —padded headboards — curtains — door curtains or portières (well-weighted and

Couched gold thread work

padded)—paper-weights and trays—jewel boxes—fire screens—book covers for precious books—bookmarkers—needlebooks —work boxes—handbags—beachbags— belts—lunch mats—runners—tablecloths —lampshades—tea cozy (or, for a different shape, a coffee-pot cozy)—egg cozy for both a single egg or several eggs—Danish style soft toys—babies' crib covers—christening robes—bonnets—bibs—children's clothes—adults' clothes (much discretion must be exercised here; consider the fashion angle and avoid "artsy-craftsiness")—special greeting cards. I would like to add an idea that is Scandinavian in origin—special cloths and centers for the table at holiday time. All these are useful articles on which the embroidery is an embellishment, but today many embroiderers are attracted by working a panel or picture, which is glazed and framed, or a hanging. These require very careful consideration as, since they serve no useful purpose but exist solely as decorations, the design is all-important.

The craft of embroidery is coming back to the position of importance it once occupied. Influence from Europe has been considerable, especially from Scandinavia, where the heritage of traditional peasant art has been undisturbed by any industrial revolution, where nearly every woman embroiders, and where good materials and designs have always been obtainable. Embroidery as now taught in schools is intended to develop the student's sense of color and design and to train the taste. Classes for adults in evening schools, adult centers, and women's organizations have been backed up by articles on embroidery in newspapers, magazines, and women's journals. A succession of inspiring and attractive books on embroidery continue to be published, and there are frequently exhibitions of modern embroidery in large cities.

Do not fail to visit embroidery exhibitions whenever you can — illustrations in books can never be the same as the actual work seen at close quarters. Be on the lookout for new books. You can request them from your local library, and if, when you have seen them, you decide that they will help you, buy them, especially those giving technical information. Many new churches have been built in recent years, and contemporary architecture needs contemporary furnishings, so some of the most exciting modern embroidery is ecclesiastic. Exploring churches in strange towns and villages may be rewarded by a fine altar frontal, a seat cover, or a kneeler.

All this is very encouraging, but still a beginner may be uncertain how to start on the creation of an original design and doubtful that she will be able to carry it through to completion. "Oh! I cannot draw" is so often heard. While an ability to draw certainly helps, lack of it does not prohibit you from doing embroidery because there are many other ways of evolving a good design. In fact, skill in realistic drawing can sometimes be a handicap as a strict pictorial treatment is not suitable for the limitations of embroidery. Here I am leaving out those examples of embroidery, laboriously worked in long and short stitch, that set out to imitate paintings, for the admiration which they evoke is purely on account of the industry and patience involved. They, however, do not exploit the various stitches fully.

TOOLS AND MATERIALS

In every craft no design can be attempted without some knowledge of the techniques and tools particular to that craft. Stitches are the words, so to speak, the various methods are the grammar, and the tools make it possible to work correctly. So first, collect your tools and materials:

Stitchbook. The few stitches shown here will do to start with, but later acquire a more complete vocabulary by buying yourself a stitchbook.

A selection of varied needles. It is important to use the right needle for the job in hand because the ease and pleasure with which you work depends on it. Fine and coarse needles, with round eyes and long eyes, crewel needles, some thick chenille needles, and tapestry needles (blunt ended) all in various sizes are required.

A thimble. If you have grown up without having learned to use a thimble, as so many women have, it will certainly be difficult to get used to one. Perseverance, however, will pay off because no rhythmic, regular stitching can be done without one. Though a fine needle is more accurate, you must remember that the needle has to make a hole sufficiently large to draw two thick-

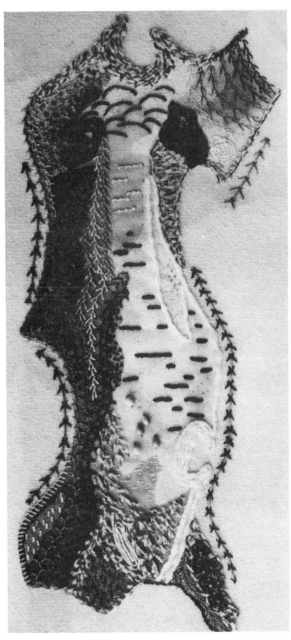

"Silver Birch Bark." This panel uses various stitches and threads.

nesses of the thread through it. Too long a needle, for example, a darner, is awkward to use with a thimble, so use a chenille needle instead.

Fine embroidery scissors are absolutely necessary. They must be really sharp and cut well right to the tip.

Medium sized scissors for cutting larger things than thread are necessary.

Embroidery frames. A small ring embroidery frame, called a tambour, will be useful when you first start to embroider. Avoid ring frames of plastic, which have a tendency to slip, or frames without a screw for adjustment. If the material in the circular frame slips, or if the outside ring is too large, bind one ring with a strip of binding or tape.

Instructions on dressing a frame are given in many good books on embroidery. The ultimate luxury when working is to have the frame fixed to a stand; this also looks quite interesting when standing in a room in the same way as a spinning wheel does. (Frames are a good idea for a gift, and they will give life-long pleasure.) Square frames have pegs and holes for adjustment.

Markers. Chalk (dressmaker's), or the same substance in pencil form; a fine sable brush (No. 0 or 1); and tubes of watercolor, chinese white and black are necessary for marking fabrics.

Paper. Drawing paper, graph paper, and tracing paper are needed for embroidery work. The latter is useful for laying over your work when trying out corrections.

Background fabric. The choice of background fabric is all-important because it sets the mood and the style of the work. A fabric with a really interesting texture and color can arouse your creative spirit. Select a material not too cheap in quality, or you will be discouraged by the result. Never buy inexpensive background fabrics—your time is too precious to waste on poor material. The idea that anything will do to start with is completely wrong, as even well-executed stitches will fail to achieve a completely successful piece of work. This is just the stage when you need all the help a good material can give you. The background fabric should be firm or it will pucker and be less easy to hold. And it shouldn't be too tightly woven, like poplin or grosgrain, or the needle will not pass through it easily, especially if the thread is thick. If you have to tug each stitch, this will dis-

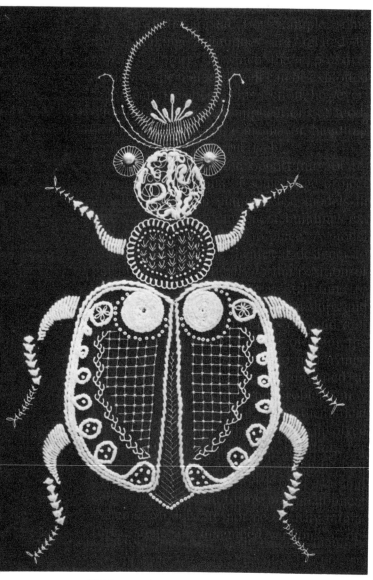

White work on a dark slub background featuring varied thicknesses of thread.

dery had necessarily to be chiefly on a pale neutral background because natural fibers such as linen and wool were usual, and these could not easily be dyed in the length, and silk, which could be colored, was rare and consequently costly. Time has further darkened the fine examples of embroidery in our museums, so it has come to be accepted that embroidery tended to be on natural-colored backgrounds.

Suggestions for background fabrics are: woolen fabrics, which are most excellent and sympathetic, such as flannel, velour, and smooth woolen dress materials; dress linen; good quality dress cottons; and even weave linen. Felt has neither warp nor weft threads to strengthen it and has moreover a boring texture. Cloth with an even weave or easily counted thread is helpful for getting stitches evenly spaced on a sampler. (This kind of fabric aids in the counting of threads and serves as a prop to your morale and helps you along.) Burlap is difficult to work with for embroidery because its uneven surface can be a hindrance. However, a good quality and evenly woven type is suitable.

Threads

Assemble your palette of threads; and remember, a good collection is inspiring. Fine and thick, smooth and rough, silky and woolly, and also some experimental threads such as string, raffia, unusual and knobby knitting and weaving yarns, metallic threads, mohair, and angora all should be included. Some regular embroidery threads follow:

Stranded cotton comes in skeins of divisible threads of six strands; it is mercerized and therefore moderately shiny. Stranded cotton is made in more colors than any other thread. It is worth searching for the special muted tapestry color range.

A single thread is easier to manage than a stranded or multiple thread, and knotted or looped stitches are unsuccessful using

turb the rhythm and pleasure of stitching. The fabric should not be stretchy or too loosely woven. Avoid furnishing fabrics, especially rayon, unless of expensive quality. These mostly have a loosely woven surface, and the stitches will sink into them. Also, they are too often coarse in texture.

Make a firm stand against muddy and neutral colors to start with; you will find that your ideas appear quite different on, say, a deep, rich colored background worked in lighter tones. Historic embroi-

several threads in the needle. It is hard to see why stranded cotton is so universally used. The advantage is that it can be used in any number of threads from one to six. Probably the real reason that it is so popular is that many shops are able to offer it, and it comes in more colors.

Coton à broder is similar to cotton thread, but it is used as a single thread because it is thicker. Coton à broder is easier to use than cotton thread although it does not have quite as many colors.

Soft embroidery cotton comes in skeins and is thick, smooth, soft, and completely matte.

Pearl cotton comes in balls and is shiny, medium coarse, and twisted. It is sold in two thicknesses (5 and 8) and comes in many colors.

Linen thread is colored, not very fine, loosely twisted, and uneven.

Lace threads are very fine and come in white and natural.

Perlita is a very heavy, shiny, and cord-like thread.

Fresca is an even thicker thread than Perlita and is matte. Both this and Perlita are in limited colors.

Crewel wool is two-ply thread, best used for canvas work. Use as many threads as needed to fill holes in canvas—this varies with the chosen stitch.

Tapestry wool is a four-ply thickness thread. Other wools are: knitting wools and double knitting crochet yarns; uneven yarns such as bubbly poodle. Only looped mohair and angora can be couched.

Twisted embroidery silk is very shiny, loosely twisted, and of medium thickness.

Buttonhole silk is for fine, even work.

Metallic threads generally have to be couched.

A comprehensive range of colors and threads is collected only with difficulty. If you know other embroiderers living in your area, members of a local class, for example, then try persuading your local shop to stock a wider selection, or at least the vari-

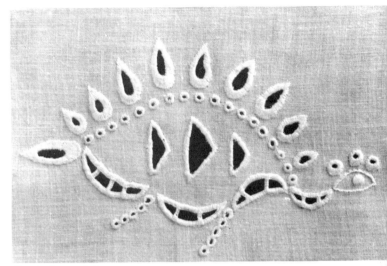

Broderie anglais

ous shade cards from which thread supplies can be ordered. Alternatively, write for your own shade cards and order what you need through the very knowledgeable and reliable people who run postal services for embroidery material supply.

A note regarding threads: if threads are kept for a long time in a tangled mass, constantly turned over, and rubbed together, they will suffer. Mercerized cottons lose their luster, silks get snags, and wools get matted. So keep threads in good condition, either in boxes or, a better idea, in plastic pages of separate colors, or, though it is more trouble, in a roll-up cotton holder.

Beads

Develop a squirrel-like addiction for small beads, sequins, bugle beads, cords, and simple braids. (Elaborate braids do not mix well with handworked stitches.) These can be added to your stitches to give contrast and interest. Your friends' button boxes, junk shops, curiosity shops, and old evening dresses are some sources for beads. You can sometimes buy bags of mixed beads or "sweepings" from the wholesale firms who supply the couture trade. This is far cheaper than buying in separate packets, in which you get far too many beads of one kind.

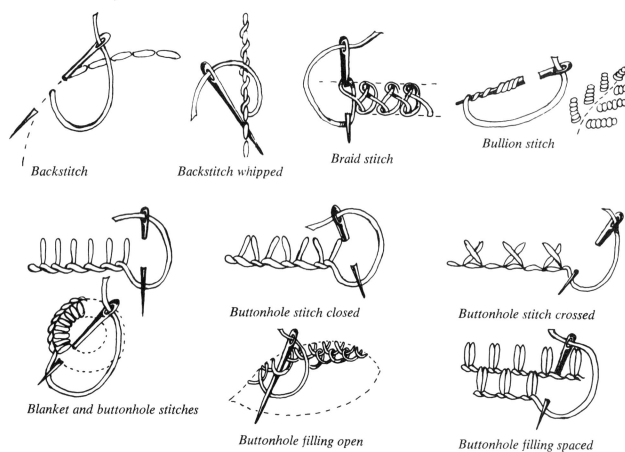

Backstitch

Backstitch whipped

Braid stitch

Bullion stitch

Blanket and buttonhole stitches

Buttonhole stitch closed

Buttonhole stitch crossed

Buttonhole filling open

Buttonhole filling spaced

Stitches

Instead of the usual dull sampler of stitches, chalk out a simple motif of, say, a sprig of flat leaf shapes and/or a flower on a piece of fabric about 7 inches square and try out several stitches on it. You can test your sense of arrangement and color at the same time. An axiom to encourage beginners is: no stitch in itself is difficult to execute and some are extremely easy—the hard part is the even repetition. Practice makes perfect. Never work a fresh stitch straight onto a piece of work as the relationship between the texture of the background, the thickness of the thread, and the chosen stitch will be different every time. Also you need to practice a little to get the stitch going evenly. Look through your stitchbook and make a collection of stitches that appeal to you on different fabrics with assorted threads. The same stitch looks quite different in a thick thread compared with a thin thread worked in the same size. Looking through this collection

later will, perhaps, give you an idea for a complete design. Consider the suitability of the stitches for the work in hand; for instance, a few of the most handsome stitches do not take washing and ironing. Others will not stand up to wear or friction, such as the kind they will get on a cushion or chair seat. But these may be possible on a hanging or under glass.

Surface stitches are those that are not influenced by the weave of the background and can therefore go in any direction on the surface of the fabric.

Line stitches are those in which the needle travels in a single line:

Running back	Many variations of these can be threaded and whipped singly or in blocks
Pekinese	Based on backstitch. Contrasting color can be used for the interlacing thread
Stem	Quick and flexible but does not turn sharp curves easily

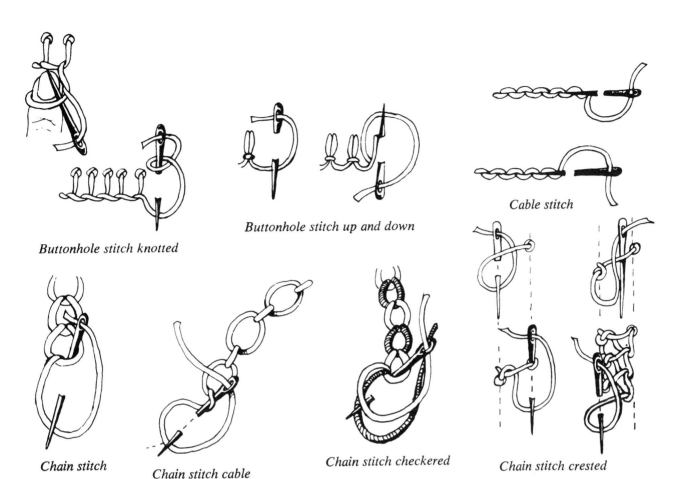

Buttonhole stitch knotted

Buttonhole stitch up and down

Cable stitch

Chain stitch

Chain stitch cable

Chain stitch checkered

Chain stitch crested

Chain	Can be whipped or back-stitched	Twisted chain	Pretty
Magic chain	Worked with two or even three colors	Feather	Single (like slanted buttonhole), double, or triple
Cable	Worked from left to right	Braid	Worked from right to left, makes an effective border
Coral	Worked from right to left		
Couching	One method is shown here, but it is not difficult to devise other ways	Rosette	Charming tassel-like effect
		Chevron	A close cousin of herringbone stitch

Band stitches are wide stitches worked across two lines. Many have an interesting shape or silhouette. Heavier than the previous group, they can be in parallel rows to make good fillings but generally look better with a narrow space between each row.

		Cretan	Versatile, open or closed, can be graduated
		Fishbone	Can be graduated, open or closed
Buttonhole	There are two types generally used: one is identical to the blanket stitch but is worked with stitches close together; the other is called the tailor's buttonhole and is worked like the latter but is given an extra twist	Leaf	Like fishbone stitch
		Fly	Either vertical, sprig-like, or horizontal points
		Thorn	Lovely for sewing down a metal thread or cord that cannot be pulled through fabric
		Wheatear	Lacy
		Satin	Appears deceptively easy —the needle just goes in and out—but actually one of the most difficult stitches

Chain stitch double

Chain stitch heavy

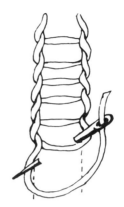

Chain stitch open

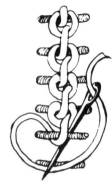

Chain band raised

Chain stitch rosette

Chain stitch twisted

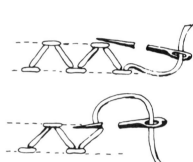

Chevron stitch

	with which to get good results
Herringbone	Worked from left to right
Loop	Can be adapted to fill a shape
Scroll	Only suitable under glass, space stitches evenly
Wave	Worked from right to left, may be used as a filling or a border
Couched	Contrasting thread can be used
Seeding	Keep stitches of even length but place at random
Raised honeycomb	Avoid too heavy a thread
Raised chain band	Single thread. By making the horizontal bars longer, several parallel bands may be worked on them
Guilloche	Single thread. Comprises stem stitch, satin stitch, an

interlacing stitch, and French knots

Interlaced band	Also known as herringbone ladder filling stitch
Tête de boeuf	Pretty filling stitch

Filling stitches are mostly best worked in frame.

Detached buttonhole	These stitches can be executed in two colors to get a graduated effect, but there are pitfalls and sometimes results look messy
Cloud filling	
Wave	
Couched	
Seeding	Like satin stitch, deceptively difficult
long and short	
Raised honeycomb	*(See Band Stitches.)*

Stitches can be classified into "families" as follows:

Flat stitches. Running, back, stem, long and short, fishbone—closed and open—leaf, chevron, arrowhead, thorn, cross,

124

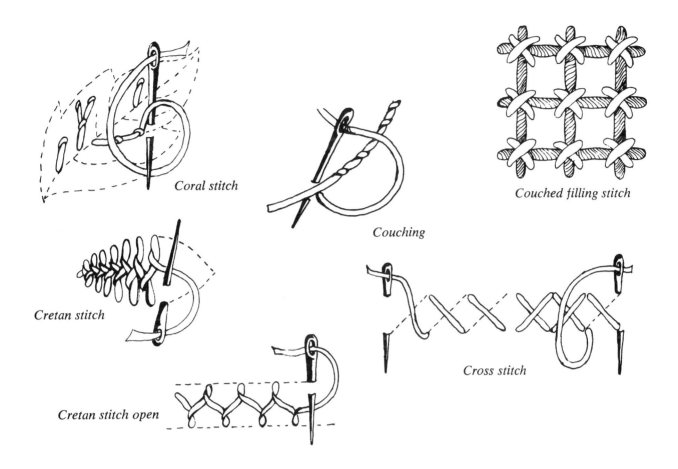

Coral stitch

Couching

Couched filling stitch

Cretan stitch

Cretan stitch open

Cross stitch

couching, feather, buttonhole, closed feather, loop, scroll.

Looped stitches. Buttonhole, crossed buttonhole, closed buttonhole, spaced buttonhole, cretan stitch, up and down buttonhole, detached buttonhole filling.

Chained stitches. Chain, magic or checkered, twisted chain, open chain, broad chain, double chain, rosette, crested, cable chain, braid, wheatear, tête de boeuf.

Knotted stitches are most frequently worked with a single strand of firm thread. French knot, bullion knot, coral knot, double knot.

Composite stitches. Interlacing, Maltese cross, Pekinese, threaded back, cloud filling, twisted lattice, cretan filling, raised, honeycomb filling, sheaf, raised chain band, guilloche, interlaced band.

KINDS OF EMBROIDERY

Workers of various tastes and abilities can find a method to suit them. You can work finely or boldly, in work of one color such as "white work," in which the texture of stitches makes the design that does not rely on color. You can stitch in the entire background as in canvas work, or work to the counted thread. The latter imposes limitations and a discipline that helps the stylization of the design, and many people feel safer with an even count of thread to help them.

Traditional methods of stitching have been given vitality today because people are experimenting with the old rules. For example, white work—so called because it was always worked with natural-colored linen or cotton and matching threads — is now often worked in strong colors with contrasting threads. The scale of stitches in one piece of work can be varied, or two or more methods can be combined. The following notes suggest some of the many ways in which embroidery stitches may be used.

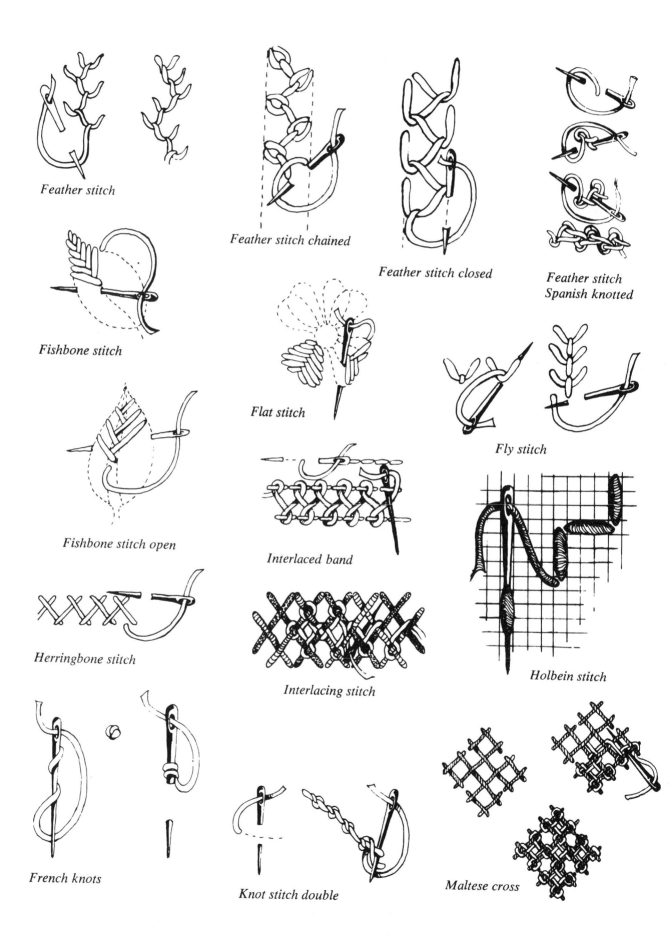

Feather stitch

Feather stitch chained

Feather stitch closed

Feather stitch Spanish knotted

Fishbone stitch

Flat stitch

Fly stitch

Fishbone stitch open

Interlaced band

Holbein stitch

Herringbone stitch

Interlacing stitch

French knots

Knot stitch double

Maltese cross

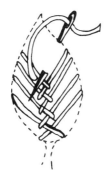

Leaf stitch

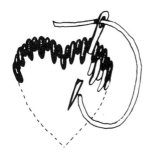

Long and short stitch

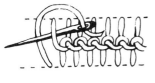

Loop stitch

Pekinese stitch

Running stitch

Running stitch laced

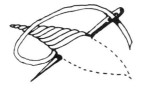

Satin stitch

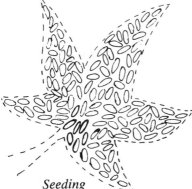

Seeding

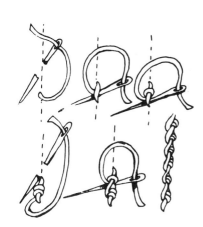

Stem stitch

Scroll stitch

Sheaf stitch

Tête de boeuf stitch

Portuguese stem stitch

Thorn stitch

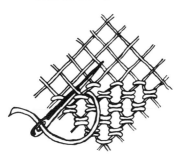

Twisted lattice stitch

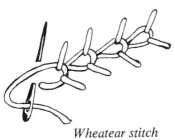

Wheatear stitch

127

Counted thread

First we will consider methods based on the counted thread. For this technique, it is preferable to use a cloth with the warp and weft threads of even thickness. You should be able to count the threads, and it should not be so tightly woven that a blunt-ended needle (called a tapestry needle) cannot pass between the threads. This needle is always used to avoid piercing the background threads or the sewing thread. These fabrics are specially made, ranging from 16 to 34 threads to the inch, and are listed in embroidery catalogs. Try them out and do not attempt to work on one too fine for your eyesight. You can obtain a magnifying glass to hang around your neck, or half-lenses in three magnifications to clip on to your existing glasses. Some people find an engraver's glass useful—this is a magnifying glass on a gooseneck stand. It is better not to work too long with these aids, but they are certainly useful to get a stitch started or to sort out a mistake.

Drawn thread

This technique is used primarily for patterns built up of lines of openwork, and it is much used for table linen. Threads are withdrawn either from the warp or weft. This weakens the lines of cotton, so threads are replaced decoratively to strengthen them. Where the lines cross, a square hole is left, and this is filled with webs to prevent the openwork from being torn by the tip of the iron. Contrasting colored threads are rarely successful. Drawn thread work does not make many demands on design abilities —just space the lines well.

Drawn fabric, or pulled work

The second name of the title here is the more descriptive one for this technique. No threads in the background are withdrawn, but the background threads are pulled apart by different stitches to make patterns of holes. A great variety of textures can be obtained by working on a loosely woven

Net embroidery

linen or cotton. The sewing thread should match exactly or be nearly the same thickness as those of the fabric. Again, a contrasting colored thread looks confusing.

Hardanger

This technique originated in Hardanger Fjord in Norway and is a fairly coarse type of work. Formerly white work, today we often stitch in white on a colored background. Finely woven linen or cotton must be used, but the best results are obtained on specially woven Hardanger cloth, the threads of which are woven in pairs. Pearl cotton, either no. 5 or no. 8, is used, and the design is built up with rectangles of satin stitch called kloster blocks, generally over four or five threads, using the thicker no. 5 thread. Spaces of four threads are left between the blocks; the threads on the inside of the blocks are cut and those of the spaces left. This leaves open squares, which are sometimes filled in with looped stitches, and the remaining background threads are woven into bars using no. 8 thread. Picot

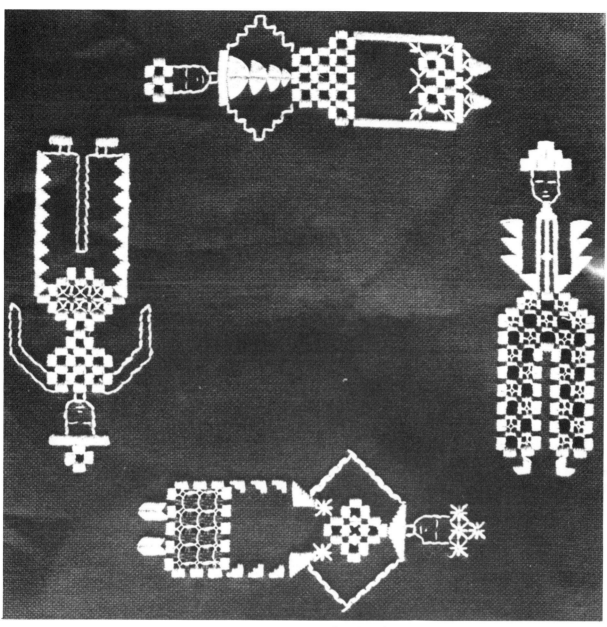

The central motif of a tablecloth done in Hardanger work.

loops can be added. In spite of the heavy technique, the finished effect can be lace-like. Designs have perforce to be geometric and traditionally have always been so, but it is possible to stylize a flower, figure, or bird motif with charming results. Surface stitches worked on the counted threads can be introduced, but the best designs exploit the light and dark character of the holes cut in the fabric.

Cross stitch

The entire design is carried out in cross stitch over an even number of threads. Of course, all the crosses must cross in the same direction, but unless the work consists of fairly solid masses of stitches it tends to look thin and straggly. Denmark is the real home of this work, and traditional Danish embroidery of this type specializes in deli-

129

Pattern darning.

cate, naturalistic flowers finely worked. A bold stylized design can look effective in one color on a contrasting background, say, white thread on a deep blue or red fabric. From the fashion angle, this could be acceptable for use on a dress.

Assisi work

This is allied to cross stitch in that the design is outlined in double running stitch and the background is filled in with a long-armed cross, Italian cross, or simple cross stitch in another color.

Patterned darning

This is a sort of damask; the embroidery thread weaves in and out of the background in a regular pattern. Each part of the design has a different texture, and the weaving threads follow the warp or weft. Tone contrasts can be obtained by heavy or light filling. In addition to plain even-weave linens and cottons, a coarse fabric and one rather finer, huck toweling, are inviting to work on, because thick threads such as soft embroidery and pearl cotton can be woven through the surface loops and knots only, making easily built-up borders. This stitching technique is good for dressing table runners, place mats, guest towels, and the like.

Needleweaving

This technique is very limited in use because it is composed of borders and rectangles only on the straight of the grain of the cloth. It is generally found on brightly colored peasant costumes in natural linen or sometimes worked finely in white on white cloth. Threads are withdrawn from the background in wide bands, the ends being neatly darned in. Next the top and bottom of the border are hemstitched, dividing the threads into equal number of groups. These groups are woven with contrasting threads in figures of eight blocks. The weaving thread passes from one block to the next in steps, leaving vertical slits between each and making a geometrical pattern.

Needleweaving has possibilities as dress decoration on linen or coarse woolen dress material. The wool would have to be of the handwoven type or the threads would not be strong enough to withdraw. It is also suitable for end runners, curtains, place mats, and aprons. It is not suitable for curves.

Blackwork

This work was first introduced in England in the sixteenth century, and we see it on the clothes in Elizabethan portraits. A black thread is used on white linen with fine lacy filling stitches worked on an even number of threads horizontally, vertically, or diagonally. The worker can follow designs in books and then devise his or her own patterns. Today you can try out color on color or light stitches on a dark background. Avoid a design of small shapes because you will not be able to fit in enough repeats. Formerly rather naturalistic curved shapes were outlined with heavy outline stitches such as chain, double knot, or twisted chain, and then the shapes were

Blackwork using three thicknesses of thread to give a shaded effect.

simply filled in with blackwork patterns, presenting a nice balance of light and heavy fillings. Today the designs are composed of shapes with more regard for the angular nature of the work, using as many as possible horizontal, vertical, or diagonal lines. The designs look more interesting if they are not always outlined.

131

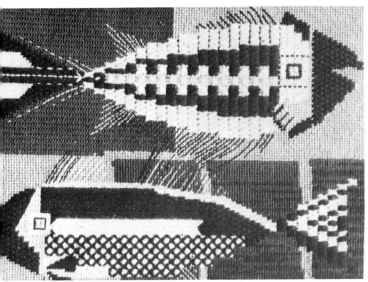

Canvas work using eight different stitches.

Double running, or Rumanian, work

This is a holbein stitch giving a lacy effect or that of delicate ironwork. It is a running stitch under and over an equal number of threads. On the return journey, the stitch is reversed to fill in the spaces so that the work looks the same on both sides —useful for table linen, which must look good on the back. To start and finish, the thread is neatly darned in along a line of stitches. Traditionally the thread is black on white linen, and the design is embellished by squares of one stitch on each side filled in with satin stitches in, say, red or bright green or yellow. The diagonal direction is worked in right-angled steps. It is best to work out your design on graph paper before you begin.

Canvas work

This work is often erroneously called tapestry work. True tapestries were woven on a loom. Here the method differs from other embroideries because the entire background must be filled in. It is worked on strong, open-meshed canvas, fine to coarse, from 10 to 32 threads to the inch. Some of the coarser counts are woven with double thread. Canvas work is very hardwearing and so is used for chair seats, church kneelers, handbags, footstools, and similar articles. Many people think of this work as entirely worked in a single slanting stitch

(tent stitch, called gros point when on double canvas, or petit point when on single canvas), but there are at least fifty canvas stitches, producing the most diverse effects. Embroidery shops have ample stocks of ready-made packs complete with design, canvas, and wools. The canvases are either already painted, in which case you just fill in with the colored wools provided, or they come with a chart to be counted out on the canvas (very tedious), or a design ready trammed—the ultimate in uncreative, repetitive work since all that is required is to work tent stitches over already laid colored threads. How much more rewarding to make or adapt your own ideas!

To begin your own canvas work, draw the design on paper in thick black ink, lay the canvas over it, and paint the design on with ball point, felt pen, or oil color. There is no need to work the design on graph paper, for the stitches will make their own outlines. However, it is very boring to use the same stitch over the whole of the work when there are so many to make variety of texture.

If the article you are making is to be sat or kneeled upon, it must be very firm; it is better to use 2-ply crewel wool because then you can vary the number of strands in the needle according to the stitch. Tent stitch on, say, 16-thread canvas would need three strands, but rice stitch or long-armed cross stitch would need four. Try out all your stitches on a sampler and keep it by you for reference. Tramming (the laid threads referred to above) is not necessary unless you work with single 4-ply tapestry wool on double canvas. Wool is usual, but some sparkle can be added by working a few points such as centers of flowers or eyes of animals in mercerized cotton or silk.

Cut work

This technique is interesting for lampshades, but it must be backed with an opaque pale or white fabric, or one of the new plastic materials, so that the light from the lamp will not glare through. It is used also for table linen and cushions, and in colors it is suitable for dress decoration. For this work use a firm linen or cotton that will not unravel easily when cut. The design must be composed of masses, crowded into the area to be filled, with not much background left. The shapes are outlined with plain buttonhole stitch to match the background, with the head of the stitch on the outside (so avoid thin shapes or there will not be much left). Then the background material is neatly cut away. If the background spaces are large, the results will be unsuccessful. It is necessary to bridge the cut spaces with worked bars to keep the work firm for washing and ironing. These bars must be worked before the background is cut away.

Broderie anglais

This is a more delicate form of decoration. The design is built up of very small holes, or eyelet ovals or rounds, connected by fine lines of whipped stem or chain stitch. The material is fine, firmly woven cambric or fine linen, and it is worked with tiny running stitches. Then, very small eyelets are pierced with a stiletto, and the edges finely and closely overcast over the running stitches and raw edges. Larger circles and ovals are cut horizontally and vertically in a cross and again overcast with the material turned over to the back. Any surplus material is then cut off.

Build up your own design with masses of eyelets—if you use them sparsely and rely on stitched lines, the effect will be feeble. It can be used on babies' and children's clothes (when worked boldly in color) and also for women's dresses. Lampshades and table linen look interesting when worked in unexpectedly rich colors.

Net embroidery

This is another counted thread method.

Fine or coarse net is tacked over the drawing of the design, and the design is then darned onto the net in various stitches. You can use fine net for such articles as delicate table mats, babies' dresses, and wedding veils, or coarse net worked in very thick thread for curtains. Two things to remember: the thread is wholly visible so stitches that cross elaborately on the wrong side look muddled (herringbone, for example, looks like figure eights) and much can be done with tartan arrangements of straight lines. Starting and finishing are awkward, so do much of the design in a continuous line. Avoid small isolated motifs or spots. Hexagonal nets are used that have three straights on the grain, so the lines of the stitches should follow these. Contrasting colored threads are less successful.

Shadow work

This is worked on transparent materials —cottons, organdy, nylon, organzas, voile, very fine cambric, and linen for tablecloths, lampshades, babies' clothes, pillows, coverlets, blouses and fine dresses, and for the charming cloud cloths—large organdy cloths thrown lightly over laid tea tables or buffets to keep them fresh if they have to be prepared some time in advance of the function. The cloth can be lightly decorated with shadow motifs and the edges weighted here and there with china beads, though I cover these with padded cloth so that they will not damage delicate china.

This embroidery is composed of long, narrow shapes or circles worked entirely in close herringbone stitch, also called double backstitch. The embroidery is worked on the wrong side so that on the right side one sees the outline in black stitches and the shadow of the crossing of the threads. It looks particularly lovely worked in white thread on white, or in white on pale or darker colors, or in bright colors on a pale background, because then only the back stitches are vivid with the cross threads

133

Quilting on fine embroidery linen using padded linen quilting.

close together or the padded look will not survive and it will become flat and stiff. Do not use contrasting thread or thick embroidery stitches—a running or backstitch is best. Quilting can be done in a frame. The traditional quilted bedspreads were worked in large frames, the designs being scratched on the cotton surface around traditionally shaped templates.

Smocking. Originally, smocking was a decorative way of releasing fullness needed across the back and chest of a working garment and at the same time keeping the work elastic. To achieve this, the stitches must be worked zig-zag across two lines. Smocking survives today in young children's dresses. Occasionally fashion permits its use for women's clothes—around the waists, wrists, neck, and bodice. Smocking is done before the garment is made up. If the band of smocking for a baby's dress comes below the armhole level, it is neater and easier to deal with if the rectangle of material for the front and back is smocked straight across, the armhole cut into it and then the armhole seam double machine sewn.

Smocking must not look skimpy — you should allow three times the finished width to make smocking. First, prepare the work by putting in lines of dots. These can be marked by a ruler or by an iron-on transfer. It is fun (and quick) to use a checked, striped, or spotted fabric; then, provided the pattern is woven, you do not need to mark dots for smocking. If printed on, your dots rarely will be on the weave of the fabric anyhow. Next, put in a gathering thread along each line of dots and draw up tightly —pull it to set the pleats and release slightly.

If you have a cloth with a distinct weave so that you can keep a straight line, iron the smocking dots on the back of the fabric because sometimes they can be messy or show on the front. Pick up a small stitch under each dot on the back; then the draw thread will lie at the base of the pleats and

muted by the background. Connecting lines in the design can be in stem or backstitch. To prepare the cloth, the design is pinned under the transparent material and then painted with a fine brush and watercolor.

Quilting, smocking, and patchwork

These techniques originally were functional methods and not strictly embroidery.

Quilting was used originally to give added thickness to coverlets for warmth; a layer of combed out or carded lamb's wool was enclosed between two layers of cloth and then stitched in lines to hold it in place. The stitching soon developed into decorative patterns and today, in addition to wool, you can use nylon or dacron wadding, which do not go flat when washed. For quilting avoid choosing a realistic design because the wrinkles of the padding will confuse it. Do not put several lines

134

is less likely to be caught up in the embroidery. If, on the other hand, you have a smooth fabric and the dots must be on the front to act as a guide line, then iron lightly and pick up a large stitch under each dot so that again the draw thread will not get caught up by the smocking.

Test the heat of the iron carefully before ironing on the smocking dots. Too cool an iron and the dots won't mark—if this happens in a few places fill in the gaps by pencil. If the iron is too hot the dots will run and make a mess.

After you have pulled the thread through the fabric, you can pin the gathered-up work to a stiff paper or stay, especially if the smocked area is to be curved around a neck. Then twist the long ends of each pair of draw threads in a figure eight manner, around pins at the end of every two rows. You are now ready to start smocking. The first row is better if it is nonelastic, so work two lines of stem stitch from pleat to pleat, carefully adjusting spacing and tension. This stitch, being nonelastic, sets the width for the rest of the work, which has to have stretch and give so all subsequent lines are worked up and down in various ways.

There are very few different actual stitches in smocking—variations on stem stitch, chevron, and feather stitch are mainly used. Variety is obtained by the direction of the stitches. Because the general appearance is quite complicated, avoid using too many colors or any attempt to embroider flower forms.

A neat and decorative edging for a smocked sleeve or top of a waist on an an apron or dirndl skirt is to hem the edge and smock through the hem. By doing this the cuff is elastic, and you don't have to finish with a binding. A skirt or apron top will need a stay band of the material to prevent stretching.

Patchwork. Early patchwork grew out of the necessity of utilizing small scraps of valuable cloth. In the nineteenth century it was a favorite occupation of groups of ladies—a large bedspread, for example, being an ideal community work since each person could make up a section, which was later joined to the back side of the work.

In patchwork, the cloth of each patch has to be tacked over a stiff paper or thin card shape, which must be accurately cut from a metal template. The patches can be squares or equal-sided triangles or combinations of both—the most popular is the five-sided hexagon, which builds up like a honeycomb. A three-dimensional effect can be obtained by using the diamond template and dark-, medium-, and light-toned cloths. The most difficult to use is the scale, or shell, pattern. Use a razor blade and cut on a piece of thick cardboard, which, being grainless, is better than a wooden cutting board. Good quality stiff notepaper, old playing cards, etc. can be used for the paper shapes. The patterns can be built up geometrically in motifs. Make a large number of patches in each of the colors you are using; then arrange them before you start to sew. Do plan your bedspread, cushion, or tea cozy before you start. A haphazard collection of patches never looks good. The patches are joined by oversewing neatly on the extreme edges on the back. Try to use thread to match at least one of the sides you are joining.

Do not mix different types of cloth. Keep the work all cotton or all wool or all silk. Templates for wool should be large. Use plain colors or very fine patterns, unless you have fun with a printed pattern by cutting one little motif to come in the middle of a patch. Make a careful choice of your colors. You can embellish your patchwork by embroidering a tiny motif in the middle of some of the patches.

There is another form of patchwork called log cabin, which is formed by overlapping folded strips of cloth. If the colors are graduated in tones, this technique can look unusually subtle. But unless very well done, it can have an untidy appearance.

Shadow work by the author.

DESIGN

So far, all that has been discussed has taught the embroiderer the means of expression. But what are you going to say? Technical ability does not produce a design. And to make a design is difficult for those who are not gifted or trained as designers. But the more the embroiderer practices stitches and methods and experiments with a variety of threads on different fabrics, the more ideas will germinate, because stitches do a lot of the work and make much of a simple design. Never use

136

your thread just to draw the lines of a motif. For example, if you are developing something feathery or furry — the plumes in a bird's tail, angel's wings, a fox's brush, or a girl wearing a shaggy coat —then employ stitches such as fly, feather, and herringbone. Other stitches, such as buttonhole, backstitch, chain, or couching, will suggest the firm, hard edges of buildings or furniture; the holbein stitch or interlacing will suggest ironwork, the legs of a bird, or of furniture. Stem stitch should be used for something firm but slender, consider open chain or closed feather stitch.

Knobby twigs, tree bark, crustacea can be done in coral knot, double knot, or Portuguese knotted stem stitch. Centers of exotic petals and leaves can be executed in border stitches with a rich complicated silhouette, such as raised chain, band, crested chain, or wheatear. For surfaces of water, meadows, patterned robes, use wave filling, trellis, or the honeycomb stitch.

Throw a handful of exciting colored threads onto an interesting piece of cloth. Take out and add colors until you feel they are right. Try a very few strong colors backed up by neutral tones and see what results. That yellow woolen with those lovely greens and oranges could develop into a giant tiger lily, a stylized lion, or an interesting group of haystacks with patterns of plowing around them. Keep the shapes simple and flat. Now get the best references you can—drawings, photographs of the real thing. Reject secondhand ideas of design (which we have seen so many times before), and remember that in embroidery and the crafts in general, a realistic rendering is disastrous.

Design, briefly described, is a matter of assembling some shapes in a given space in a satisfying arrangement. So it is essential to start by setting out the shape you have to fill. Draw it to the exact size or smaller, but in proportion, on brown or tinted paper. Then in newspaper (for contrast), cut out quickly and roughly the shapes of your

motifs and arrange them on the brown paper. You can move them around until they are right, and then with a thick, soft pencil or a felt pen, scribble any lines or textures. Newspaper is plentiful, and by using it, you won't be inhibited to cut up and start all over as you would if you used more costly paper.

Cut out flowers — their shapes are so variable; birds — adding wings and tails; animals — refreshing your memory from zoological or natural history books; things seen around the house—quaint little chairs, vases, coffee pots, utensils, garden implements; the flat façades of interesting buildings. Look at the proportions of windows, arches, domes and steeples and assemble a group of them. Children's books today are a great source for motifs. They show a high standard of design in excellent and unusual colors. Children's own drawings have a directness and can express simply the basic character of the subject, which can often be translated into an embroidery design.

Study the best of modern commercial art. Make a well-edited collection of your own or your friends' Christmas cards. Start a scrapbook to which you can constantly be adding ideas.

At this point it will be useful to know how to enlarge a design, either your own or one you have copied or traced. You will need to know also:

1. How to dress a square frame.
2. How to transfer a design from the paper to the cloth.
3. How to stretch a finished embroidery professionally.
4. How to mount a finished embroidery.

All these methods can be found in most of the numerous good books on embroidery.

William Prince

musical instrument making

THERE MUST BE MANY PEOPLE who have thought of the pleasure it would give to be able to make and play one's own musical instrument, but have never attempted such a venture because it appears to be much beyond the scope of the average home craftsman. There are, however, many instruments that range in quality up to professional standards that have been constructed by painstaking amateurs who have had no training in the art of the luthier. If you can use woodworking tools reasonably well, I can think of no more rewarding task than to apply your talent to the making of a musical instrument.

GUITARS

It is doubtful if any other instrument in musical history has had the popularity that has been accorded to the guitar during the past ten years, so it must be the first to be discussed. To produce the range of notes, a guitar has shallow metal strips inserted at varying intervals across the fingerboard. These are called frets, and all instruments so designed are called fretted instruments. On the classical and flamenco guitars there are usually 19 or 20 frets. On the wire-stringed instruments, which include electric, cello-style, country and western, and Hawaiian steel guitars, there may be up to 24 frets.

Like most stringed instruments, the guitar has an open sound chamber over which is attached a soundboard. On this soundboard depend the vibrations of the strings, which are transmitted through the bridge, which rests upon it and which in turn produces the music. The soundboard, therefore, is the most important part of the instrument and must be fashioned with great care. Soundboards are made from quarter-cut, straightgrained spruce or fir from Europe or North America. The remainder of the soundchamber of the guitar is made of hardwood to give the stability that is necessary for amplifying the sound. Concert guitars are made of rose-

Prima balalaika made by the author. The soundboard is Canadian spruce; fingerboard is ebony; fingerplate is Indian rosewood.

wood, although in many instruments European walnut, maple, Cuban mahogany, and pearwood have been used. The necks of the guitar are, of long practice, made from what is commonly called Spanish cedar. The lightweight mahoganies are also used.

The flamenco guitarist's instrument is like the concert guitar in shape, but it is often fitted with wooden pegs instead of

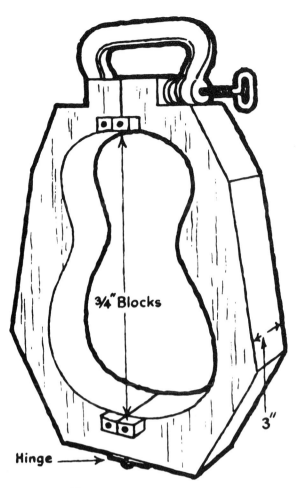

Guitar mold.

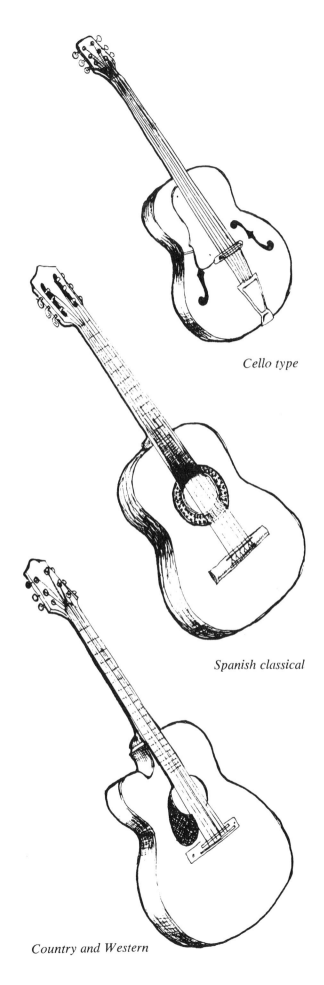

Cello type

Spanish classical

Country and Western

metal machine-heads. This is traditional, but it is in keeping with the lightness of construction that is an essential feature of this kind of instrument. Instead of rosewood, the body of the flamenco guitar is made from the wood of the Mediterranean cypress tree, which is very light and imparts the special timbre that is required in the music.

To make a Spanish guitar, you need a mold some 3 or more inches deep with the inner section cut out exactly to the shape of the completed sound-box. It is usually of softwood and may be made from solid timber or built up of laminations glued together.

First the ribs (sides) of the guitar are prepared, a bare $\frac{1}{12}$ inch in thickness. After soaking for 10 or 15 minutes in water, they are bent over a hot iron and fitted into the mold. There they are stamped or wedged into place and allowed to dry out.

139

Guitar neck

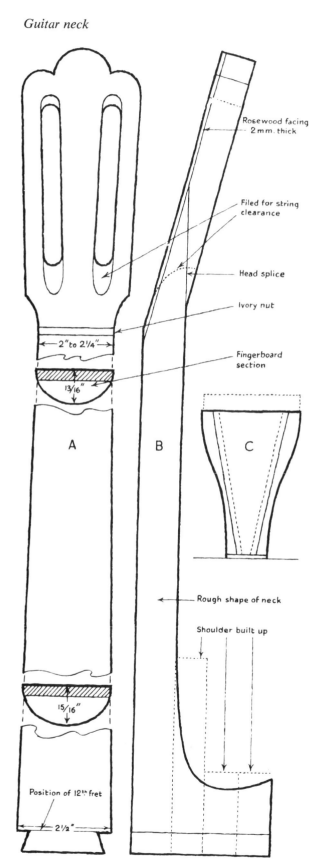

2" to 2¼"

13/16"

A   B   C

15/16"

Position of 12th fret

2½"

Rosewood facing
2 mm. thick

Filed for string
clearance

Head splice

Ivory nut

Fingerboard
section

Rough shape of neck

Shoulder built up

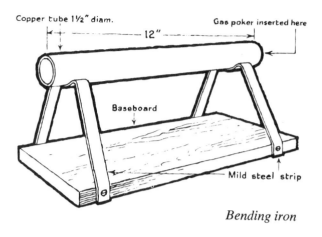

Copper tube 1½" diam.

12"

Gas poker inserted here

Baseboard

Mild steel strip

Bending iron

The next process is to glue onto the ribs blocks of softwood at the shoulder and tail ends of the body. Into the shoulder block will be dovetailed the neck, after the sound-box is finished.

Next, fillets of softwood, about 3/16 inch by ¼ inch, are bent and glued inside the back and front edges of the ribs. These are to give a sufficient gluing surface, on which will be fixed the back and soundboard of the instrument. The back and soundboard are prepared to about 1/12 inch thickness and then roughly to shape some 1/16 inch larger than the finished size. They are given a slight curvature by gluing to them the supporting struts, which have been shaped beforehand. For the back there are three struts spaced about equidistant at right angles to the center line. The soundboard has two similar struts, above and below the sound-hole, but the large area over which the bridge is glued on the outside is strengthened by a number of small, thin struts placed in the shape of a fan. They are fixed after the bridge has been glued in place. First the back, then the soundboard (after cutting out and decorating the sound-hole) are glued in place while the assembly is in the mold. The body of the guitar is then removed from the mold, the edges trimmed, and the hardwood binding fitted to front and back edges.

The neck of the Spanish guitar is often made from wood about 1/16 inch in thick-

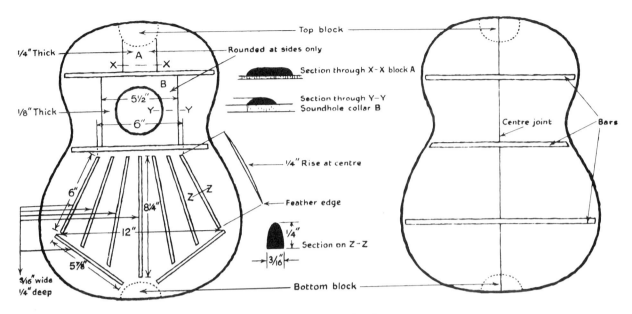

Section through X-X block A

Section through Y-Y
Soundhole collar B

¼" Rise at centre

Feather edge

Section on Z-Z

Top block

Rounded at sides only

Centre joint   Bars

Bottom block

Soundboard and back

ness with pieces glued together to make the heel, to the depth of the body, and the head is joined on and cut to shape afterward. The slots for the passage of the strings and the holes for the machine-heads are made at the same time. The neck is made with a dovetail, which is then joined into the shoulder block.

The guitar fingerboard should be prepared ¼ inch or ⅓ inch in thickness and should extend from the nut to the soundhole. The fingerboard is marked out and the fret positions scored across before it is glued into place. After the frets are fitted the whole instrument is sandpapered to a fine surface before polishing or varnishing, and attaching the nut, machines, and strings.

This general outline may be used as a basis for making other instruments, such as a plectrum, or folk guitar, Hawaiian guitar, electric/acoustic guitar, ukelele, tenor ukelele, tenor guitar, and flat-back mandolin. Although the round-backed mandolin and the balalaika are made by a different process from that described, both these instruments are within the scope of the home craftsman.

Guitar decorated in engraved marquetry of tortoiseshell, ivory, and pewter with floral patterns and figures.

141

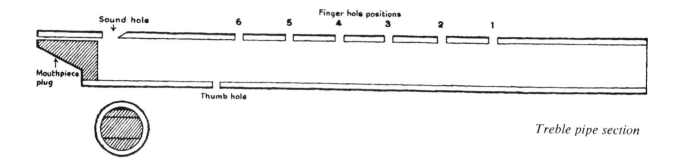

Treble pipe section

WIND INSTRUMENTS

Quite a variety of simple but sweet-sounding wind instruments may be made by the sparetime craftsman, and the materials used can be so cheap as to permit experiments in order to produce perfect articles. Instead of using the laborious techniques of hollowing wood from a solid piece, such as is necessary in the making of clarinets, oboes, and kindred instruments, we can find suitable tubing in wood, plastic, or lightweight alloys that will well serve our purpose. Depending on the bore of the tube, you can make pipes and recorders pitched at treble, alto, tenor, and baritone, thus being able to form a full consort of instruments. A start could be made with a treble pipe as follows:

From a piece of jointless bamboo with an internal diameter of about ¾ inch cut cleanly a length of 11⁵⁄₁₂ inches and made a hole, ¼ inch by ⅙ inch, some 1¼ inch from the mouthpiece end. To this hole, which has its shortest measurement across the tube, should now be cut a sloping channel that follows the curve of the bamboo and ends in a fairly sharp edge on the inside. The angle of the slope will depend on the thickness of the bamboo wall, and about a 40° angle should be tried at first. The final angle may be decided after the mouthpiece has been made and tried.

In order to set the pitch of the instrument, the mouthpiece must now be made. This is done by cutting away the end of the tube so as to leave about one third of the rim, where the lips are applied. The lower saw cut is made ¾ inch from the end of the tube and less than halfway through its diameter. It is joined by a slanting cut from the end to remove the waste material. A plug of cork or balsa wood is now fitted firmly into the mouthpiece, being shaped externally to match the tube and extending inside to a point a little higher than the sound-hole. From the sound-hole to the upper part of the mouthpiece should be cut, in the tube, a straight, shallow channel (about ¹⁄₂₄ inch), and this will correspond with a shaving that will be taken from the top of the plug.

It is usual to have these pipes tuned to C or D, and the pitch is determined by the length. When a clear tone is achieved, tune the pipe with the aid of a piano. If it is sharp, reduce the length slightly until the pipe plays the desired note correctly. Now measure the distance from the end of the pipe to the center of the sound-hole and put a mark a quarter of this length from the end of the pipe. This will be the first hole. Then from the sound-hole center measure 2¹⁄₁₆ inches and mark the position of the sixth hole. The remaining four holes are marked at equidistant intervals between the first and the sixth. Each position is bored and tuned separately before starting the next one. A small hole is made and gradually enlarged to produce the required note. The last hole, which is for the left-hand thumb, is made on the side opposite to the finger holes at a position a fraction of an inch nearer to the mouthpiece than the sixth hole.

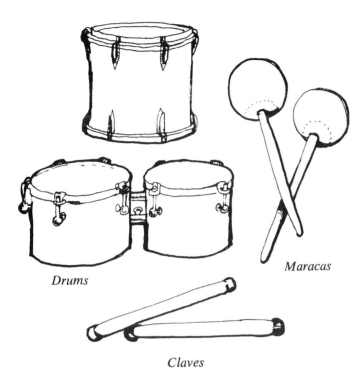

Drums

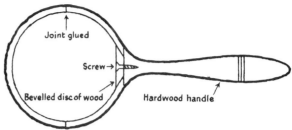

Maracas

Claves

Section through a maraca

Joint glued

Screw

Bevelled disc of wood

Hardwood handle

A final smoothing with flour-grade sandpaper and a coat or two of clear varnish to the exterior surfaces — except the mouthpiece—will complete the instrument.

SIMPLE PERCUSSION

Percussion effects give the amateur, perhaps, the greatest scope for ingenuity, and from cheap components can be contrived the most exciting rhythms. Indeed, some famous jazz bands have built their reputations around the sound of metal thimbles striking the corrugated surface of the old-fashioned washboard.

Simple but effective drums can be made out of many hollow objects. Small round wooden casks, heavy plastic and pith-fiber drain pipe, and heavy cardboard packing tubes can be made into drums and bongos. Drum heads, which are obtainable from musical supplies dealers, are soaked in water to make them pliable and then fastened over the upper end of the drum. Tuning varies by the length of the drum; the longer the cylinder, the lower the pitch. By sawing the tubes into different lengths, one

can make a very versatile rhythm section.

Another simply-constructed percussion instrument is the marimba. This instrument may be made from hardwoods or softwoods. To get the most pleasing results may involve some interesting and rewarding experiments. If you have some material about $1\frac{7}{12}$ inches by $\frac{7}{12}$ inch, cut two pieces about $21\frac{2}{3}$ inches long to form the side pieces of the marimba bed. To the narrow edge of each piece, fix a piece of thick twine at each end with a tack. The twine must be stretched taut from end to end. Stand the pieces side by side, with the twine uppermost, about $5\frac{5}{12}$ inches apart at one end and $10\frac{1}{4}$ inches at the other. To hold them in this position, lightly tack a piece of lath across the ends.

The keys of the marimba are made from the same material as the sides, and you will require eight pieces for this one-octave instrument. The keys will lie flat across the bed spaced about $\frac{7}{12}$ inch apart. The natural key of C is a good one to start with, so cut the first key, which will be the lowest one, long enough to protrude a few inches over each side of the bed at the wide end. Sound it with a light wooden hammer and tune it with the piano to C natural. It will probably be too low at the start, and the tone is sharpened by shortening the key slightly or paring away on the underside between the sides of the bed. Remember it is simpler to sharpen the keys than to flatten them, so start off each one with a good overlap.

Following the same procedure, make each key up the scale until you have the full octave. Now, take off the pieces of lath and sound the keys, making adjustments to the angle of the bed pieces until the best alignment is found. Then permanent pieces are fixed at the ends to complete the bed. Holes are bored through the keys at the center of the point at which they rest on the bed and through these are gently hammered wire nails to keep the keys in position. The nails must not in any way restrict the vibration of the keys.

A great variety of percussion instruments are used in Latin American bands, and some of these effects may be easily copied. Coconuts make excellent maracas. With a fine-toothed saw, cut the nut across into two halves; remove the flesh; and dry and smooth the shell with sandpaper. Attach a wooden handle to the end, either by gluing into a hole or screwing on from inside. Inside the shell place a few split peas or similar seeds and glue the halves together. Decorate the maracas with enamels anyway you like. Other hollow objects could be used in the same way.

The Latin American rhythm sticks called claves are made from pieces of hardwood about 7 inches long by 1 inch in diameter. They are played in pairs, one being cupped loosely in the hand and struck with the other one.

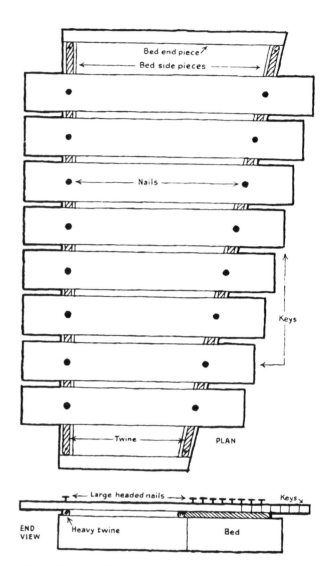

A simple marimba

Derek Waters

natural materials

AMONG THE PLEASURES in this area of crafts is the discovery of the materials to be used. Quite often you will come across some natural object and store it away until the need for it arises. Certain flower arrangements require material that is gathered months before use and dried. When a tree is being felled, it is often possible to beg a piece from the woodsman, but before you can get to work with your chisels, the timber needs to be seasoned. Under normal circumstances, this progresses at the rate of one inch per year—from both sides—so pencil the date of felling on your green timber when you get it. Sometimes the unexpected acquisition of a piece of wood—unusual in shape, color, or size—may start the creative urge in the mind immediately. On the other hand, the material may be in store for months, or even years, before another factor stimulates some craftwork.

WHERE TO LOOK — WHAT TO LOOK FOR

When you look for materials, fields and forest preserves offer fine opportunities for discovery. Since man first began to cultivate the land there have been ceremonies at harvest time, which included making symbols and decorations. Recently there has been an interesting revival of the rural craft of making corn dolls. The top section of the ripe straw is used for these. Wheat is best, but oats, rye, and even grass can be used to make the various traditional designs. Woodlands are worth searching, especially if they are somewhat neglected. Fallen branches are some of the things to look for. Hold them up in the air; turn them this way and that to see the shape they make in silhouette. Look for interesting contortions, configurations, and branchings as you rotate the wood.

Where wood has lain for some time, the bark may be loose or rotted away, revealing the wood underneath. Sometimes bark beetles have been at work and have engraved remarkable patterns for their breeding

Cockerel made from dried seeds and leaves.

chambers and feeding channels. Bark, with its texture, color, and shape, can also be collected and used for material arrangements.

Flower arranging is a very popular craft today. All kinds of flowers, foliage, fruit, and even vegetables found on the domestic scene can be used in arrangements. They may be used for fresh flower displays and sprayed with a variety of colors and finishes, such as gold, pearl tones, and blush tints. Or they may be picked, placed in

145

Driftwood found on the seashore is weathered into interesting shapes and textures.

Toy made from a lobster's claw.

sand or vermiculite in a dark dry place, and allowed to dry, and then brought out to be displayed all winter. Pick wildflowers and dry them too.

The woodlands will provide other things for displays. Spring is the time to look among the trees for flowers that bloom before the leaves grow and reduce the amount of light reaching the ground. If chemical sprays have not had too extensive an effect, there will be an abundance of flowers to collect in the summer meadow and from its edges. Come the autumn, leaves turn brown and gold, seeds and berries are brightly colored to attract the birds; all of this makes a rich harvest for the collector. Fungus, found in a surprising variety of forms and colors during the fall, can be used for brief displays; the shapes in-

spire drawings and the making of molds from which some permanent forms can be cast in plaster of paris. Remember, however, that some fungi are extremely poisonous, even when dried. When collected, fungi should be kept away from children, and your hands should be thoroughly washed after touching them.

Winter is seldom regarded as the best time of year for collecting, but often berries persist on the trees and shrubs. And it is easier to appreciate unusual branch shapes when they do not have leaves on them. Twigs, with variations of bud shape and formation, can be collected and arranged. Evergreen branches from pine, spruce, and other needle and cone type trees may be gathered all year around.

Leaves that have lain on the ground

146

for a few months may have become skele-tonized; poplar leaves are particularly good examples. These can be collected, pressed, and arranged on paper. A more sophisti-cated display can be made under glass or plexiglas for tabletops or finger panels for doors.

Where seeds, cones, and twigs are gath-ered to make figures, pieces of wire can be cut to act as branches for the various items to form a figure. The ends of the wire can be either stapled to a piece of wood or passed through such a base to secure the figure.

It is in those places where there is water that some of the best materials can be discovered. By riverside and sea there is usually an abundance of debris, which is constantly changing. Particularly after storms, both the riverbank and seashore are worth searching. The abrasive action of sand and pebbles smooths most things that spend any length of time in the water. In the case of wood, softer areas are worn away more rapidly, resulting in in-teresting textures, and edges and corners are rounded. Unusual shapes are produced, which need only a little embellishment with sandpaper, files, and small saws to make them suitable for anything you want to make. These wooden forms can either be freestanding or become parts of mobiles. Sometimes a long, sinuous branch can be hung from its center of gravity to turn slowly in the air and offer many different views to the observer below.

Among beach finds, you may come across the white oval shapes of the cuttle fish bone. These can be carved and filed to make low relief shapes. A penknife is a useful tool for this material—which is very much like salt to work, but does not have the ever-present danger of crumbling like the latter when attempting features that make part of the material too thin.

Collecting pebbles is a fascinating hobby. Often the colors are less bright when away from the water, but brightness returns if

Traditional corn doll.

the stones are stored in a jar of water or if clear varnish is brushed on them. Stones can be broken open with a hammer and chisel to reveal unsuspected colors and pat-terns, which can be used quite successfully in mosaics. A pattern can be decided upon and sketched onto a piece of blockboard. The stones are best fixed with an epoxy adhesive. Plaster of paris is used to fill in the intervening spaces between the stones. Alternatively, the mosaics may be planned to go on patios or garden walls, and for such activities, a mixture of sand and ce-ment should be prepared (in the propor-tion of two of sand to one of cement) with enough water to make a stiff, pliable mix-ture. Then, the pebbles are pressed into place and allowed to set.

Shells are plentiful on the beach, and a large collection can be made to supply any

147

*Eroded driftwood is good for natural
sculpture, but it may need a little finishing off.*

number of projects. For example, when making a small figure, a dogwhelk might be chosen for the body, a periwinkle for the head, and a limpet for the hat. In utilizing shells like this, problems arise when fine detail is required. There are small shells on beaches, but it may be necessary to use small beads for eyes and other features. Paint can also be employed to provide such details. Use an epoxy or contact cement to hold items to shells and to hold shells together.

Certainly the natural environment has much to offer the craftsman, not only because of the cheapness, variety, and abundance of material available but also because it offers a continual challenge in selecting and modifying each item to suit a particular purpose.

Michael Grater

paper

AS THE BASIC MATERIAL OF A CRAFT, paper might not appear immediately promising. It is flat. It is not strong; and while it comes in a variety of colors and types and has many uses, which we take for granted, we rarely think of it as a material for sculpture or modeling.

If you take a sheet of paper of any sort and hold it, as a craftsman must hold his materials, you are very unlikely to get an immediate inspiration. You can demonstrate this by actually taking a piece of exercise or drawing paper, or even wrapping paper, about the size of this page. To make anything with this piece of paper you would have to begin by understanding something of its constructive potential—what is possible with it. If you try to stand the paper, for example, upright on a flat surface, it will fall down. If, however, you fold the paper through the middle from top to bottom, it will be possible to stand the shape you have made on edge, like a greeting card. Whether it will stand firmly or still appear to be hopelessly limp will depend on the quality of the paper you start with. If your present example is not adequately firm, you will need to try again with paper of a slightly heavier quality. If the folded paper will stand unsupported, you will see that, in a simple way, you have controlled the material. You have introduced a strength factor; and if you look closely at it, again as a craftsman must look at his work, you will see that you have also done something to its appearance. You will now have two surfaces, or planes, meeting at the center fold. If you look carefully you may be able to see that, although you have not changed the nature of the surfaces, they will now be slightly varied in tone or shade according to the way the light is falling on the paper.

What you have done is a simple craftsman's technique. You could have crumpled the paper up, which would have been a way of manipulating it, but the resultant ball of crushed paper would be imprecise

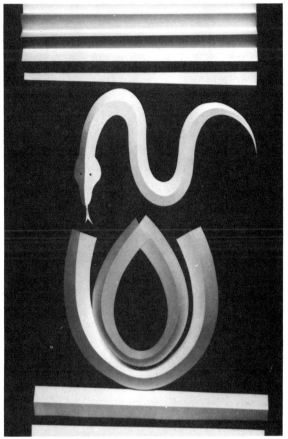

Fig. 1

and probably not a rewarding treatment for future use in modeling.

However, the simple fold is an example of a controlled technique that can be repeated and takes into account the nature of the material. It is a technique that can be applied in many ways because it shows an appreciation of what the material can be made to do. It is the appreciation of material that forms the basis of work in any craft.

For working with paper there is no special quality requirement. Any paper can be used if the craftsman can control it and make it do what he wants. If he has ability and understanding in a few simple techniques, the craftsman will appreciate whether the material is usable or not.

149

Creative modeling in paper is obviously best attempted with good quality material. But it is not necessary to go to a great deal of expense. There are a number of techniques that have been refined by craftsmen working with paper. These can be learned quickly and easily and can be applied in work with all sorts of paper.

Scoring and folding

If a fold in a piece of paper will give it strength and will add visual interest, it is desirable that the act of folding can be controlled with some precision by the craftsman. Any sort of a fold in paper is assisted by scoring the surface along the line to be folded.

To demonstrate this, you should cut two long, narrow strips of paper of equal size. You should now aim, by controlling the material, to make these strips stand upright. You can fold the first one freehand through the middle from top to bottom. In the second example, you should lightly cut the surface of the fold, using a straight edge as a guide and taking care not to cut right through it at any point. A knife or a scissors blade can be used.

After scoring, you will find that the cut will open slightly as you fold away from it. When you have mastered the technique, it should be possible to make a precise and unbuckled fold which, compared to your first example, is likely to be crisper and cleaner in effect than the unscored fold.

The curved score. In paper modeling it is often useful to have a curved fold, for example, on the surface of a leaf or a flower petal. The curved score should be made freely. It is not possible to use a straight edge, so it must be practiced. For a simple exercise, you should cut a number of identical leaf shapes and try various straight or curved scores on them, comparing the effect of the folds that you are able to produce. This technique can be practiced in many different ways (Fig. 1).

As a more interesting exercise, after mas-

Fig. 2

tering the latter technique, you might make some freestanding figures. These can be cut in stiff paper or cardboard preferably on the fold so that they are symmetrical when you open them. They can be developed as characters, with drawn or painted decoration, or as more elaborate cut paper shapes (Fig. 2). Colored or patterned papers will add to the visual effect of the finished work.

Fixing

For paper modeling any method of fixing can be used that gives an adequately strong fixture with the minimum of difficulty. There are three main methods, used either singly or in combination:

Fig. 3

Gluing. Any of the modern white emulsion or household paper glues can be used. These stick on contact between surfaces and are usually available in plastic bottles or tubes. They are so efficient that the only real problem is to keep any messy excess off the front of the paper.

Stapling. An immediate and permanent fixture can be made between any number of papers with the use of a hand stapler, which pushes and folds a small wire staple through the material. There are many different sorts currently available.

Slotting and flapping. When it is necessary to fix one shape to another, it is sometimes useful to cut the shape with an extra flap that can be inserted into a slot cut at the point of fixture. The location of the slot can be established by holding the shape with the flap against the background and marking its exact position before cutting. The advantage of this method is that its use will result in an invisible fixture with the flap hidden and, if necessary, glued out of sight.

Cutting. The ability to cut paper neatly and accurately is obviously an essential skill for the paper craftsman, but again there is no hard and fast rule about how it should be done. Either scissors or a sharp knife can be used. The type of craft knife that can be bought with replacement blades is likely to prove most useful for any type of scoring or cutting. It can be used in combination with a cutting surface made from a sheet of cheap cardboard, which can be replaced when the surface becomes too rough from constant use.

Raising form

The basic problem of working with paper as a modeling material, since it starts by being flat, is to raise any adequate sort of form or shape. In the first application of the scoring technique, a simple form was established by the two planes meeting at the fold of the paper. This particular technique, as you will have seen, can be used in many ways for modeling, either as a single fold or in multiple arrangements. There are other simple methods of raising form in flat paper.

Overlapping. If you take a flat piece of paper, square or disc, and make a single

151

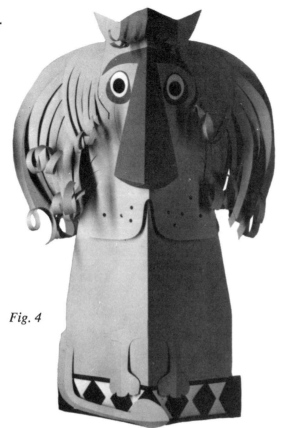

Fig. 4

Fig. 5

cut in it from the outer edge to the center, it will be possible to overlap the sides of the cut. As you make the overlap, the paper will take on a new form. From a disc, for example, the form will raise as a cone. This is a technique that can be developed and applied in various ways. In Fig. 3 a disc is treated variously with the cut to center and with scores so that the techniques combine to make an overall visual effect.

Curling. Another method of raising form from the flat is to establish the sort of mass effect, less precise but still visually attractive, that can be achieved by curling the paper. If you take a strip of paper and run a blade along one surface, from one end to the other, you will disturb the tension on the surface, and the strip will tend to spring into a curl. This is a technique that will require a little practice.

Begin by cutting a number of strips of varying widths and practice by holding each of them in turn at one end and, starting at this point, running a knife or scissors blade along the underside of the length. The blade should be controlled with your thumb at the top of the strip as your hand

Fig. 6

Fig. 7

moves along it. It is a simple scraping movement, which you might have to practice, and in some of the earlier attempts, you might find yourself tearing the strip. You will do this less often as you get the feel of the technique and will appreciate how much pressure you must apply to make the paper curl. As in all craftwork, the craftsman must learn to rely on his touch along with his knowledge of how much manipulation the material will stand before its usefulness is ruined.

The curling technique is one that can be used in many ways to add attractive visual effect to paper models, for example, in the hair (Fig. 4).

Surface treatment

When you have appreciated the need in paper modeling to raise simple form, you will be able to investigate the further opportunities that may be used to make the modeling interesting. There are various surface treatments that may be used. Painting and drawing are, of course, methods of treating a surface, but for modeling there are other simple techniques.

Cut texture. Cuts into a paper surface can exploit the development of pattern and the play of light over the surface. If you take a piece of paper and make a number of V-shaped cuts in the surface, you will be able to raise the cut shapes so that they throw small shadows. This visual effect can be developed in many ways by altering the shape or arrangement of the cuts.

Applied texture. An alternative method to cutting into a surface is to vary its visual effect by adding a pattern or texture of folded papers. If you cut a number of simple fish shapes, you can experiment with some of the potential of applied texture. Paper folded in various ways to produce shadows can be fixed to the surface, either in continuous strips or as a single shape repeated in patterns (Fig. 5).

Basic forms

The various techniques that you have considered so far can be explored in many

153

paper

Fig. 8

essentially three-dimensional, which can be exploited creatively with added papers using some of the techniques already described (Fig. 6).

Other simple freestanding forms can be made from the triangular or square prism. For the triangular prism you will need to fold the paper into three equal sides, allowing a flap at the edge for an overlapping fixture. Square and rectangular prisms can be made in the same way with four sides and can be used as basic forms for further development (Fig. 7).

By experiencing the techniques described, you will acquire an adequate starting point for the development of a craft skill in working with paper. As a material, paper is cheap and readily available, and anyone should be able to obtain pleasure and satisfaction from controlling and exploring paper in all sorts of interesting ways and, more important, in making the paper do exactly what you want it to.

Masks (Fig. 8) are a simple statement concerning the way flat paper may be used. You may have seen more ambitious examples of what the professional paper craftsman calls paper sculpture. This sculpture has a wide variety of commercial applications. Any example of this that you come across might be visually impressive, but its impact is less meaningful to the young craftsman than a simple understanding of the material and what is possible with it.

In craft there is no particular merit in virtuosity or complex expertise. And in paper craft there is in fact a disadvantage in overcomplication. Where the material is simple, it will support simple end-products that are crisp and uncluttered and easy to look at. The potential of this craft is lighthearted. It is a fun activity that is open to anyone who can gather some paper, something to cut it with, and some means of making it last.

ways in three-dimensional paper modeling. When you are trying to make a shape in any three-dimensional craft, it is quite unlikely that it can be very rewarding to rely merely on accident. The material you are using is likely to have potential in certain basic shapes. You can establish the simplest of these in paper by rolling a flat sheet into a cylinder. This should be secured at the top and bottom. In this instance, you are likely to find that stapling will be the most effective method. The cylinder you make will be a freestanding form,

154

Leon Metcalfe

plaster and polystyrene plaques

THIS SECTION IS CONCERNED WITH the making of plaques from two essentially different yet readily obtainable materials—plaster of paris and polystyrene. Certain basic knowledge is, however, common to both materials, and this should be fully appreciated before work commences. It includes such considerations as size, shape, design, and color. Useful working sizes for plaques fall in the range of 6 inches to 12 inches across, but it is necessary to consider the thickness of the work in relation to the overall size. Strength and a certain amount of aesthetic satisfaction can come from a well-proportioned piece of work, and the thicknesses for the sizes given above should range between ½ inch and 1 inch.

Basic shape can enhance and influence the appreciation of the completed work, and in this respect it is best to keep to simple geometric shapes such as circles, squares, rectangles, and pentagons. Avoid fine points and angles because these are fragile and difficult to protect unless the plaque is mounted on a larger rigid backing. When the design of the motif or decoration is under consideration, simplicity is again the key factor, and bold, simple designs and colors will always be found to be most successful.

PLASTER

Plaster of paris is cheap and can be obtained in white powder form from most hardware or building materials stores and sometimes in very small quantities from pharmacists. It is mixed with water to a creamy consistency and poured into greased molds, in which it will set quickly. Metal box lids, which are made in a variety of shapes and sizes, form useful molds, but others may also be made from flat plastic sheeting or cardboard. The basic white color of plaster of paris can be changed at the mixing stage by adding a powder paint color. This will then be the base color for the plaque. Before the plaster has set, it is advisable to introduce a reinforcing agent.

Plaster plaque

The larger the plaque the more important this becomes. Any form of open-weave material, such as gauze bandage, is useful for this purpose, and strips of this should be pressed down into the mixture so that they are completely submerged. A final strip of material can be looped and the ends inserted into the plaster for hanging or mounting the completed work. The grease in the mold should enable the plaque to be turned out easily, when it will be ready, after cleaning and smoothing, for the addi-

155

Polystyrene plaque.

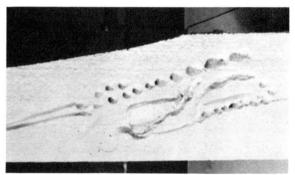

An example of experimental routings and burnings into an expanded polystyrene sheet.

tion of the chosen design. The smoothing of the surface can be accomplished with fine sandpaper, and sharp corners can be rounded off into pleasant curves.

A bas-relief technique is imposed on the surface of the work by means of linoleum block cutters or similar small cutting implements. Plaster can be decorated with almost any type of paint, ranging from powder color to enamels, depending on whether a matte or shiny surface is required, but care should be taken that the plaster is quite dry before painting. A final protective layer of varnish can be painted over the completed plaque.

POLYSTYRENE

Polystyrene is widely used as a packing agent for fragile goods, and this source should not be forgotten because it can be the cheapest way of obtaining the material. Most hardware stores and building materials suppliers stock both sheet polystyrene and also prepared wall tiles. Tiles are most useful for plaque-making because they require no initial cutting or shaping and they have neat beveled or grooved edges.

To cut a basic plaque shape from sheet polystyrene, a hot knife is the best tool to use. The blade of the knife can be heated

in the flame of a gas jet or sterno. Alternatively, use the heated tip of an electric soldering iron. The cellular structure of this material does not lend itself to fine, detailed work, and this should be avoided.

Sketch the basic design of the plaque on the surface of the polystyrene with a felt pen and hatch those areas of the design which are to be removed to produce a bas-relief effect. These low-relief areas can then be burned away by using an electric soldering iron or the heated knob end of a steel knitting needle.

Painted decoration of the design can be added using most types of paint except cellulose, which has an unfortunate effect on the polystyrene. Any final dressing of the work can be done either with the hot soldering iron or with fine sandpaper or emery boards.

John Lancaster

plastics

THE RANGE OF THREE-DIMENSIONAL materials available to artists has extended considerably during the past decade, and this has provided them with a wider range of spatial expression than was previously available. It is certainly not uncommon today to find sculptures executed in metal, wire, glass, neon, plastics, or a combination of materials such as these, which are relevant to a machine age in which technology, engineering, and mass production play dominant roles. Of course sculpture in more traditional wood and stone, which have been used from the time primitive man started to be creative, still is being executed.

The new synthetically-produced materials commonly referred to as plastics (a term derived from the Greek word *plastikos* meaning growing, developing, and forming) consist of formless matter that can be given molded or modeled form by craftsmen and artists using a variety of techniques. Because methods of producing the material have been improved, costs have, fortunately, been reduced and this has brought a comparatively cheap material within easy reach of the sculptor. It enables him to work at speed on three-dimensional works that are light in weight, and he now has the facility to produce standing structures or relief panels on a very large scale. William Mitchell, the architectural sculptor, has had considerable success in designing and making decorative reliefs for both interior and exterior walls of new apartment and office buildings and has used materials such as polyurethane, polystyrene, cold cast bronze, and cements, which he has found to be so appropriate to this work.

I am convinced that the most sensible approach to creative work is an empirical one based upon experiment and self-discovery. The artist must accept a material for what it is and go on to discover for himself just what he can do with it. At the same time, he must be willing to admit the unexpected, or what Freda Koblick, the sculptor, calls

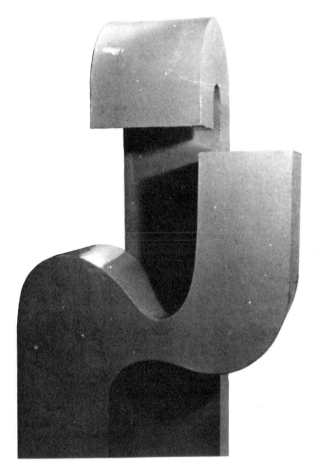

"Two Yellows," a completed sculpture in laminated fiber glass.

unplanned happenings, for these add excitement and can lead to further interesting, creative work. However, the sculptor must be acute enough to recognize the significance of such happenings and make the best use of them. New discoveries can foster discernment as the artist sees shapes arise from the formless material, as well as stimulating the urge to make further experiments and investigations. Forms will emerge that are not predetermined, or with their inspirations rooted in the work of earlier cultures, and the artist's own crea-

157

tions will be original. He must, initially, allow himself to react to materials and be prepared for a reciprocal reaction to occur. His thought and design processes will be stimulated as he comes to terms with more involved problems; his self-discovered techniques and ways of working will be extended as he gains confidence in manipulating materials, and he will gradually come to terms with technical processes that will enable him to pursue his craftsmanship further. Reading of appropriate technical literature should be supplemented by visits to workshops in which plastics are used in the production of sailing dinghies, canoes, caravans, or even household utensils. Firsthand knowledge can be acquired by watching craftsmen at work, and the discussion of technical procedures with them can be an invaluable supplement to the experience of the person who is struggling alone. Indeed, the amateur will often receive off-cuts and scrap materials quite cheaply from such workshops, and this can considerably extend his range of personal experimentation.

One easily obtainable plastic material is foam rubber, which may be purchased from local hardware stores in both thin and thick colored sheets. It is soft, extremely pliable, and has not as yet been fully explored as a sculptural material. This means that the field is open for sculptors who are prepared to experiment with three-dimensional foam rubber forms. It can be cut, squeezed, pulled, burned, and twisted into the most incredible shapes, and it is possible to fix it in a semipermanent position with thread, glues, and wire. The additional use of wood, wire, plaster, or cement will give added permanency to an otherwise flexible, temporary kind of plastic, and, as a further development, the resulting shapes may be cast in other suitable materials.

Expanded rigid polystyrene, which may be bought from local builders' merchants in large and small sheets, is excellent for quickly conceived structures. It may be so

Detail from the main door panel of a cathedral.

manipulated that its nature is changed, but once again the experimental approach should be emphasized. The artist may try squeezing, sawing, tearing, routing, and hitting with a sharp or blunt instrument; he may burn it with a soldering iron or cut it with a hot wire, which will cut through it cleanly. In producing the forms the sculptor has in mind the surface of that expanded rigid polystyrene may be textured by the application of certain adhesives that dissolve where they touch and leave interesting pattern qualities on the surface, which may be further enhanced with paint, stains, and dry color. When making large constructions it is possible to attach sheets of this material by means of glues and fixing wires (U-shapes made from soft florists' wire) pushed through the expanded polystyrene like nails into wood. The addition of thin coats of plaster will add a fairly substantial outer skin, and, indeed, such coverings strengthen sculptures, which still remain light and easy to handle.

Coating a polystyrene structure with plaster.

Relief sculpture.

Yet another interesting way of working in plastics it to rout or burn shapes out of the expanded polystyrene sheet and then use this as a mold into which cement or metals are poured. The molded forms take on the sculptured shapes, and their accidentally-produced surface textures—which can often be most pleasant — become part of the finished structure.

Styrofoam is a light plastic that is produced industrially by expanding polystyrene with methyl chloride gas. It is good for mold making because the molten metal will cause the Styrofoam to vaporize in the casting process, but it must be pointed out that there is a slight danger to health in using Styrofoam because it contains a quantity of the methyl chloride gas, and care should be taken when trying this method. (*See* precautionary notes issued by the manufacturers.)

In conclusion, it must be stressed that the most interesting and often the most exciting plastic imagery results from an un-

Expanded polystyrene relief panel. The letter shapes were cut with a hot wire.

inhibited way of working that is not bound by the restrictions of traditional craft techniques. The artist should not be over-cautious. He must be prepared to make mistakes and to learn from these when producing three-dimensional work in a field that is relatively new and still open to individual developments. There are few restrictions or barriers to be surmounted, and this in itself should give the greatest encouragement.

159

printmaking

"Man with Newspaper." Etching showing aquatint.

THE PRINTMAKER need not be contained within the limitations of one particular method; he can select from four main techniques, which come under the collective title of printmaking. These are wood-cutting, etching, lithography, and silkscreen printing, with many variations and extensions of each process. A combination of two or more processes may sometimes be used to create a single print image, but usually the technique selected as an area of specialization is that most suited to one's particular requirements.

Printmaking can be defined thus: an autographic means of programming the production of a number of copies of a single image for the purpose of distribution. This means that a print is created using a preliminary plan; if the print is to be in four colors, then a separate plate or block must be made for each color, and the colors must be registered in the correct position on the printing paper. The main interest of most artists and designers lies in the special graphic qualities of the print processes; that is to say, an artist would select a printmaking process to achieve an effect not possible in any other medium. For example, lithography is best used for its soft and atmospheric qualities; etching is concerned mainly with linear and sculptural effects; woodcutting and silkscreen printing are basically used for hard-edged designs and broader tonal qualities.

Lithography is a chemical process, while the other three are based on mechanical principles. On a professional level prints are usually made with the aid of special printing presses and equipment, but there are many techniques that can be used at home or at school without presses or expensive equipment. The first two sections, relief and stencil printing, are mainly concerned with processes that can be carried out without the use of a printing press. The following is a brief outline of each printmaking process:

RELIEF PRINTING

Woodcuts and linocuts fall into this category. The nonprinting areas of the block are cut away with a sharp gouge or knife; the parts of the block that remain are in relief and will therefore receive printing ink from a brayer rolled over the surface. This process is the oldest and perhaps the best known of all the printmaking media; most people have at some time made a linocut or a potato-cut — a basic form of relief printing. In schools linocuts are often used for repeat or multiple images and also for printing directly onto fabrics. A print taken from a relief block is recognized by the characteristic simplicity of the cut or gouged shapes and the tonal weight of the image, which is inherent in the medium. Block printing is a craft that requires a certain amount of control, especially in the use of cutting gouges.

STENCIL PRINTING

Silkscreen printing is founded upon the

The etching press in operation.

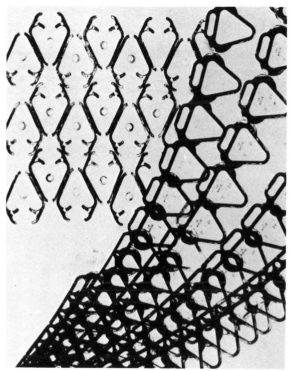

Offset print from a plastic electrical plug.

INCISION PRINTING

This process is really a reversal of the relief process because the areas of the plate that are taken away act as a reservoir for the printing ink, the parts of the plate in relief being wiped clear of printing ink. A metal plate made of zinc, steel, or copper is covered with a fine layer of specially prepared wax ground; this is done while the plate is hot so that the wax can be rolled into an even layer with a leather-covered roller. The wax ground surface of the plate is held upside down in a hand vise and smoked black with lighted candles, taking care to rotate the candles continuously so that the wax is not scorched or burned.

The drawing is made using a steel needle, which exposes the base metal through the wax ground. When the drawing is completed, the back of the plate is protected with an asphaltum-based varnish, and the plate is immersed in a bath of diluted nitric acid. The acid bites into the metal in those areas from which the wax has been removed

basic principle of stencil printing and was developed by the fabric industry as a means of producing printed designs on woven material. A piece of silk or organdy is stretched tightly over a wooden frame. The frame contains the printing ink that is forced through the weave of the stretched material by a rubber blade called a squeegee. Parts of the weave are first blocked out with a water-soluble glue or paper stencil so that the ink forced through the weave forms a positive image on a sheet of paper beneath the screen. The stencil or glue blocks the weave in those parts of the design that are to remain clear.

161

Inking up a lithographic plate on the press.

ing care not to remove the ink from the incisions. Finally, the plate surface is wiped with the palm of the hand until the drawing appears as a crisp line on the shiny surface.

Then, the plate is warmed again to keep the ink moist and laid on the steel bed of the mangle-like printing press. A sheet of damp printing paper is laid down on top of the plate, followed by a sheet of blotting paper to absorb the excess moisture and a set of felt lengths that help to force the paper into the incisions on the plate when the bed, under great pressure, moves through the steel rollers. As the paper is forced into the incisions, the ink is transferred to the paper. When the print is lifted from the plate the inking procedure must be repeated to take further copies.

A wide tonal range can be obtained by using lines of varying depth. A two-color print can be made by filling the incisions with one color and rolling a second color over the surface of the plate. Tones can also be made by melting particles of fine resin dust onto the plate, the resin forming a pitted texture that will retain printing ink. This process is called aquatint.

PLANOGRAPHIC PRINTING

In the process of lithography the image is taken from the surface or plane; metal tools are not required, the drawing being made with a brush and ink or a wax crayon. It is perhaps the most spontaneous of the printmaking processes since one can paint directly, using the medium with the same degree of lucidity that one might use with paints on a canvas or with ink in a sketchbook.

The process of lithography is founded upon the mutual repulsion of grease and water. Originally drawings were made on blocks of calcerous limestone quarried in Germany and particularly receptive to grease. Now zinc and aluminum plates have almost replaced the use of stone except in special establishments. The plates are mechanically grained and chemically treated

by the drawing needle. The wax ground forms an effective acid-resist in the remaining areas. The depth of the line to be bitten can be controlled by removing the plate at various stages to paint out delicate lines with varnish. When the etching stage has been completed, the plate is taken out of the acid bath and washed with water before clearing away the wax and varnish with turpentine substitute; the plate is then ready for printing.

The incisions on the plate (the drawing) are filled with a heavily pigmented ink, while the plate is kept warm on a hotplate. A leather pad is used to force the ink into the incisions, and the surface of the plate is then wiped with a pad of fine tarlatan, tak-

162

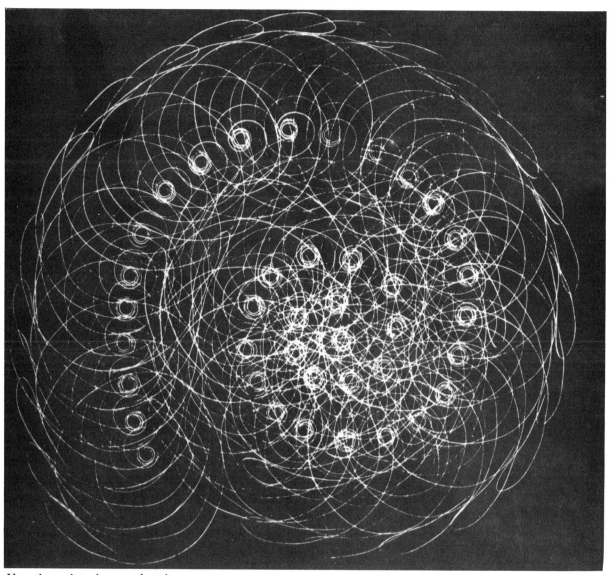

Negative print of a metal spring.

so that grease and water will have anchorage on the surface of the plate. Crayons and ink are made from greasy substances such as soap and tallow; the ink can be diluted with either distilled water or turpentine to make halftone washes on the plate. Any mistakes made at the drawing stage can be corrected during processing.

When the drawing has been completed, the whole surface of the plate is covered with a fine film of liquid gum arabic. The gum arabic desensitizes the plate and acts as a protective stencil to contain the grease drawing. An area of grease penetration forms beneath the drawing and, as the gum hardens in the surrounding areas, provides a smooth aqueous surface. The grease draw-

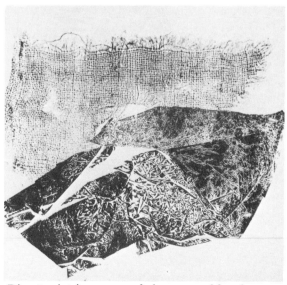

Direct print from crumpled paper and hessian.

163

ing is dissolved with turpentine, leaving only the area of grease penetration within the grain of the plate; this is strengthened with asphaltum solution before the plate is finally washed clear with water and evenly dampened with a sponge.

A roller charged with a special printing ink is rolled over the surface of the plate; the ink on the roller will adhere only to the grease image on the plate because the fine film of water applied with the sponge will cause the ink to be rejected on the remaining areas. When the image has been built up to full strength with printing ink, a sheet of paper is placed on the plate and the first print can be taken. Successive prints can be taken by redampening the surface of the plate and rolling up with ink.

Color lithographs are made using a separate plate for each color. The colors are registered by means of a small mark that appears in the same position on each plate and is also to be seen at opposite edges on the printing paper.

BASIC PRINTMAKING TECHNIQUES

The following techniques are among the ones most widely used today.

Collage relief blocks

The first requirement for a collage print is a printing plate made of cardboard, chipboard, or tagboard. The size of the plate will determine the image area of the completed print. A good plastic adhesive is needed for securing found materials to the base and for coating various materials to give them a suitable surface for the retention of printing ink.

No cutting tools are required for this system of printmaking; any article or piece of material that will readily accept a layer of ink from a printing roller can be arranged on the baseboard and finally secured with the adhesive. The height of the collected fragments on the block should be as equal as possible. Certain objects are quite unsuitable for this method; however,

coarse woven fabric, cloth, and lace are particularly suitable. String and rope can be formed into patterns on a board that has been coated with adhesive and left in the arranged position until the adhesive dries. Most cloth and similar materials should be totally immersed in the adhesive before being laid down onto the baseboard. Leaves, silver paper, and flattened-out packages are also useful in creating a collage.

When the collage is completed, sufficient time should be allowed for the adhesive to set to a high degree of hardness; otherwise the roller will tend to lift off certain fragments as it is rolled across the surface of the block.

An interesting extension of this collage technique is the use of the adhesive itself for retaining impressions of textured materials. The baseboard is given a very heavy coating of adhesive, and, when it is almost dry, objects can be pressed into the surface; the imprint will remain as the adhesive hardens and will print as a negative image. One can work to a particular theme using this method—signs of past events, footprints, tire marks, etc.; or mechanical objects—flywheels, screws, nuts, and bolts.

Descriptive printmaking

A great deal of in-depth research has been carried out by Michael Rothestein in the extension of relief processes. In a recent lecture, he described the uses of printmaking techniques for visual narrative. By taking apart a commonplace object, such as a wooden crate or a tin can, it is possible to produce a visual description of each surface, or facet, inside and out, by rolling up the surfaces with ink and taking prints. In this way we develop a total understanding of the object more accurately than if a pencil drawing or photograph is made of it. A search for suitable objects could be centered around industrial-waste areas, where any number of found artifacts would be suitable for graphic analysis.

Inking up a relief block on the bed of an Albion press.

One of the simplest methods of making trial prints is the use of an offset technique. For this method, a large gelatin roller is necessary in addition to a standard size inking roller. The surface of the object is rolled with ink, and the gelatin roller is allowed to rotate slowly over the inked surface until the limit of the rotation is reached. The image is then transferred from the gelatin roller to paper.

Woodcuts and linocuts

The woodcut or linocut drawing is usually made directly onto the surface of the block or on a sheet of thin paper that can be pasted in reverse onto the block. At the drawing stage one must decide if the drawing is to appear as a negative or positive image in the completed print. For a positive image, you must cut around the contours of the drawn line; for a negative image, the line itself is removed. A brush or felt-tip pen is ideal for drawing on the block; a pencil or pen line is difficult to interpret in terms of even the finest cutting gouge.

In cutting the block always direct the movement away from the body. A wooden bench hook is useful for keeping the block steady. Broad, flat gouges are used for clearing away large areas of the block, and the

165

Surface print of grass, leaves, and a safety pin.

finer V-tools are employed for detailed cutting. Lino is much easier to cut if it is warmed slightly. Lino can be etched by using a diluted solution of caustic soda, which is painted on the surface of the lino directly. The areas of the lino to remain smooth are protected with an acid-resist varnish. The caustic solution forms a granular texture on the lino. Rubber gloves should be worn to protect the skin from the solution, which can be quite harmful. A variety of timbers can be used for woodcutting; the most popular wood is parana pine, although some of the harder woods are more suitable for detailed cutting. Pear has a particularly good surface.

Printing by burnishing. There are several types of inexpensive printing presses available, and very often a visit to a printer's sale is a worthwhile expedition. Bookbinders' nipping presses are also good for

giving a direct pressure, as is the Farley proof press, which has a simple roller pressure.

Burnishing is the simplest technique for taking prints, but it can be tedious if a large number is required. The ink should be rolled out into a fine film on the inking slab before a fine layer is rolled over the block. Over-inking will spoil the print and cause some of the finer textures to fill in. A sheet of printing paper with an absorbent surface, such as a soft Japanese rice or mulberry paper, should be placed carefully onto the inked block, and a metal weight of some kind should be placed on top to prevent the paper and block from moving. The burnishing is done with a wooden spoon or similar object, using a circular movement as pressure is applied. The metal weight can be shifted from corner to corner as the burnishing progresses, and a corner

166

of the paper lifted to judge the effectiveness of the burnishing. The tonal qualities can be controlled by the amount of pressure applied with the burnisher. A clean, hard printing roller and a flat, cold iron are alternative tools for burnishing.

Printing in color

To make sure that the color is registered accurately onto the sheet of printing paper, a simple registration system can be planned. The best method is to make a registration sheet that can be used throughout the printing of all the colors. The sheet should have a margin over the size of both the block and printing paper. Lay marks are drawn on the sheet for the correct positioning of the block and paper. For burnishing techniques a more substantial registration system is necessary, comprising a wooden base with slats of wood fixed to the surface for positioning both block and paper.

When the first color has been printed, sufficient time should be given for the ink to dry before printing the second color. The effects of overprinting are lost if a wet color is printed over a wet color. Printmakers are limited in the number of colors that they can use and tend to take full advantage of overprinting; for example, yellow overprinted on blue makes a green at the area of overprinting, but the yellow and blue retain their value as color primaries where they are printed directly onto the white paper. If a set of four blocks is used in producing a print, it is advisable to make a set of color proofs, amending the colors if necessary.

Large blocks may use quite a lot of ink; when rolling large areas of color make sure that no roller marks are left in the ink.

Monotypes

The fact that only one print can be made from this process makes this technique less popular than others, but it is an ideal medium for exploring preliminary graphic ideas. There are two basic methods:

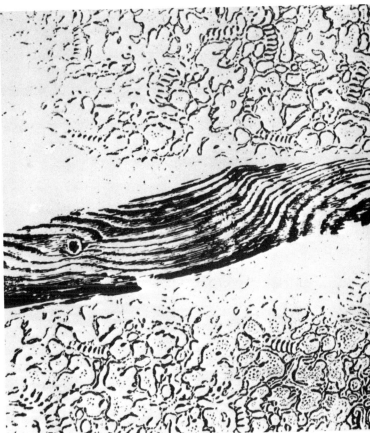

Print from plastic adhesive combined with wood grain.

In the first a slab of glass is covered with a fine layer of ink, which should be blotted several times with wastepaper so that it is not too tacky. A sheet of bond paper is then placed carefully on the glass, and the drawing is made with a ballpoint pen or pencil. While drawing, the hand should not rest on the paper at any time. The point of the pen or pencil forces the paper into contact with ink remaining on the glass, and the ink adheres to the underside of the paper at the point of pressure. When completed, the drawing is lifted from the glass, and the inked drawing will appear on the reverse side, together with perhaps an overall half-tone film of ink, which is difficult to avoid but often lends to the tonal composition of the print. The glass can be cleaned with turpentine, and a different color may be used for further additions to the print.

167

The second monotype method is to paint directly onto a clean slab of glass with dilute printing inks or oil paints; the ink can also be dribbled or smeared with a cloth. When the drawing reaches a satisfactory state, a sheet of paper is pressed onto the glass to remove the surplus ink or paint, and a final print is taken on an absorbent paper, burnishing with a soft cloth.

Stencils

The basic stencil process is an interesting one that is too often ignored and is open to development, although it has been replaced to some extent by silkscreen printing. The stencil is made preferably from a thin card such as an oiled manila card, which is very strong and will not be broken up by the viscosity of the printing ink. The shapes are cut away with a sharp knife, and the stencil sheet is placed on top of the printing paper. The ink is rolled through the cutout shapes to meet the printing paper surface. A soft rubber composition roller is recommended for this purpose.

Silkscreen

One of the main reasons that silkscreen printing has achieved a prominent position in the field of experimental techniques is that it is a highly versatile medium that does not require the use of machinery. Most of the materials can be purchased inexpensively in any town.

Although silkscreen is a medium founded on the basis of simple apparatus, it is possible to produce a wide scale of tonal values with this technique. The printing frame is constructed from wooden slats 2 inches by 2 inches. In making the frame a margin of at least 2 inches above the print area should be allowed to act as an ink duct. The frame can be joined with metal brackets, nails, or a standard woodwork glue.

For basic experiments, the frame can be covered with organdy, a material that is available in most fabric stores or departments, but for fine precision work a good

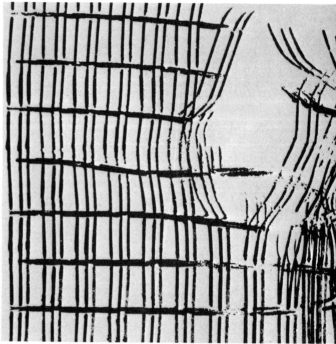

Direct relief print from a metal grid.

quality Swiss silk is recommended. There are a number of ways of stretching the organdy or silk tightly over the frame. The use of a staple-gun is the quickest method but has the disadvantage that the staple marks eventually damage the frame. The material should be stretched like a canvas, tacking the center pieces first and then tensioning the remaining sides. This must be done without causing the material to tear. It is possible to stretch silk using gummed paper tags only, but the most ingenious system that I have seen is the use of a bicycle inner-tube stretched around the outer edges of the frame; the silk is then tacked over both frame and inner-tube and is finally tensioned by inflating the tube with a bicycle pump.

When the silk is firmly stretched over the frame it should be washed with warm soapy water to remove any dirt or grease. The print area should be centered and indicated with a pencil line on the silk screen. The remaining areas should be masked off with gummed tape both outside and inside the frame. The gummed tape can also be given

Using a squeegee on a silkscreen.

a coating of shellac to seal the edges properly.

The screen itself is hinged to a baseboard with an attached support bar to keep the screen in a raised position when laying down printing paper. The squeegee is made from a length of wood that has a rubber blade slotted in on one edge. The width of the squeegee should overlap the width of the print area so that an even layer of ink can be forced through the weave of the screen. After the screen has been prepared, a stencil can be made by one of the following methods:

Paper. A stencil can be made from any type of thin paper, even newspaper. The shapes can be cut away with a knife or torn out to give a softer edge to the printed image. The thicker the paper stencil, the heavier the deposit of printing ink, so that even for flat areas a thin paper such as newsprint is quite adequate. One should bear in mind that the shapes cut or torn away provide the apertures through which the ink is forced after penetrating the weave of the silk, thus forming a positive image on the paper beneath the frame.

Newsprint or paper stencils are fixed to the open screen just as the printing commences. A sheet of printing paper is placed in position on the baseboard with the stencil on top; the screen is then brought down on top of the stencil and a film of printing ink is dragged across the screen area with the blade of the squeegee. The ink will pass through the open stencil shapes to the printing paper, and the remaining ink will cause the stencil to adhere to the screen. Since screen ink dries rapidly (about 10 minutes), the stencil is firmly fixed to the screen, the only disadvantage being that the silk cannot be used again.

A special stencil paper is marketed by a number of graphic supplies firms. This is a thin paper coated with gelatin. It is transparent and can, therefore, be placed over an original design in order to trace the main shapes of the color to be printed. The shapes are cut out with a knife or razor blade. The stencil paper is attached to the screen by laying the gelatin surface of the paper in contact with the underside of the screen. A hot domestic iron is run over the silk on the inside of the frame, causing the gelatin to melt and adhere to the screen. There are also several different types of self-adhesive stencil papers that are quite useful.

Glue. Water-soluble glue stencils can be painted directly onto the screen with a brush, filling the weave of the screen so that the printing ink will not go through the screen wherever the glue blocks the weave. A number of manufacturers produce effective water-soluble screen fillers, and interesting effects can be achieved by spattering glue onto a wet screen or by diluting the glue with water to obtain half-tones. The main advantage of this technique is that the screen can be used several times, provided that the screen is cleared of ink and the glue removed with warm water.

When you are working on the screen, the original design can be placed underneath the screen and the main outlines traced onto the silk with a soft pencil. When the painting-out of shapes with glue has been completed, hold the screen up to the light to check for pinholes that may need retouching with glue.

Wax Resist. For direct linear work, a wax lithographic crayon and lithographic drawing ink can be used to draw and paint on the screen. Make sure that the screen receives a heavy deposit of ink and crayon pigment so that the weave is filled. On completion of the drawing stage the whole screen surface is coated with screen glue and allowed to dry. The drawing is then dissolved with turpentine. The screen will thus be clear wherever the drawing is dissolved and blocked in the surrounding areas by the glue, which is not disturbed by the turpentine. This means that at the printing stage a positive image will appear on the printing paper because the line drawn with the wax crayon or ink is eventually the only clear part of the screen weave.

For poster work transfer dry lettering can be burnished to the inside of the screen and protected with the special fixative to prevent damage when using the squeegee. Most of these methods can be employed for printing on fabrics (*see* Fabric Printing), but a special ink dye is required for permanence on fabric, and the screen should not be hinged for printing.

Printing. Preparation for silkscreen printing is a critical task because once the actual printing operation begins, it must be done without pause or interruption; the fast drying ink will clog the screen if it is left for even a half an hour, and it may be very difficult to remove.

Organize the printing table so that paper is easily at hand and have the ink, ready mixed, in a spare container. Ideally it is a good plan to have an assistant to handle the paper while you are doing the squeegee work on the screen. The paper can be registered on the baseboard with simple paper tabs as lay-guides for two corners of the paper. With the paper in the correct position on the baseboard, rest the screen flat on top so that the paper is sandwiched between the baseboard and the screen. Then spread the ink in a line on the margin opposite your standing position and within the gum-paper margin. Holding the squeegee with two hands, put the rubber blade immediately behind the line of ink and drag the ink toward you, remembering that the ink must be forced evenly through the screen mesh. The squeegee action should be sharp and brisk, and it should be held at an angle of approximately 45°. Before lifting the screen, make sure that the squeegee does not fall on the screen into the ink; then lift the screen and remove the paper, which will contain the printed image. Register the next sheet of paper and move to the opposite side of the screen for the next screening. Add more ink to the screen as may be necessary.

When the printing is completed, place a wad of newsprint underneath the screen and scrape out the surplus ink with a palette knife; finally clean the screen with turpentine and soapy water.

Additional colors can be overprinted the same day. By the time you have cleaned up your first screen the prints will be ready to receive the next color. Colors can be either transparent or opaque. The ink can be extended by adding reducing medium.

Stuart Robinson

puppets, masks, model theaters

PUPPETRY IS MORE THAN A CRAFT. Not only can it be enjoyed as an improvised activity, but it can be studied as a serious craft with most advanced techniques. It is particularly useful with shy and retarded children as an excellent way of releasing the inner tensions that often produce and foster such disabilities. As imaginative play, it affords a true example of integrated work in the classroom because it involves different methods of creative expression, including painting, modeling, storytelling, acting, speaking, lighting, and effects that will delight both the creator and the beholder. All this is involved, yet the operator is hidden from the spectator.

To start with, quick methods and simple materials are essential because it is the use of the puppet that is important rather than the making. Whichever type of puppet is employed, it should evolve from the actual materials available. This will make it seem logical and individual with a life of its own. From these characteristics the puppet will perform in a certain way that will give rise to a sequence of action and to the plot, which will be the result of free play. Since it is so important to retain the spontaneity of performance, a script of cues rather than a written dialog will give the best results. The best way to start puppetry is not to plan and produce scripts but to make a puppet and use it. Everything else will grow from this. It is not until the fun of making and playing has been experienced that it becomes possible to make a puppet to suit an existing character or play.

It is useful when planning a public performance to have one member of the group as a producer and cue prompter (actions rather than words), who will guide the flow of the action, look after lights, curtains, and special effects, such as music and noises, who will see that properties are available and generally will manage without imposing too much control. The producer can often be a link-man, narrator or commentator, who brings the audience into

Puppet with paper pulp head.

the action. He or she can see that the performers speak out clearly and loudly and that the backstage workers keep their directions to a whisper.

It is quite feasible to start a group project, integrated work, or center of interest from a number of puppets. A group of explorer puppets, each of whom goes off,

171

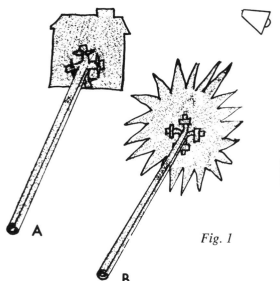

Fig. 1

Fig. 2

finds something, and enacts his voyages and discoveries with other characters in one scene of a production, is a possibility. Research and written records will be needed; pictures, scenery, models, and writing can all be easily linked to a real, live performance. Each separate scene may use different kinds of puppets appropriate to the action. More than one stage can be set up, and the action can flow from one to another. There is no end to the possibilities arising from the imaginative use of puppetry. The following sections give the basic techniques and ideas. The only extras necessary are imagination, enthusiasm, and inspiration, the stock-in-trade of most children and many teachers.

SHADOW PUPPETS

To make shadow puppets you will need the following: a bright light from a window or a reading lamp; a picture frame covered with some semiopaque material, such as an old sheet, thin white cotton, linen, or tracing cloth. Whichever material is selected, it should show clear shadows but not the performers who are behind. The frame can be held or fixed to a table with G clamps or tied between chairs. You also will need some manila-envelope weight paper, stiff dark paper or cardboard, a stapler, scissors, a paper punch, Scotch tape, paste, push-through paper fasteners, black book cloth, colored cellophane paper.

Method

Cut or fold the manila paper into any simple shape. Use a stapler or sew on a support of folded stiff paper, wire, or card (Fig. 1).

With the light behind and either above or below you, hold the shadow up to and touching the screen. As you press the puppet against the screen, the shadow appears darkest; as you hold it farther away it will seem lighter and larger. Play with the shadows on the screen, letting them fly, fall down, move away, and so on. Set up a mirror at an angle so that you can see the shadows as you work the puppet (Fig. 2). Invent simple situations as the puppets suggest and voices to suit them.

Now devise two characters and some suitable props, cutting or tearing shapes from stiff tagboard. Facial features, such as eyes, nose, and mouth, can be made with a paper punch. Play against the screen with shadow puppets and allow a small incident or plot to develop. Simple scenery can be fixed to the screen with Scotch tape and can include colored cellophane for eyes, buttons, faces, sun, flowers, and so on.

Moving shadows

To make the shadow figures move try only a few joints at first, one or two per

Fig. 3

figure because you have only two hands to hold and to manipulate the puppet. One hand can hold a wire from the body, and the other can hand work the legs that move together with the head on the second wire. After further experiment, you will discover that four or five supports can be operated by one person at the same time.

Permanent shadows

For these use a stiff cardboard that can be cut cleanly, such as shoe and stocking boxes. Cutting directly on the cardboard without preliminary drawing gives a much livelier result than does drawing an exact outline. Allow sufficient circular overlap at joints, and place these to give the maximum amount of controlled movement. Push-through paper fasteners are the easiest form of fastening, and punched holes are uniform enough to allow free movement.

After jointing, the supports to hold and work the puppet must be added. Galvanized or copper wire (about 16 gauge), thin wood rods, umbrella or cycle spokes also are needed (Fig. 3). Fasten the wires and rods to the appropriate part of the figure. The holding support, which will take the weight of the figure, must be very firmly attached by sticking and sewing to give rigidity. Sometimes legs or other parts can be left free to dangle. Where it is necessary to prolong the life of the puppet, cover it with a dark matte bookcloth, using a rubber cement.

Further experiments

As you progress, a more rigid or permanent screen that allows greater scope for experiment will soon become necessary. Tagboard may be combined with plywood, wire, metal sheet (such as zinc, aluminum, or tin), or clear acetate. The last material can be colored with thinned oil paint, colored tissue, or colored inks. It can also be used as a full-size sheet of transparent scenery with the setting painted on in opaque black ink and/or transparent colors and then placed immediately behind the screen.

Strong lights are useful as suns, moons, car headlights, bonfires, etc. Tinsel, sequins, pieces of mirror with edges protected by Scotch tape, and similar material hanging near the light source produce a magic sparkling background. Puppets can recede and advance right up to the screen. Necks can be made of expanding material. Heads and other parts can be controlled separately from the rest of the body, and figures can come apart if joined correctly.

Shadow puppets should be stored flat, taking great care not to allow the supports to tear away from the actual body. Ideas for play production and an all-purpose stage are discussed later in the chapter.

GLOVE PUPPETS

To make glove puppets, you will need some pieces of plain or patterned fabric (old large handkerchiefs, curtain and dress samples) about 18 inches square; assorted size elastic bands; Magic Markers or felt pens; cardboard tubing cut to about 1-inch or 1½-inch length rings; assorted trimmings: beads, brooches, curtainings, net, lurex pieces, fasteners, feathers, embroidery silks, gummed paper shapes, ribbon scraps, etc.

Method

Place a cardboard ring on your first finger, cover the whole hand with a piece of cloth (Fig. 4), slip rubber bands over the card ring head and down the neck, and

173

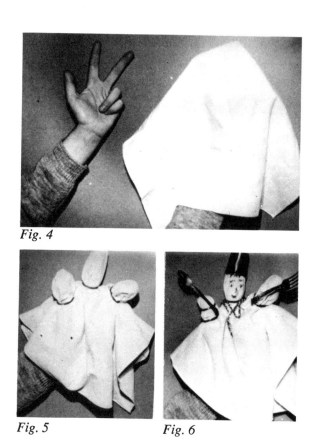

Fig. 4

Fig. 5   Fig. 6

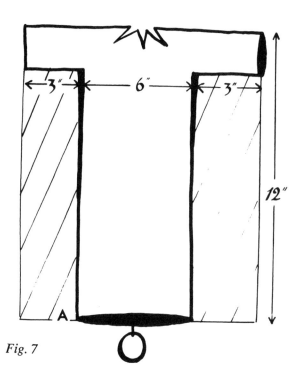

Fig. 7

other rubber bands over the thumb and second finger (Fig. 5). Use a ball-point or felt pen to draw on eyebrows, eyes, a nose, and mouth (Fig. 6). Trim the puppet with beads or other suitable decoration; make a paper cone hat; use wool, string, or unraveled plastic scouring pads for hair. Fasten waistcoats, coats, and aprons with glue, push-through fasteners, staplers, or needle and thread. Make props from pillboxes, doll's pots and pans, cups, brooms, and cutlery, small bead boxes and similar items.

This glove puppet is excellent because of its versatility, but inevitably it comes to pieces after the performance. A more permanent glove puppet may be made as follows. The body is the operator's hand. The clothing is a simple T-shirt glove as shown in Fig. 7. The head can be made from a match box; pulp cup, flower pot or egg tray; milk or yogurt containers; old rubber or tennis balls; plastic containers; old

sponge or plastic foam pieces; carved potatoes; or soap. Eyes can be made from beads, buttons, fasteners; hair can be made from wool and string. Even a paper bag can be used for a complete puppet. The head can be further improved by making a tube of paper to fit the forefinger, crumpling or winding paper strips around it, pulling a nylon stocking over the head to obtain a much smoother skin effect, and fixing this into the neck of the glove. The nose may be pulled out from the paper of the head and stitched in place; scraps of felt or buttons can be sewn on for the eyes and mouth; features can be drawn or painted.

This type of glove puppet is one of the easiest to make and the quickest and most satisfactory to use since it is easy to alter and is lightweight.

Permanent glove puppets

The T-shaped glove shown in Fig. 7 may be joined to a wide variety of heads, which are shown in Fig. 8. Whatever material is used for the actual modeling, it may be built upon a modeling base (A), such as an old light bulb, plastic or glass container, ball, stone, potato, paper-stuffed toe of an old sock, stocking or leg of a pair of tights

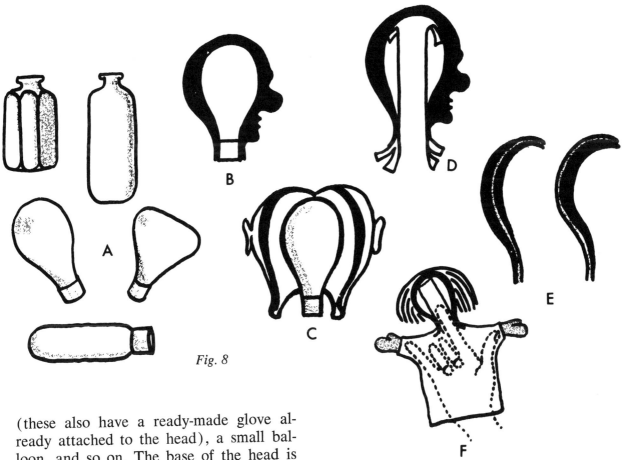

Fig. 8

(these also have a ready-made glove already attached to the head), a small balloon, and so on. The base of the head is best greased, oiled, or painted with a liquid detergent before covering with a ¼ inch or ⅓ inch layer of the modeling material (B). Allow the head to dry out between layers if the layers will be thicker than ½ inch total. When dry, cut heads up center (on other than sock, stocking, tights or balloon bases), remove base (C), insert a finger tube (D), stick the slit in the head back together or paste over with pieces of thin paper or bandage. Allow head to dry and attach to glove (F). In the case of sock bases, remove the stuffing when the head is dry; with a balloon base let down balloon and pull out.

Prime the face with white or slightly tinted emulsion paint or tempera color and use felt markers for features; string, cotton wool, rug wool, plastic pan scrubbers, frayed out cotton, straw, etc. for hair, eyebrows, mustache, beard, etc. Ears, noses, and chins can be modeled or stuck on afterward, as can sequins, buttons, or paper fasteners for eyes.

Modeling materials for heads

1. Sawdust heads from a mixture of wheat paste, water, and sawdust.

2. Styrofoam balls covered with strips of cotton sheeting dipped in watered down Elmer's Glue-All and applied around the ball in layers.

3. Paper pulp heads can be formed by making pulp from newspaper or soft paper torn into small pieces and soaked in well mixed wheat paste.

4. Sawdust and paper pulp mixes may also be used.

5. Two ovals or circles of colored felt stuffed with cotton wool around a tube and sewn together.

6. An old mitten converted into a head or glove.

7. Egg-shaped balls of Styrofoam or balsa wood carved into a head with a finger tube inserted and then dipped into a watered down Elmer's Glue-All mixture.

8. Paper or cloth pieces or strips built

175

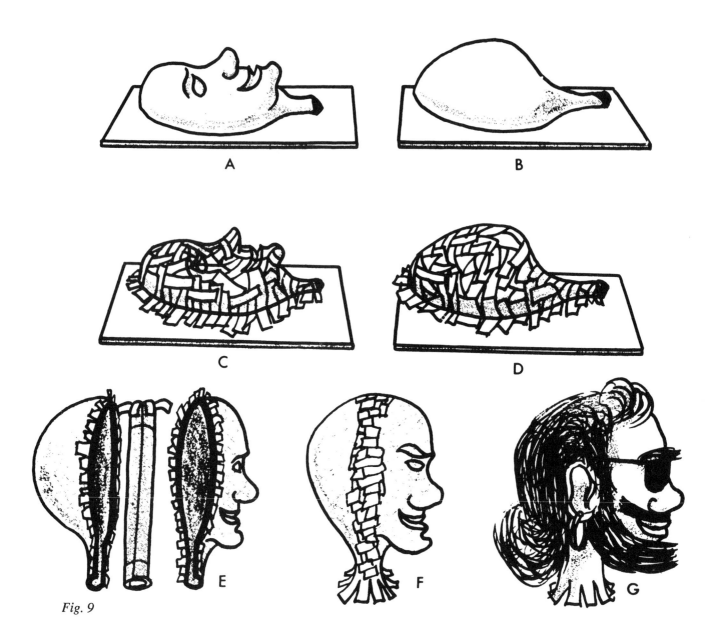

Fig. 9

around the modeling base with wheat paste. This technique may also be used by building up directly on the finger tube, although this gives a slightly heavier head but is, of course, much tougher than other types.

A very tough permanent head may be built by modeling on plastic or clay as in Fig. 9. First model the head in two halves (A and B). Then, rub the head with vaseline or oil, press on strips of thin cloth (bandage, butter muslin, old handkerchiefs), work in a layer of paste (wheat paste), and build up alternate layers of pa-

per and cloth strips pasted into a skin, six or more layers thick. Build up features as required (C and D) and leave to dry. After removing plastic or clay, insert a finger tube (E), join head together (F), and paint, add hair, etc. (G).

When not in use for a short time, hang glove puppets upside down from hooks set around the stage frame, using a curtain ring sewn at the lower back hem of the glove. Store glove puppets by pulling the glove inside out and back over the head to reduce friction on the face paint.

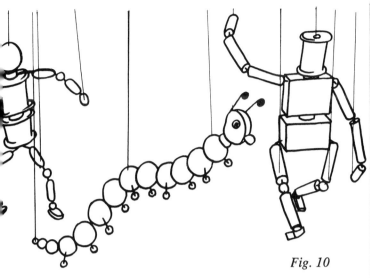

Fig. 10

STRING PUPPETS

For string puppers, or marionettes, you will need thread, string, peanuts, beads, foam rubber lumps, matchboxes, thread spools, balls, cans (avoid jagged edges or holes), small weights, Scotch tape, decorative scraps of material and trimmings, felt markers, rubber bands, small screw eyes, tagboard, Le Page glue dotter, paper clips, colored foil, and cellophane paper.

Methods

String together about a dozen peanuts or beads or any other items listed previously to form a figure. Keep joints loose with washers to give free movement. Clip on simple clothes with rubber bands and use small pieces of scrap metal to give sufficient weight to feet, hands, or seat to enable the puppet to move correctly (Fig. 10).

Cut out a flat head, body, arms, and legs from tagboard; loosely tie these pieces together with short knotted ties, and hang and move with two lengths of string or thread. A simple rolled paper shape puppet is shown in Fig. 11. It is made from stiff paper cut and rolled to make cylinders and cones or folded in cubes or other geometrical forms. Fasten the shape with Le Page glue dotter, Elmer's Glue-All, or Scotch tape and add some weighting as necessary.

Fig. 11 Puppet made from paper cones.

Advanced string puppets

Controls for string puppets should be made from a smooth soft wood, such as deal, which will take hooks, eyes, and screw holes easily and does not require complicated tools. Other strings may be fitted for special purposes, including mouth strings, elbow strings, and strings to special properties such as hats, standing-on-end hair, and juggling items.

Stringing the puppets is best done from   177

a jumping stand, a rod, a bar, or a specially made gallows, adjustable to various heights. For the actual string, use macramé thread or fine fishing line. It should be noted that some types of nylon and rayon can be difficult to knot securely.

The point at which you hang the control for the puppet must be at the overall correct height from the stage floor when the puppet is in use. The usual practice is to fix the head string(s) to the control at a point well above the eye level of the audience. Take care that there is sufficient play to allow your puppet to sit or lie down and still keep your hands and the control out of sight. In using a detachable leg bar, keep it on the peg or hook. Make arm strings slightly overtaut to prevent arms hanging lifelessly at the sides of the puppet when your fingers are busy with other things.

In stringing the puppet work in this order—head, shoulders, arms, legs, and then any other strings. The simplest control and the fewest possible strings is a golden rule. Walk-on characters can often get by with head strings only. The strings should all be taut when the figure is standing normally. To keep the string taut use a small screw eye or pass thread through a hole and knot on the other side. (A drop of Duco cement on the knot will avoid the tragedy of knots becoming untied during the performance.) Take the thread right through the clothes to the screw eye beneath.

Much trouble with marionettes often arises from poor weighting of the hands, feet, and hips. Hands that are too light tend to float about; feet that are not correctly weighted will not walk properly, and the puppet will not be able to sit down unless hips are heavy enough. Hands and feet may be cut out from sheet lead and covered with plastic or wood. At the hips attach sheet lead around the seat.

It is difficult to make a marionette walk smoothly. Practice in front of a long mirror, although, of course, in a performance you will have to judge from above. If the strings

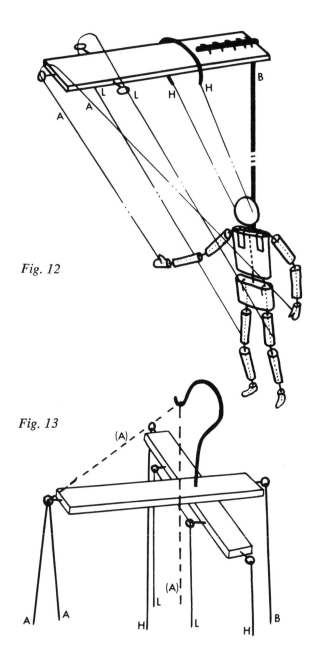

Fig. 12

Fig. 13

become tangled, do not cut or unscrew the eyes, but concentrate on releasing one string only, and this will often release the rest. When your puppet is strung and ready for use, it will need to be hung from a rack. On the stage back there should be a rail or hooks to take the puppets waiting their turn.

If you have to pack up your puppet and you wish to prevent tangling the strings, then: hold the control and gently turn the puppet around several times, so twisting the strings together. Next take the control and carefully roll it down the strings until it lies on the puppet. Secure the strings and control around the puppet with a large elastic band or tape. To undo the puppet, simply work in the exact reverse of the way in which you wrapped it, and your puppet should be ready for use.

Newspaper string puppet

The materials required for a 15- to 18-inch newspaper string puppet (Fig. 14) are: two or three newspapers, tissue paper (paper handkerchiefs, toilet paper, etc.), macramé thread, wheat paste, Le Page tube glue, 2¼ yards of ½-inch wide white tape, elastic bands, beads or washers, odd scraps for clothes, hair, etc.

Head. Cut 2 feet 6 inches of tape and tie at halfway fold with about 1 foot of macramé thread (A). Fold half a page of a large newspaper to give a folded strip about 12 by 3 inches (B). Paste this around the tape just below the knotted fold; leave the threads hanging out and about 8 inches of tape below (C). If necessary, hold the newspaper in position with rubber bands until dry. Fold another half page of a large newspaper to make a folded strip 6 by 1½ inches and paste over the top (leaving threads out) as shown in D. Build head and neck up by pasting on paper strips about 4 inches by 2 inches. Use alternate layers of newspaper and tissue to build the required size. Pieces of thin rag, muslin, etc. also can be used to fill out the nose, eyebrows, and chin. Leave thread coming out at ear position and tapes hanging out below neck (E). Exaggerate any prominent features. This is not always necessary, but it is usually a good idea.

Upper body. Separately fold two or—for a flat puppet—three pieces of newspaper as you did for the head, and wrap around a ruler, pasting as you wrap (F). Withdraw the ruler, leaving the center hole clear of paste. Use rubber bands down the body to hold together during drying.

Lower body. Follow the same procedure as in the upper body, but use a folded strip of newspaper 12 inches by 2 inches to produce a smaller section (G).

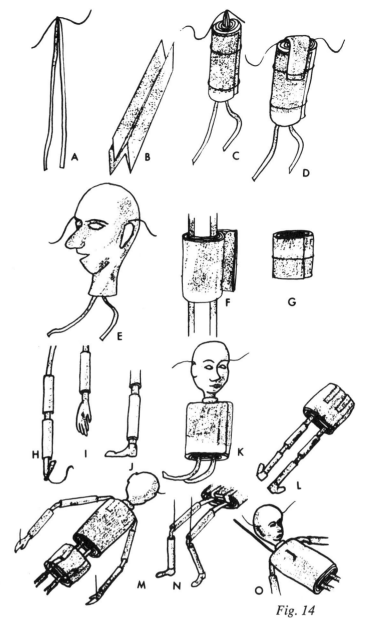

Fig. 14

Arms and legs. Take four 12-inch pieces of tape and eight single strips of newspaper each 12 inches by 3 inches. Crease each tape in half and stretch out. Fold and paste strips of newspaper around the tape as shown in H. Each strip gives half an arm or leg. Leave ½ inch for the elbow and knee joints.

For arms, fold one end of tape in half and tie 6 inches of thread at fold. Use pasted paper to build up hand over folded tape (I); put a small piece of lead inside hand if possible.

For legs, fold over tape as with arms (but do not tie on a thread). In foot put, if possible, a small piece of lead, a small metal button, ball bearing, metal bead, or similar heavy scrap to help weight feet (J).

179

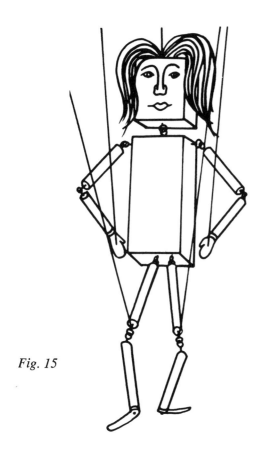

Fig. 15

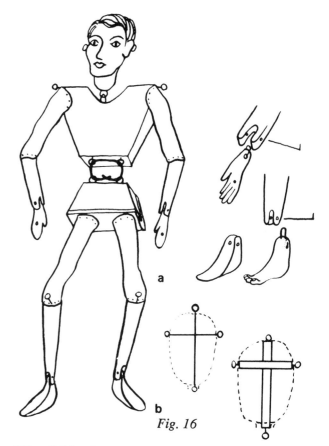

a

b

Fig. 16

Putting together. Thread head tapes down through a bead or washer and then through the upper body (K). Thread leg tapes up through lower body (leaving ½ inch between top of legs and body) over top and glue down on back of lower body (L). Thread head tapes that are hanging from upper body down through lower body leaving about ½ inch space at waist; fold remaining tape around the bottom and glue up back of lower body (M). Glue loose ends of arm tapes into the slits on top of shoulders, leaving ½ inch tape free for shoulder joint between upper arm and upper body (M). Use an awl or compass point to make a hole in each upper leg just above knee and tie 6 inches of thread to each leg (N). Now paint puppet and dress. Fix stiff wire to back of puppet by drilling a hole through upper body and inserting wire, or take down neck and bind on to body with thread (O). Attach end of wire to control and string puppet as described previously.

Wood block puppet

The materials required for this 15 inch wood block puppet (Fig. 15) are: pieces of wood and doweling of various sizes, sheet lead or heavy metal buttons, screw eyes, and glue.

Method. Cut out and assemble as shown in Fig. 15. Hands and feet may be modeled from balsa wood, corks, or wood-like plastic.

Wood puppet

The materials required for a 12 inch wood puppet (Fig. 16) are: pieces of wood and doweling of various sizes, sheet lead, screw eyes, wire, shoe laces, glue, short panel pins or tacks, and cord.

Method. Cut out and assemble as shown in Fig. 16. The head can be made from any method previously given. The upper arms and legs are made from a cloth tube or strips. Hands and feet are modeled from wood-like plastic built onto a base of cut-out sheet lead (B). Lead is also used to line the lower body for extra weight. It is usual to make heads solid and (C) shows the basic wire or wood armature necessary to give secure anchoring points for the string screw eyes.

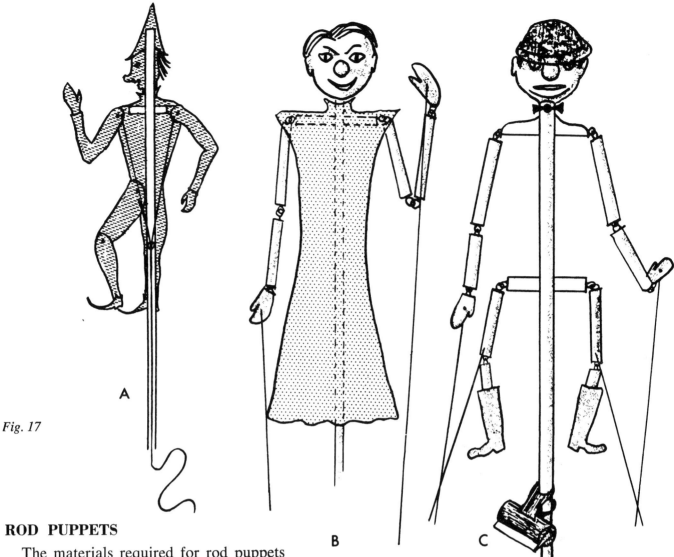

Fig. 17

ROD PUPPETS

The materials required for rod puppets are ¼ inch to ½ inch thick cardboard, round or square doweling, wire, small screw eyes, scrap materials.

Vertical wire controls. In Fig. 17 rod puppets with vertical wire controls are shown. The first (A) has a vertical support carrying the body and head and controlled by strings. (B) has a head made from a ball, potato, or plastic container, and a colored crêpe paper costume. (C) shows developments.

Glove and fully modeled head. In Fig. 18 rod puppets with glove and fully modeled head are shown. (A) shows glove puppet with arms and hands worked with rods. (B) shows a glove with fingers in legs, the body held up by a rod and the jointed arms worked by wires. (C) shows methods of attaching wires. (D) gives other ideas, animal, and each animal will prescribe its own problems to be solved.

Fig. 18

A   B   D   181

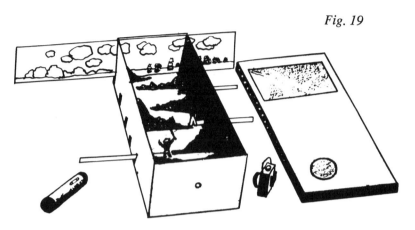

Fig. 19

Fig. 20

PEEP SHOWS AND TOY THEATERS

Everyone finds peep shows fascinating. The intriguing view through the tiny hole punched in the end of a shoe box, together with the mysterious light filtering through the colored cellophane paper covering the holes cut in the lid, can open up a miniature world of delight.

The easiest beginner's peep show uses figures, animals, trees, buildings, and all the necessary scenery cut from magazine illustrations and arranged within the shoe-box in layers receding from the peephole to the far end. The strategically arranged holes in the box top or sides allow shafts of daylight or torchlight to fall on important parts. Pieces of colored cellophane give interesting effects, as shown in Fig. 19. Some boxes have other peepholes to give different viewpoints. Others have strips attached to the figures, which slide in and out of slits cut in the box sides. A further development is the use of all sorts of pebbles, shells, sponges, twigs, toy soldiers, and the like.

Different types of boxes give different effects. If it is possible to obtain circular hat boxes, these have great possibilities for varied views of a central topic, which should have certain parts hidden from some peepholes. Long and narrow boxes give cor-

ridor views, and the insertion of small pieces of mirror set diagonally to the peephole enables one to see around corners and into buildings.

The peep show in a concertina, or folding, form has been in existence from a very early date, probably the middle of the 18th century, or even earlier. In essence it consists of a back scene, a number of cut-out sheets forming a series of layers between the back and front, and a front panel cut either as a proscenium arch or with a peephole. The concertina sides of paper or linen have the cut-out sheets joined in them, and each sheet has the middle cut away so that a sky or building strip ties the top, and the ground strip ties the base to the sides. The whole can be folded away easily. Some are so designed that the back scene is on the inside of the base of a box and the front on the box top, the whole closing into a shallow box for storage (Fig. 20).

The simplest toy theater to build consists of a box with a proscenium front with the set built up in a series of cut-out cardboard flats placed between the proscenium and the back cloth. The properties, figures, and scenery may be manipulated by wires, rods, cardboard or acetate strips from under-

Fig. 21

The Victorian Toy Theater

neath, through slits in the sides and back, or by strings from above. Narrative theaters are useful for group work in a large class. Four or five children can work on one theater, which will tell a part of the complete story. The adventure type of story is most effective for this.

If the theater is used with slide-in rod puppets, a very versatile form of puppet theater becomes possible. A simple walking device for a flat or padded push-on figure is shown in Fig. 22. In (A) the leg circle is cut out to the dotted lines position for the four legs and feet and a hole is punched in the center. The figure is cut out and the legs piece joined to body with a push-through paper fastener so that legs revolve easily (B) and (C). The figure can be made from stiff cardboard in three layers, the center layer being for the top half of the figure only. The legs piece goes between the outer layers, which have been stuck to the center layer at top. The rod for pushing the figure may be fixed at waist or above.

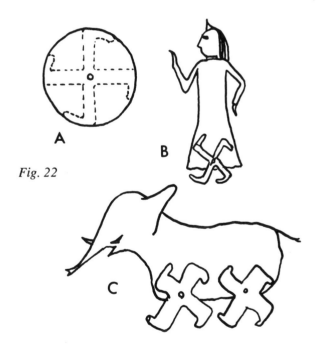

Fig. 22

MASKS

Many of the methods discussed in the glove puppet section are suitable for making masks, and reference will be made to the similarities in the appropriate section. It is not always advisable to make a full facemask. Often a half or three-quarters

183

Fig. 23

Fig. 24

mask, which allows part of the wearer's face to show, such as a nose and chin, is much more alive in use than a full mask.

Paper, cloth, and carton

Masks of paper, cloth, and carton are simply made. In Fig. 23 it is easy to see that any large and strong enough container (not a plastic one, of course) can be made into a most effective mask (A), with strings to work parts (B), inner straps to rest on shoulders (C), and a number combined (D).

Paper plate

The materials for the paper plate mask (Fig. 24) are easy enough to obtain: paper plates, scissors, stapler, fasteners, a variety

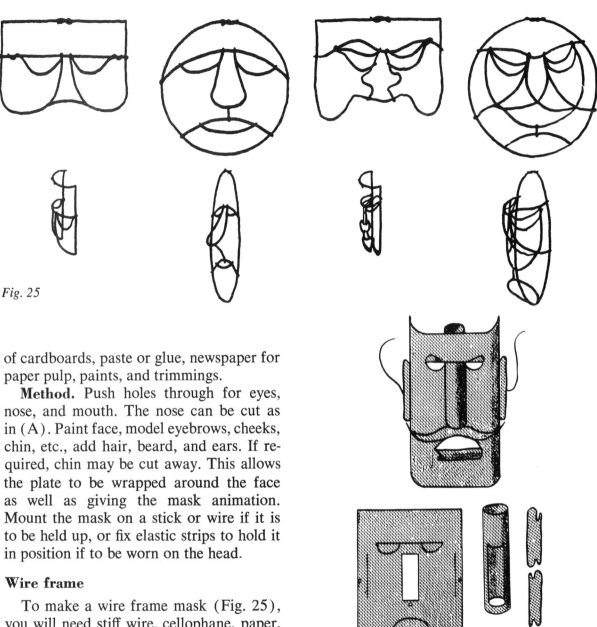

Fig. 25

of cardboards, paste or glue, newspaper for paper pulp, paints, and trimmings.

Method. Push holes through for eyes, nose, and mouth. The nose can be cut as in (A). Paint face, model eyebrows, cheeks, chin, etc., add hair, beard, and ears. If required, chin may be cut away. This allows the plate to be wrapped around the face as well as giving the mask animation. Mount the mask on a stick or wire if it is to be held up, or fix elastic strips to hold it in position if to be worn on the head.

Wire frame

To make a wire frame mask (Fig. 25), you will need stiff wire, cellophane, paper, cloth or cardboard for covering, thread, fasteners, stapler, adhesives, paint, and trimmings.

Method. Bend the wire into the required shape. A number of suggestions for full or half masks are shown in Fig. 25. Stretch fasten by sewing, sticking, stapling, or securing with fasteners. Cut holes for eyes, nose, and mouth. Turn back any resulting flaps onto the inside of the mask and fasten down. Brush mask and leave to set. Repeat pasting if necessary and, when it is dry, paint and decorate the mask.

Fig. 26

Folded paper or cloth

For this mask (Fig. 26), you will need: stiff bond paper (90 pound) or six sheets of cardboard or buckram, sharp knife, scissors, fasteners, adhesives, paint, and trimmings.

Method. The simplest forms of folded and fastened cloth and paper masks are

185

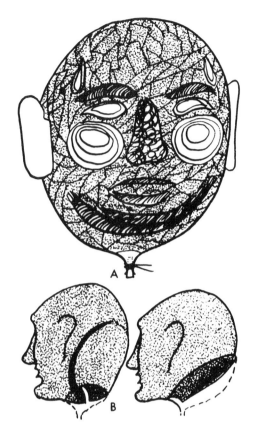

Fig. 27

constructed as in Fig. 26. Using careful slitting and cutting, together with decoration, quite elaborate but rather fragile masks may be made. A development of this type of mask is to construct the main section from a thin acetate sheet (plain or colored, fully or semitransparent). This can then have trimmings added, using epoxy adhesives, Le Page's clear adhesive, or painting.

Balloon mold masks

To make a mask, or even a head built up on a balloon, you will need large balloons, newspaper and other soft paper, old thin fabrics, paste, scrap materials, string, paint, and trimmings.

Method. Blow up a large balloon, tie the neck with string, paint with a liquid detergent or apply oil or a thin coat of grease. Tie the balloon to a chair or heavy object to hold it in place. Use long strips of news-

paper (12 inches by 4 inches), toilet paper, tissue, paper handkerchiefs, etc., to cover all over and paste on top. A second layer is prepared by soaking strips of muslin, bandage, old sheet, old stockings, or any thin fabrics available in paste. These strips are then placed crossways on top of the first layer. Repeat alternate layers of paper / cloth / paper / cloth up to eight or nine layers for a sturdy head. Use a good waterproof paste such as wheat paste, and finish off with a well-soaked layer of fabric.

Leave top third of the face for the forehead, use a crumpled piece of paper for nose, and paste fabric over in several layers. Use thick cord, string, or rolled paper covered with pasted fabric for the chin, eyebrows, and lips. Shaped cardboard covered with pasted fabric can be used for ears; extra paper/cloth layers are added for cheeks as shown in Fig. 27. Alternatively, all features may be placed onto the balloon before the first layer is spread over.

When thoroughly dry, undo string and remove the balloon from the mask. Paint and decorate the mask after cutting a hole or slitting for insertion of the head, as shown in (B). If powder paint is used for decoration, fix with a spray of charcoal fixative or rub over with a matte wax polish. For masks only, a different face may be built on the back and front of the balloon. After removing the balloon, and splitting up the sides you will have two masks.

Of course, any of the previous mixes suggested in the glove puppet section such as sawdust, paper pulp, etc. may be used here with the balloon. It is, however, wiser to start with a layer of thin fabric and finish with another one, both well soaked in paste.

Clay mold mask

To make a mask or head shaped on a clay mold, you will need the same materials as for the balloon mold mask, plus clay.

Method. Proceed as recommended in the glove puppet section using the method employing cloth strips and of course making the clay mold large enough to fit your head or face.

Use a large stone or upturned dish, cover with a thin layer of clay, and build up features, proceeding as you did for the puppet head. The mask should be designed about ½ inch larger all around than the face it is to fit, to allow for shrinkage during drying. After trimming, painting, etc. are complete, punch holes about an inch in from the edge of the mask behind the ears, and attach a piece of elastic to go around the back of the head.

Masks from the face

To make a mask from your own face obtain some aluminum foil, newspaper and scrap cloth, adhesives, paint, and trimmings.

Method. It is essential to have two people to make this type of mask. Place a sheet of foil on the face you wish to use as a mold and press in and around the features. Take care to press gently, particularly over the eyes. It is necessary to remove the foil after a few moments to insert nostril holes so that your model can continue to breathe! Use enough foil to fold around and up to the ears, try to avoid a crumpled effect, and obtain as smooth a finish as possible. Remove the foil very carefully, and if necessary secure side folds with Scotch tape. Take care not to push in the face. Sometimes it is possible to strengthen the foil while it is still on the model's face, with pieces of Scotch tape across folds or other points of weakness.

Next, paint the surface with a liquid detergent or thin oil and cover with strips of cloth (or alternate layers of paper/cloth/paper/cloth, etc.), building up as smooth a surface as possible with plenty of paste. For a very close likeness, add six or seven alternate layers of tissue paper and pieces of old stocking, preferably of the stretch variety. When dry, remove foil, paint, trim, and add elastic band, and your facsimile mask is ready.

PLAY PRODUCTION

Keep the mechanics of a production as simple as possible. Do not become over-ambitious. Use only a cue script and avoid the reading of dialogue so as to retain the free spontaneous quality so essential in puppetry. Allow the play to develop from and around the interplay between the characters. The audience will need only the fundamentals of an idea to build upon this in their imagination. Encourage the audience to join in by referring to individuals by name and asking them to warn the puppet when someone else appears, and so on. It is always important to remember that puppets, and particularly string puppets, are not meant to compete with humans. They are not just little people; they, however, can do what no human can; they can fly, leap higher, float in space, come to pieces, be entirely abstract, whatever you please.

Exaggeration, melodrama, and caricature are all well suited to puppetry. Play with the voice and try to make it suit the character. Most people have a far wider range of voices than they realize. The screen hides the operator and soon removes any feeling of self-consciousness. Music and sound effects add a great deal to any performance, and these can be very simply produced. The rumble of thunder can be reproduced by shaking a large sheet of tin or aluminum; falling rain can be produced by rattling dried peas over a piece of metal mesh or hardboard. It is possible to borrow or rent records with various sound effects of birds, trains, cars, water, etc., or the actual sounds can be taped.

Play situations

To start action with a puppet begin with simple ideas: it is sleeping but is disturbed by a dog or wasp; telephones interrupt; the puppet is a magician, a policeman, mother, teacher; has a toothache, etc.

Story starters for young children: the naughty child is found out; "It's no good, I

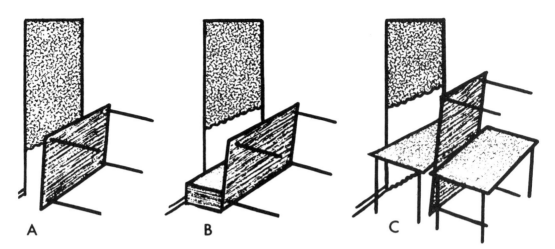

A   B   C

can't stop falling down," and so on. For older children: elephant boy; parade of the soldiers; father washes up; at the circus; a puppet revue (clowns, pianist, and so on); the birthday party, etc.

Further ideas might be developed from: nursery rhymes; fairy stories; fables; children's classics and other stories, including science fiction; poems and ballads; songs and descriptive music.

Simple stages are shown in Fig. 28. (A), (B), and (C) show an improvised stage using a table and curtain across an open door. (D) is a more elaborate form with jumping stands, a blackboard trapped between stout tables, all lashed together with string. (E) shows stage dimensions for a 12-inch puppet. Lighting points are shown at X and Y in Figs. (D and E). Obtain an experienced electrician to set up permanent lights. With young children, use cycle lamps and torches and as much natural light as possible.

A multi-purpose stage

For a multi-purpose stage (Figs. 29, 30, 31), you will need one large three-wing clothes horse, two curtains the same height as the clothes horse, and one curtain half the height of the clothes horse. These should be pleated and pinned or stapled to laths or dowel rods. When ready for use, each curtain should be as wide as one wing; the rod joined to the top of each curtain should be 3 inches wider on each side than one wing. You will also need four long rods at

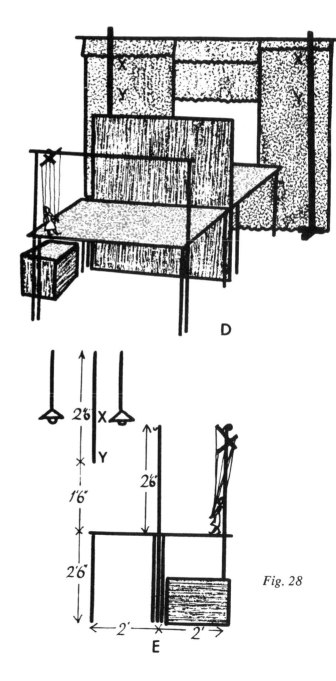

D

Fig. 28

E

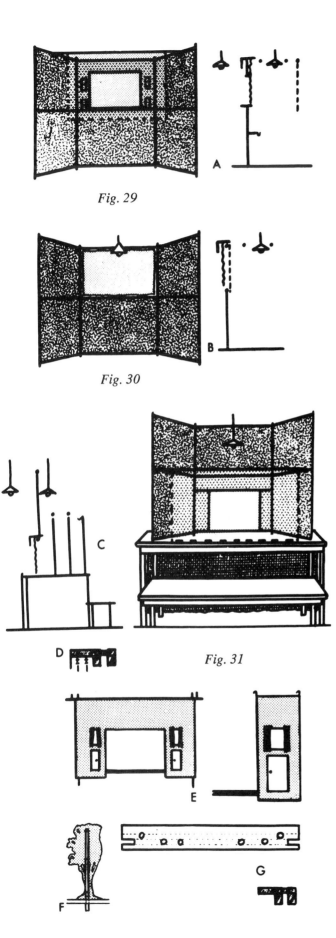

Fig. 29

Fig. 30

Fig. 31

positions shown by dots in (A) for glove puppet scenery, (B) for shadow puppet lights, and (C) for string puppet scenery, which can also stand on the floor; one shelf as in (G) with strips of wood set underneath. These lock the shelf on the front center bar for use with glove puppets. A few holes in the shelf will enable scenery such as trees, beds, and tables to be fixed so that they do not fly into the audience if knocked during the performance (F). In addition, you will need one shelf (D) with curtains and rails attached to lock on the top front bar for glove and shadow puppets and on the center front bar for string puppets. Large rubber bands will be found useful to hold the various bars in place.

Method. For a shadow stage arrange side and front curtains. Hook on curtain shelf, hang shadow screen and rod for lights (B) (Fig. 30).

For a glove or rod puppet stage, transfer shadow screen to backcloth position, hook on shelf and scenery rods (A). Side window pieces as shown in (E) are useful for by-play between glove puppets. A further useful luxury is an inside shelf to clip on below the stage shelf on which props and scenery are stored, and hooks along the front edge are used to hang glove puppets (A) (Fig. 29).

For a marionette stage rearrange front curtain by raising the half curtain to top rail, drop curtain shelf, backcloth, and scenery rods to center front rail (C), remove center shelf (Fig. 31). The marionette stage folds right away and stores flat. It can also be used for a shop or house. The various curtains are easily cleaned, and the puppeteers are hidden.

Curtains

Deep reds and blues are excellent for curtains on a puppet stage, and these should be at least twice the width of the proscenium arch so as to allow plenty of center, bottom, and side overlaps. Fig. 32 shows details of simple homemade versions.

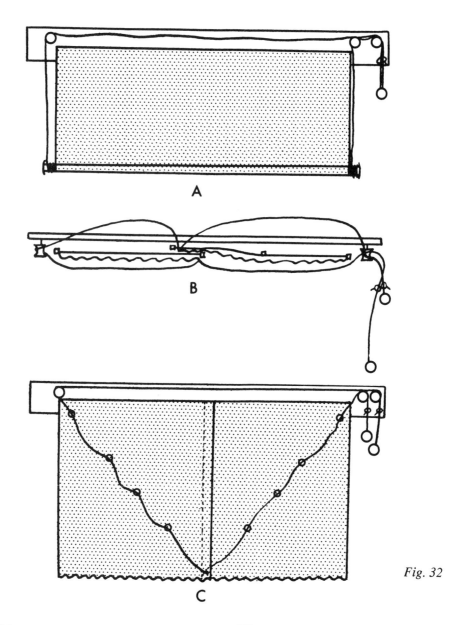

Fig. 32

If it is possible, use a plastic rail and runners; this will give a very quiet pull. The rail should be hidden behind a pelmet attached to the curtain shelf.

Fire-proofing scenery and costumes

It is possible to buy aerosol sprays or ready-to-mix powders to fireproof scenery and costumes. If you wish to make your own, mix 1½ pounds Borax, 1 pound boracic acid, and 2 gallons water. Dip or spray materials, but do not rinse. Check to see that colors are not affected before dipping the whole article into the solution.

Museums with collections of puppets

The Detroit Institute of Arts has an outstanding Paul McPharlin collection of all types of puppets and information about puppets. The following museums have collections that would be of above average interest to puppeteers:

American Museum of National History, Washington, D.C.

Cooper Museum for the Arts of Decoration, New York

Brooklyn Museum, New York

Museum of Fine Arts, Boston

Glenn Hellman

sculpture— various media

IT IS PARADOXICAL that although we exist in a three-dimensional world, most people think visually in only two. This you may at first discount as ridiculous, but ask someone with no training to make a sculptural object. The chances are that the result will be a collection of views (usually two or four), each one thought of separately, with no conception of how it affects the others, no internal logic or structure, and no understanding of how the object affects the space it exists in and defines.

The production of a self-existing object, which is the externalization of an experience in formal terms, is a rather standard definition of sculpture. People tend to have preconceived standards against which "art" is measured and judged. Unfortunately, these conceptions stand in the way of inquiry, are an excuse for mental idleness, and, as such, are barriers against a great deal of exciting and pleasure-giving experience, not only when looking at art but also in everyday life. These same preconceptions judge whether an object or situation is worth the effort of really looking and at the same time filter out those judged to be unworthy. We all need these censors—such is the complexity of life—but they should be servants not tyrants.

The process by which an experience becomes a formal idea takes place mostly in the subconscious and is generally a lengthy process. Before an experience can be used, it must be totally absorbed into the personality (when it reappears its source may be unrecognizable). This process cannot be forced. The effectiveness of the assimilation and metamorphosis depends on how well the experience is understood. (It must be remembered that an emotional experience, as far as sculpture is concerned, can only be expressed in terms of mass and space.) Beautiful objects, driftwood, stones, mechanical waste, etc. cannot be made into art just by putting them on a base and smoothing the edges (consider Marcel Duchamp!). Rather, an object must be taken

"Ritual." Antanas Brazdys.

and an idea imposed upon it. A piece of driftwood may suggest a bird if you translate your idea and concept of a bird through carving, filing, and sanding. The work must also possess sound design and form to be called a three-dimensional work of art.

For a start try these two seemingly sim-

191

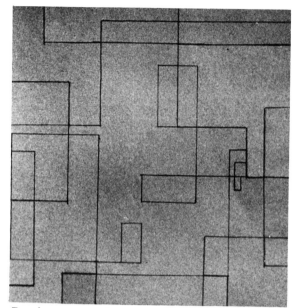

Random geometric pattern drawn on card.

The pattern extended into three dimensions.

ple exercises, which, if carried through beyond the obvious, will be found to be rather difficult:

1. Take a piece of thin tagboard, 12 inches square for convenience, and using only variations of one geometric shape, make an allover pattern, random or repetitive. Then cut the pattern so that pieces of it can be bent out on either side. You now have a two-dimensional pattern that has extended into the third dimension. Now stick on more tagboard, using the appropriate shapes, until the flat plane of the original piece is lost and what is left is a totally three-dimensional model.

2. Make a dozen or so small cubes of clay or similar modeling material (2 in. x 2 in. x 2 in.). Take one and cut into it, using only variations of the cube, to make a design in three dimensions. As you find out what happens in the first cube work on through the rest, developing in subsequent cubes ideas and forms that appear, making larger cubes as your ideas become more complex. Continue until you have exhausted all your ideas and then force yourself to try again.

It should be emphasized that these ex-

Exercise in cutting cubes of clay.

ercises are not intended to show you how to make sculpture but to introduce you physically to some of the problems of working in the round.

A craft is important to an artist in that it allows him to communicate clearly in the specific manner of his choice: it is the means only. The more the artist is the mas-

*The author builds up in plaster
using an armature of wood and burlap
saturated with plaster.*

ter of his craft, the more precise can be his statements, but craft ability should be developed alongside the exercise of creativity, not as something separate. Superior craft is no substitute for creativity, just as the finest ideas are useless unless they can be translated into some external form.

The understanding and feeling for a material or technique plays a large part in the creative process, just as the physical act of making a piece of sculpture plays a part in its evolution.

PLASTER

Plaster is a very useful sculptural material. It can be built up while wet, cast in different types of molds, and carved, as stone, from a mass. Although seldom used professionally for a final product because of its fragility, plaster can be most satisfying for studying relationships of forms both geometric and organic. When dried, plaster can be sanded, and the whiteness of this material will force you to be very critical of form. You can pour a mass of plaster into a container such as a milk carton; once the mass is set, the cardboard is torn away and the block can be easily carved with a simple knife while it is still damp. Another way would be to allow the mass to dry completely, then saw out squares or rectangles or any other shape, sand these down, and glue them together to form a construction-type sculpture.

Plaster also can be cast in a sand form. Take a suitable box and fill it with damp sand, then form a flat surface on the top of the box, and carve a low relief into the sand once a desirable negative form is achieved in it. Then, mix plaster and pour it into the sand and allow it to set. When removed, a certain amount of sand will stick to the surface, giving a sand like finish to the shape. This sand casting system limits you to relief-type sculpture; still you can learn much from this basic two-dimensional type of sculpture.

When building up plaster directly you will need an armature or framework upon which to build. Metal wire and metal mesh or coarse screening can be used. However, in this case, it is difficult to change the form once started because the metal armature is difficult to cut out or alter once the plaster is set. Another method of building up is to use coarse burlap that has been laundered or used enough to remove the stiffening. Burlap will help the plaster to be slightly waterproof. The burlap can be dipped in plaster and laid out or hung up to set. The sheets can then be cut, and shapes can be

193

built up by putting various parts together with additional wet plaster.

Working with plaster

You usually can purchase casting or molding plaster at your local lumber company or hardware store. Sand-mixed plaster used in construction of walls is not useful for most sculpture purposes. The casting or molding plaster sets in about 20 minutes. Mixing should be done in a slightly pliable plastic pail or bowl-type container. Cool water should always be used. The water should be poured into the mixing pail. Your hands should be dried before dipping into the plaster bag so as not to cause lumps from the drops of water that might fall into the bag. The plaster should be sifted through your fingers into the water until it rises to the surface. The mixture should not be stirred until all dry plaster has been sifted into the solution. You must not overload the water with dry plaster; rather when you first see that the water no longer absorbs the plaster, add a little plaster, then stop. When you stir the plaster it should be like heavy cream. From the time you stir it, you have about 20 minutes to work with it, the last 10 minutes of which are most ideal for building up. The first 10 minutes are best for pouring into a mold or form. Care should be taken not to pour any wet plaster into a drain or sink because it will set with water and nothing will remove it from your pipes. Use a bucket or pail to wash your hands and containers in.

CASTING

Plaster can be used to make a mold from a soft clay sculpture. The object to be cast should be divided in as many sections as required to pull the plaster mold off after the plaster is set. A simple head is divided between the face and the back of the head in about halves. This is done most effectively with very thin brass or aluminum shim stock available at large hardware stores. If it is not available, tin cans can be cut into 1½-inch metal squares and set up like a fence around the head and between front and back. A coil of clay is set on the top surface of the wall of metal to protect your fingers from getting cut and also to help you find the wall once the head is covered with plaster. Plaster is mixed as directed above and thrown onto the entire head front and back. This is best done by cupping your fingers to form a small container; then after dipping your hand into the plaster and filling the cup formed by your fingers, turn your hand so that the back of it is within four inches of the clay surface. Then quickly discharge the plaster from your hands onto the clay surface. On a clay work about 1 foot high, continue these layers of plaster until you have about a ¾-inch thickness. About one hour after the plaster is set, take the entire mass and put it into a large sink or pail of water. The water will soften the clay inside the plaster after about 20 minutes under the water. Cut some small wooden wedges and gently force them into the metal wall set up around the head to cut it in half. Once the two parts are separated, wash them clean and set out to dry. The next day, you can paint on a layer of tincture of green soap, available at drug stores; this will prevent the plaster that is to be put inside the mold from sticking to the walls. After soaping, put the two halves together, wire or tie them into proper position. The outside seam should be seared with clay or, even better, a layer of plaster. Now simply pour a batch of plaster into the head and pour it back out into the plaster container at least once. This procedure helps to remove air pockets. Then proceed to fill the head and allow it to set overnight. The next day, take a small chisel and hammer and chip away the mold and the plaster cast of your head will be achieved.

A form of casting that is useful for small objects is clay pressing. If done carefully, accurately, and sensitively, casts can be obtained. It is really most useful to use plaster

Fig. 1

Fig. 2

Fig. 3

Fig. 4

Fig. 5

Fig. 6

Fig. 7 Clay pressing

Fig. 1. The object to be cast, block of clay,
and talc. The talc is rubbed onto the object
and acts as a parting agent.

Fig. 2. Press object into clay up to half its width.
Dust top of clay with talc.

Fig. 3. Thin slab of clay is pressed tightly around
object and then is built up to equal other block.

Fig. 4. Completed mold with sides cut square
and top cut flat to insure a good register
when replaced.

Fig. 5. With object secured, pouring spue is
divided into halves, which are then placed
together. Make sure all edges are registered
before pinching seams.

Fig. 6. Pouring in plaster mixture.

Fig. 7. Cast object with spue still attached.
Mold is still good for further use.

as a quick reproduction of objects that cannot be worked on in their original states, that is, stone, bones, bits of machinery tools, or even other models, so that the ideas they suggest can be developed by carving and modeling.

METAL SCULPTURE

Steel sculpture probably started with Julio Gonzalez (1876-1942) and until recently had few practitioners. Although it would seem that an extensive workshop is needed for working in steel, a great deal is possible with surprisingly little equipment.

Interesting work can be done with very thin copper and lead solder using a soldering iron or propane fuel torch. Thicker metal in steel, brass, copper, bronze, and aluminum can be brazed together, that is, the use of a different alloy of metal to fuse over the parts to be joined at over 500°F. A yellow brass alloy called brazing rod will join steel, copper, bronze, or brass with a little skill and proper flux or cleansing agent, available at welding shops. If you have the use of propane fuel or a tank of acetylene or natural gas and a simple torch connection, this also will braze smaller work.

If you wish to work on metal 1/16 of an inch or thicker and of a size of more than 1 foot, you must have access to oxyacetylene welding and cutting equipment. The rest of a very basic tool kit is completed by a strong vise, a steel or wood bench, a heavy ballpein hammer, a heavy piece of flat metal to hammer on (or an anvil), a pair of vise grips, or "pony" spring clamps, and something to grind the welds with (this can be managed with a grinding stone or disc sander attachment for a fast electric drill). It is not hard to add to this list. Such items as an arc welder 100/200 amp. 100/50 volt range, angle grinder, bench grinder, bench shears, drill press, a whole selection of C clamps and grips soon find their way into the studio. As with all tools, let the need arise before buying; then you

"Head," 1964.
Steel sculpture 13 in. high.
Glenn Hellman.

get the right tool for the right job and not one that might do any number of jobs but is never actually used. The most attractive and expensive welding set or tool is not always the best.

The following selection of sculpture makes no pretense of comprehensiveness, but each does represent a different approach:

Some sculpture springs immediately from the form of the steel. "Polarity" and "2 forms II" do depend, in varying degrees, on standard steel forms for their conception. Whereas, while "Head" gains strength from being steel, its form is in no way dependent on the material. Just be-

196

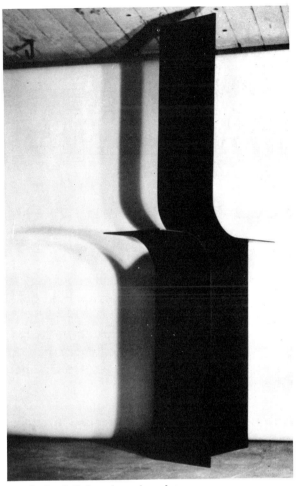

"Polarity." Painted steel sculpture.
Robert Adams.

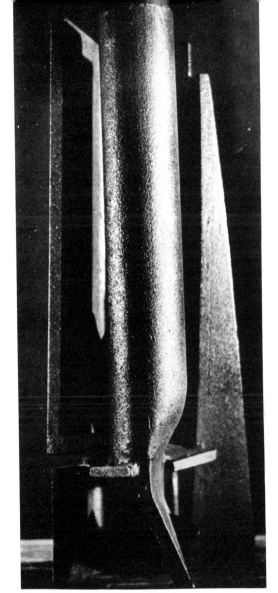

"2 Forms II." Bronzed steel sculpture.
Glenn Hellman.

cause a material is difficult, there is no necessity to become simplistic and limited in formal conception when using it. Obviously steel, as other materials, makes special demands of its own, but these should be incorporated and not allowed to dominate.

When making sculpture that requires a lot of sheet manipulation, it saves time and steel if, in the first place, a model is made and then paper patterns made from this of the more straightforward surfaces. It will be found that most working can be done cold and the rest can be done by local heating with the oxyacetylene torch. A 1-inch bar of mild steel can be easily bent in almost any curving type form by heating it red then bending. The same would be true

for sheet stock. The welding or fusing of steel requires some skill with the acetylene torch, as does the cutting with a cutting head. You should get a welding and cutting manual and practice these techniques.

Steel sculpture can be polished to whatever degree the artist chooses either with a sanding disc or a buffer. The sculpture soon will rust even indoors if not lacquered, well waxed, or oiled. For outside use, you can use the new cor-ten steel, which has a very slow rate of rust damage and turns a rich plum color out-of-doors after several years. For indoor use, you can purchase a bluing kit, the kind used by gun collectors. If the steel is properly cleaned and polished, a very rich and relatively long-lasting blue metallic look is obtained from this product.

197

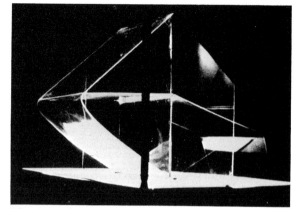

Plastic sculpture that depends on lighting for much of its effect. Stella Fagg.

"Construction in Space with Crystalline Center." N. Gabo.

PLASTICS

There are many types of plastics that will produce very effective sculptures. The clear, transparent colored, and opaque colored acrylics come in almost any size and thickness. They also come in solid rounds and tubes. These can be easily sawed with a hand or machine powered coping saw. After achieving the desired shape, the cut edges can be sanded on a machine sander or by hand. By using consecutively finer garnet paper, you can bring a surface almost to a polish; then with a cloth buff and polishing rouge, the surface will take a clear polish. This plastic can be glued or fused together with plastic solvent glues or clear epoxy. It is suggested that surfaces be held in position with masking tape, and then using a plastic solvent glue in a hypodermic needle, allow just enough glue to flow between the two edges to be glued. These sheets of plastic can also be formed by heating in a kitchen oven, until the whole sheet becomes flexible like Jell-o; at this point, remove the plastic from the oven and hold in the desired form or press over a wooden form (using oven gloves) until it has set and cooled sufficiently to hold its new position. Another interesting facet of this plastic is that it will conduct and hold light, so that if you build a box with a fairly strong light bulb inside, then cut an opening the exact size of a round bar or sheet of plastic, all of the light will channel itself through the plastic, causing an interesting glowing light, similar to the work by Stella Fagg in this chapter. By cutting or scoring the surface of plastic at any point, you can cause a light accent.

Other exciting plastics are the expanding foams in which two parts are mixed, and the material expands to many times the size of the original liquid volume, creating free-flowing forms of Styrofoam. The fumes from these materials are dangerous. Be sure that you question the hazards of using these materials before attempting to work with them.

Polyester, a thermo setting plastic, is another interesting material with which to work. It can be cast in a plaster or rubber mold, or it can be molded directly. The heavy liquid form of polyester can be crystal clear, or it can be colored with either transparent tones or solid opaque colors. A hardener or catalyst is added to the liquid, and this causes heat and subsequent hardening. By itself, polyester is not strong enough, but by using fiberglass as a reinforcing agent, it becomes very tough, durable, and lightweight.

Sculpture in marble. Brian Bishop.

STONE

Marble, limestone, and alabaster are soft stones that are easily carved; alabaster, for that matter, can be cut with an ordinary carving knife and can easily be filed. Limestone and marble are better worked with standard stone chisels, but they also can be filed and sanded to achieve the desired finish. Stone is generally thought of as a *subtractive* material, versus clay, which is thought of as an *additive* material. However, stone can be used as a construction-type material. Slabs, blocks, and other cut forms of marble or limestone can be acquired. These in turn can be drilled with a masonry bit and pinned or dowled together using epoxy or other masonry cements to become very durable and firm. Found shapes from architectural demolition can also be used in this manner to create interesting sculptures.

In your inquiries about stone, it should be remembered that monument works deal mostly with granite, which is much harder than the above mentioned stones and requires power tools to work. Stone cutters who cut sills and building stones are a better source for this type of work.

"Stone." Michael Kenny.

FABRICATION

Modern methods of fabrication can be used by the artist. The work titled "Stone" by Kenny is an example of aluminum sheets put together with rivets on an aluminum frame. Likewise, steel and other metals can be put together using nuts and bolts or sheet metal screws. Some of Alexander Calder's very large stabiles are made in this manner. Once assembled, paint coatings such as urethane or other strong waterproof paints can be used to make the work suitable for either indoors or outdoors or both.

199

Irene Barker

sewing

The first Singer sewing machine, manufactured in 1851.

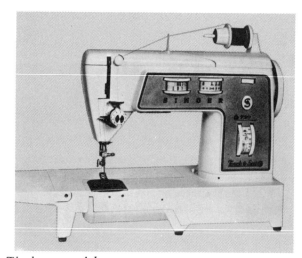

The latest model.

THREE VIRTUES are required to produce good needlework: perseverance, patience, and practice. All these are scarce in the rush and bustle of modern life, both at home and in schools; therefore they must be applied by the newcomer to the craft of sewing to projects that are quickly completed and give a feeling of success and satisfaction.

TOOLS AND EQUIPMENT

The old adage, "a bad workman blames his tools" contains great truth. A good needlewoman requires good tools, and they must be readily available and in "apple-pie" order. Nothing is more irritating than finding, when you are all ready to make a new dress, create a fabric picture or a piece of embroidery or, at a mundane level, to replace a button or mend a torn sheet, that the scissors are blunt or missing, or the only available needle is a crowbar or has an eye so fine that a magnifying glass is necessary to thread it. A well-equipped workbox (even if it is only a cardboard shoebox) is essential. See that it contains sharp scissors —not just one pair but a large pair for cutting out, a medium-sized pair for general work, a small pair for snipping ends, and, if possible, a pair of buttonhole scissors. Make sure that you own an awl and a selection of needles—sharps, betweens, and darners. A box of pins, sharp and rust-free, are also needed. Most important of all, buy a thimble. Half an hour spent in the local department store will teach you a great deal about the tools of sewing.

In addition to tools, the good needleworker needs some of the artist's tools: sharp pencils (HB and B), a ruler, a supply of plain paper, graph paper, tracing and carbon paper, newspaper, and a sketchbook for jotting down ideas and sketches as and when they occur. A set square and a protractor are also useful.

Having assembled the tools, make sure that they remain sacred. Do not let anyone borrow the scissors for jobs in the garage or garden, and prevent people from rummaging in your workbox for a rubber band, Scotch tape, masking tape, or safety pin.

PLAIN SEWING

Today, the sewing machine has reduced the necessity for plain sewing. No longer are people compelled to spend long hours making every garment and household arti-

200

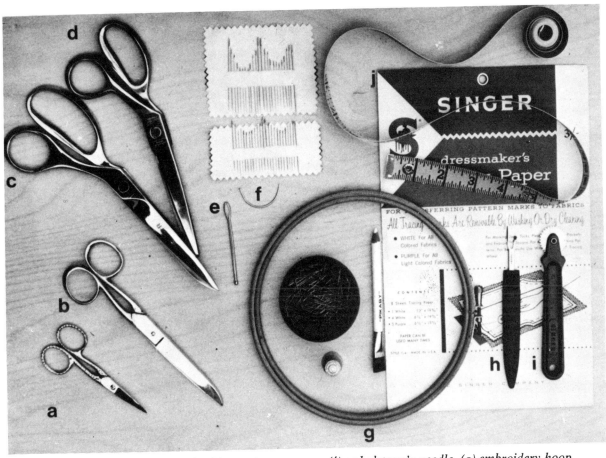

Basic equipment includes: (a) embroidery scissors, (b) scissors for general work, (c) cutting out scissors, (d) pinking shears, (e) spring awl,

(f) upholsterer's needle, (g) embroidery hoop, (h) stitch remover, (i) tracing wheel, and (j) tracing paper.

cle by hand with minute and even stitches. In spite of this, a knowledge of plain sewing is still of value because articles made by machine frequently need hand-finishing. Hand-sewing, though, still brings to mind pricked fingers and slow, hard labor. This need not be so if the fabric and needle are correctly positioned and a thimble used. Thimbles are made in metal and plastic. The metal ones are preferred as they are safer and more durable. The thimble is worn on the second finger of the sewing hand, and must fit comfortably. Position the hands as shown in Fig. 1, and use the top of the thimble to push against the eye of the needle so that the entire needle is inserted into and through the fabric. All that

is now required to complete the stitch is for the thumb and forefinger simply to pick up the needle and pull through the thread—all the expected effort and sore fingers prevented by the correct use of a thimble. With practice, it is possible to sew to an even rhythm.

Avoid a too long or short thread; too long wastes time in pulling through and is liable to knot, too short means frequent casting on and off and rethreading. A comfortable chair and good lighting, preferably daylight, are also aids to plain sewing. Obviously, it is impossible to arrange all sewing in daylight hours, and it is worth purchasing or making a special table lamp that can throw light onto the work below

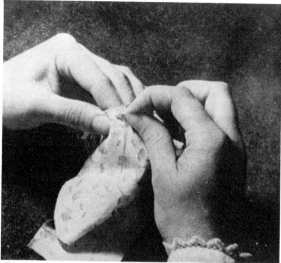

Fig. 1

Fig. 2

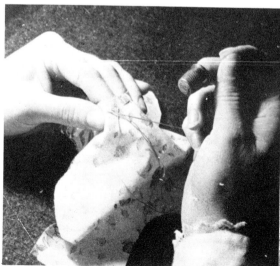

Fig. 3

eye level to prevent eyestrain. Some of the plain sewing stiches are:

Tacking, or basting. This is a quickly-worked temporary stitch that holds the fabric in place and prevents slipping while the permanent stitching (hand or machine) is worked. A line of tacking may also form a guide to mark the exact line of the permanent stitches. Tacking holds a garment together for the initial fittings. Never commence with an unsightly knot; two firm stitches on the spot are better. Adapt the size of the stitches to the fabric and to the strength you require. Where possible, avoid machine sewing over the basting thread because this makes removal of the basting difficult.

Running stitch. This stitch has three main uses. It can be used to join two pieces of fabric; it can be worked and then pulled to form gathers; and it can be used as a decoration, in which case it becomes an embroidery stitch. It is worked from right to left; the stitches should be small and even and the space between the stitches equal to the stitches themselves. One stitch at a time is wise in spite of the temptation to pick up half a dozen on the needle at once. Commence with two stitches on the spot.

Backstitch. This is another stitch that will join two pieces of fabric. It is slow to work but very stong. When worked perfectly it has the appearance of a line of machine sewing and, indeed, is the hand-sewing stitch that machine sewing replaced. Many bitter tears have been shed by young misses slaving over backstitch. In years gone by, lines of backstitch were used to ornament the cuffs and collars of hand-made shirts!

Begin with two stitches on the spot and work from right to left. First, take one running stitch forward, with the next stitch go back (hence the name) with the needle point into the end of the first running stitch, preferably down exactly the same hole in the fabric; now take a stitch forward equal

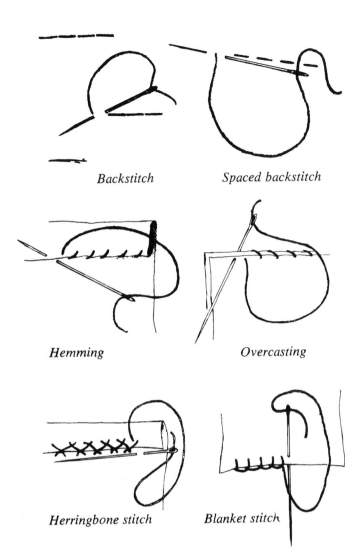

Backstitch　　　　*Spaced backstitch*

Hemming　　　　*Overcasting*

Herringbone stitch　　　　*Blanket stitch*

to twice the length of the stitch. Repeat.

Spaced backstitch. As its name implies, this stitch is worked in precisely the same manner as backstitch except that the needle does not go back into the previous stitch. It is not quite as strong as backstitch, but it is more unobtrusive. It is used to insert zippers by hand when an almost invisible effect is desired.

Hemming. This stitch is used to fix a folded edge. It may be the folded edge of an actual hem, or the folded edge of a bias tape strip, facing, or bindiing; or the folded edge of a cuff, a pocket, or a mundane necessary patch. Commence at the right-hand end of the piece to be hemmed by running the thread inside the fold and taking two small stitches on the spot on the fold itself. Hemming is a V-shaped stitch. One side of the V is formed by the thread and the other side by the inserted

sloping needle. The stitches must be small and even.

Slip hemming. This type of hemming is the one usually used on dress hems because when it is well worked it is almost invisible. It gets its name from the fact that the needle slips along inside the folded edge, only emerging to make a minute V-shaped stitch, visible just below the fold.

Herringbone stitch. This stitch is worked on a once-folded edge to finish and hold in place the raw edge. This stitch too may be used for decorative effects. Work from left to right. Commence by running the end of the thread under the folded edge and work two very small backstitches on the spot.

Oversewing and overcasting. These two are the same. Their names vary according to where and how the stitches are worked. Oversewing joins two folded edges together and can be worked on the right or wrong side. Overcasting is worked on a raw edge to prevent fraying.

Blanket stitch. Loop stitch is often called blanket stitch and is worked from left to right. It can be worked over a raw edge, a once-folded edge, or a twice-folded edge (a hem), or it may be worked as a decorative stitch. The edge of the fabric is held with the thumb on top and the stitch taken with the needle pointing toward the worker. In this way gravity forms a loop, and all that is needed is to pull the needle through the loop thus formed. These days few people blanket stitch their own blankets, but many other applications will be found for this useful stitch.

Buttonhole stitch. This stitch is frequently confused with the blanket stitch, but a buttonhole so worked would not be as satisfactory as if the correct stitch were chosen. Buttonhole stitch has a knot instead of a simple loop as in the blanket stitch. It is worked from left to right usually on a raw edge, which should be uppermost in the hand, and the rows of knots that are formed, side by side, protect the

203

The screw in the buttonhole scissors can be adjusted according to the length of the cut required.

raw edge from fraying and wear. Insert the needle to required depth, and taking the double thread from the eye of the needle, go around and under the point, counter-clockwise. When the needle is pulled through this twisted loop, a figure eight can be observed in the thread. When this eight is pulled tight, a knot is formed. The buttonhole stitch also is used to attach snap fasteners and hooks and eyes, three or four stitches in each hole.

BASIC PROCESSES

Some of the basic sewing processes that you should be familiar with are:

Buttonholes

Buttonholes are most conveniently cut using special buttonhole scissors. These have a special blade with a hollowed edge that allows the hole to be cut without damaging the edge of the garment.

Another method of cutting the buttonhole is to fold the fabric in half, snip the center, open out, and extend the snip to a slit the required length. A buttonhole may also be cut with a sharp pointed pair of scissors by swiveling the point of the blade until a small round hole forms and then ex-

tending this to a slit. The size of the buttonhole should equal the diameter of the button plus one eighth of an inch. Buttonholes may be worked horizontally or vertically on garments. Sometimes on a checked or striped fabric it may be necessary to work them diagonally to blend with the pattern on the fabric.

Buttonholes are almost always worked on double fabric. They usually have a round end, which takes the pull of the button and a square end which is orna-mental and keeps the buttonhole in shape. Feminine garments button right side over left side, and garments for men and boys button the reverse way (probably a hang-over from the day when pistols were kept in the inside left breast pocket—hazardous, I should think, but convenient for a fast right-hand draw).

Seams

A seam joins two pieces of fabric. There are four seams in general use, and it is important to be able to choose the most suitable for a particular purpose.

Plain, or open, seam. Place the two pieces of fabric together, right sides touch-ing, making sure raw edges are level. Pin, baste, and stitch (hand or machine) par-allel with the raw edge. The commercial pattern companies make the seam allow-ance ⅝ inch wide.

Using the point of an iron, open the seam flat on the wrong side. The raw edges must be finished by overcasting, blanket stitch, machine sewing the edge, zig-zag stitch using a swing needle machine, or—the friend of those in a hurry — pinking shears.

French seam. This seam completely en-closes the raw edges; it is strong but leaves a ridge on the wrong side. This limits its use to thin fabrics.

Place the two pieces of fabric together wrong sides touching, right sides on the outside. Pin, baste, and stitch. This now appears as if a mistake has been made as the raw edges are of course showing on the right side of work. Don't panic, but trim the raw edges as narrow as you dare or as the fabric dictates. Press open this trimmed seam. Turn the fabric so that the wrong side faces you. Fold back the seam along the stitching, thus enclosing the raw edges. Pin, baste, and machine sew just below where the raw edges can be felt, or seen if held up to the light.

Machine sewn flat seam. This seam is well named; it is strong as it has two rows of machine sewing and all the raw edges are enclosed. It is used on garments that take hard wear and washing: for instance, shirts and blouses, pajamas, jeans, workman's clothes, overalls, and some children's garments. Like the lapped seam, which follows, a machine sewn seam is all worked on the right side.

Place the two pieces of fabric together wrong sides touching, right sides outside. Take the full seam allowance and sew the seam. Trim the seam allowance at the back of the garment. Press the seam open. Turn the wider seam allowance from the front, into a hem over the back. Sew the edge of the hem with the machine. The finished seam is quite flat on both right and wrong sides.

Lapped, or overlaid, seam. This seam is used to join yokes and to set frills. The stitching of the seam may be close to the folded edge or sometimes well away from it so that a mock tuck is formed to outline the stitching.

Basically, one piece of fabric having a folded edge and called the overlay is placed flat on the second piece, called the underlay. These pieces are then stitched together on the right side. On the wrong side, finish the raw edges by one of the methods described for plain seams.

Disposal of fullness

All dressmaking from simple garments for beginners to the grandest creation has one main problem—to convert flat fabric

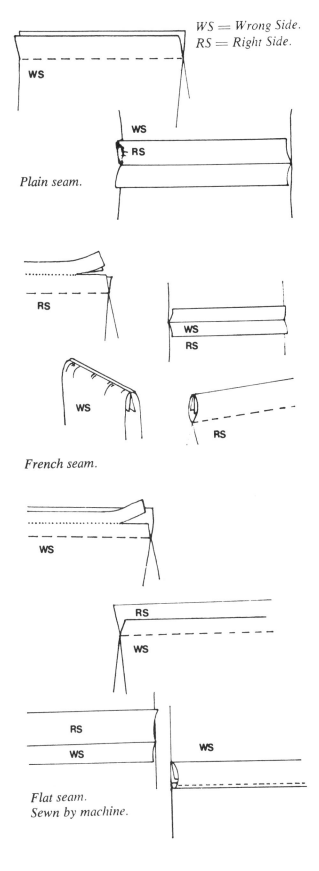

WS = Wrong Side.
RS = Right Side.

Plain seam.

French seam.

Flat seam.
Sewn by machine.

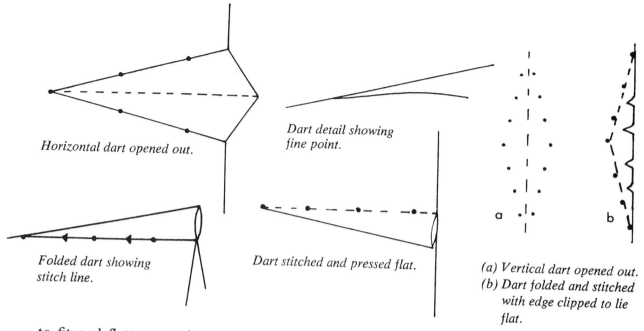

Horizontal dart opened out.

Dart detail showing fine point.

Folded dart showing stitch line.

Dart stitched and pressed flat.

(a) Vertical dart opened out.
(b) Dart folded and stitched with edge clipped to lie flat.

to fit and flatter round people, to change two dimensions to three. This problem solved, the garment also has to be comfortable and to allow movement. Obviously, sportswear needs more movement space than formal wear. There are four processes that dispose of fullness: darts, pleats, tucks, and gathers.

Darts. A dart is a fold of fabric that is stitched down, tapering to a point toward the fuller part of the figure. The point of the dart must be as fine as possible so that the finished dart when pressed is smooth and inconspicuous. The last few stitches at the point are parallel to the fold, and the very last one is off the edge.

Horizontal darts are pressed downward and vertical darts toward the center of the garment. In a thick fabric, cut the dart open and press it flat. Sometimes a dart is pointed at both ends; then it must be snipped at the center to allow it to be pressed flat.

Pleats. A pleat is a fold of fabric of any width held in place by another piece of fabric at a right-angle to it. This may be a bodice, yoke, cuff or band. Pleats can be left unpressed to hang in loose folds or pressed to give sharp edges. There are three main types of pleating: knife pleats, which have their folded edges pointing in one direction; inverted pleats, which are in fact

two knife pleats pointing toward each other; and box pleats, which are two knife pleats pointing away from each other. A quick way to solve a pleat problem is to take a length of paper and fold and crease to obtain the desired effect. When the paper is opened out it is easy to measure how much fabric to allow.

Gathers. To gather literally means to draw together or collect in a mass, like a bunch of flowers, all the fine stems held vertically. Gathers are really minute pleats and may be worked by hand using running stitches. Cast on very strongly a knot and several stitches on the spot. Use thread that will not snap when pulled. Work if possible across the weft threads. Two or three rows ¼ inch apart are better than one. Hold all three threads and pull gently but firmly, easing the gathers along with your thumbnail.

Sewing machine gathering is less irksome. Set the machine to a long stitch, 6 or 8 stitches to the inch. Work two rows on the right side, the first on the seam line and the second a ¼ inch away from it nearer the raw edge. Pull the threads on the wrong side. These gathers are easy to arrange and do not slip as much as handworked gathers. The amount of fullness is dictated by personal preference, fashion, or the amount of fabric available—"cutting your coat ac-

Knife pleats.

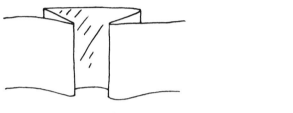

Inverted pleat.

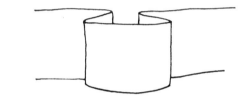

Box pleat.

Dress using a combination of box and knife pleats.

Dress using knife pleats and inverted pleat.

cording to your cloth." Half as much fabric again as the finished width gives slight fullness, twice as much is an average, and three times as much is generous.

Smocking is rows of gathers worked by hand with great precision, which are then held in place by versions of stem stitch.

Tucks. A tuck is a fold of fabric of any width that is held in place by a line of stitching (hand or machine) along its length. Tucks hold fullness in place, act as a decoration, or serve both purposes at once. Tucks may be evenly spaced or arranged in groups, and tucks of different widths may be used together. Tucks can be separated by rows of applied lace or narrow fancy ribbon or rows of embroidery done by hand or machine. The finest tucks are called pin tucks, and these appear on baby garments and on blouses and lingerie made from fine fabrics.

Work the tucks before making up the garment. Measure and mark very accurately because even a slight discrepancy repeated on every tuck will greatly alter the size of the finished garment. Released tucks must be securely finished at the release point.

FABRIC

Woven fabrics are constructed from two sets of threads. Those that are set longitudinally onto the loom are called the warp, and those that are woven horizontally across the warp are known as the weft. The two firm edges formed where the weft threads turn at the end of each row of weaving are called the selvage.

By folding the warp threads until they are parallel with the weft threads a fold is obtained that is referred to as an on the bias fold. Strips of fabric cut parallel to this fold are called bias strips. These strips are most useful because they will stretch slightly and can be eased around curves without puckering or distortion. They are used to bind or face curved edges, for instance, necks and armholes. Bias-cut cloth binding is sold ready cut and folded in a great range of colors; it is then called bias binding.

Today's fabric departments are an Aladdin's Cave and a continual temptation to the needleworker. They are, too, a reminder of the old parlor game, "animal vegetable, or mineral." Until the beginning of this century, choice was limited to the four natural fibers: wool (sheep, goats, and other quadrupeds with spinnable coats), silk from obliging tame or wild silkworms, cotton and linen of the plant kingdom. Now scientists produce from wood pulp, coal, cellulose, and other chemicals a bewildering array of synthetic fibers. Some resemble in handling and appearance the traditional fabrics. Sometimes, the synthetic fibers are blended with natural ones to give a special property; for instance, resistance to creasing and shrinkage, easy washing, durability. Rayon, nylon, and Dacron are some of these man-made fibers. Further confusion can be caused by one fiber having a different name in other countries. For example, Dacron is marketed as Terylene in England, Terital in Italy, Tergal in France, and Trevira in Germany.

Frequent visits to well-stocked fabric retailers are of value. Study the price tags on the end of the rolls; they will state, besides the price per yard, the fiber content of the fabric, often expressed in percentages, sometimes with hints on laundering or a definite order "Dry Clean Only." It is worth keeping a notebook for fabrics. Pin or stick in pieces and relevant information—price, where purchased, purpose, how much was used, and date, fiber content, and any special treatment that it may require.

After establishing the animal, vegetable, or mineral of a fabric, there are two methods of construction, by weaving or by knitting. The knitted fabrics are usually called jersey. Patterns can be woven or knitted into the fabric to produce an unlimited number of surface textures, or the fabric

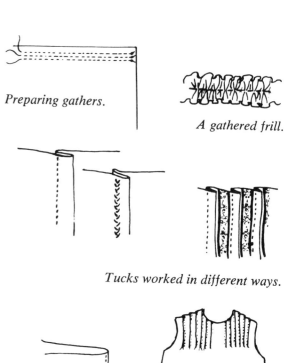

Preparing gathers.

A gathered frill.

Tucks worked in different ways.

Pin tuck.

Tucks used to hold fullness.

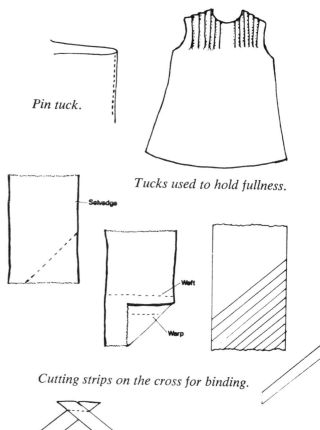

Cutting strips on the cross for binding.

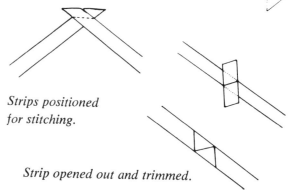

Strips positioned for stitching.

Strip opened out and trimmed.

may be printed with patterns. Some of these are perennial—dots, checks, stripes, and flower designs; others, the annuals, follow the vagaries of fashion, being *avant garde* one moment and out-of-date the next. This is a trap for the hoarder. To buy fabric because it is irresistible or "such a bargain" and then to store it too long is dangerous.

Most fabric departments have a section for remnants at bargain prices. They are reduced because they are at the end of a roll, a discontinued line, or have some small flaw in weave or print. These counters are a treasure trove, but don't always expect your sewing to be economical. Obviously, a more expensive fabric will have advantages over a cheap one in appearance and wear, apart from that self-confident glow that comes with indulgence in luxury. Some extravagances are economical in the long run.

In the stores, furnishing fabrics and dress fabrics are usually sold in different departments. This segregation must not inhibit choice. Many a successful dress (remember Scarlett O'Hara in *Gone with the Wind?*) was intended for curtains, and some dress fabrics may well be used for home furnishing ideas, particularly table cloths, mats, and cushion covers. Ticking, when its feather proofing is washed away, is very useful for this. The humble unbleached calico, when dyed or printed, may be put to uses for which it was not originally intended. Remember curtain fabrics often shrink. Check with the retailer and, if uncertain, preshrink fabric before sewing.

SEWING MACHINES

"The sewing machine is man's greatest contribution to life." (Gandhi)

Choose a sewing machine with care. A machine correctly used and maintained will last more than a lifetime. Many 19th century pieces are still performing Trojan service. Send away to several leading manufacturers for brochures; visit, if possible, a sewing machine retailer where you may watch demonstrations and try machines for yourself. Adopt the same attitude to this purchase as to a car; after all, it will last much longer. Some retailers will allow trial periods at home. Visit friends and relations and try out their machines. Don't underestimate your own ability to improve in sewing technique. Many beginners rush to purchase a hand machine and then realize too late the advantages of speed and two free hands, which are obtained with an electric model. Make inquiries about servicing and availability of spare parts. Buy the best you can afford.

Hand machines

Hand machines are used on a table. Make sure that it is a strong one. Treadle machines are always mounted on a stand. Electric machines may be used on a table or on a stand. Many machines are sold as portable—just try it; some require a very strong arm indeed. Remember, electric voltages, plugs, and sockets vary around the world, so if you are a traveler be prepared with a transformer—or settle for a hand model. The second decision is between a straight stitch machine or a swing needle machine. The former will stitch forward and reverse and will efficiently perform all general work.

The swing needle machine will do straight stitching, but, when adjusted, the needle will work from side to side producing the zigzag stitch, which is invaluable for finishing raw edges, buttonholes, and a host of other time savers. An automatic swing needle machine will also produce patterns. The machine must be set for patterns by dials, levers, or by inserting cams. New Singer sewing machines have "dial a stitch."

Care for your machine. Do not allow it to become too hot, too cold, too dusty, too dry, or too damp. It will repay you in trouble-free stitching if you oil it lightly and regularly, brush away dust and fluff, particularly around the bobbin and the nee-

Variations on a simple child's dress:
(a) Dress using contrasting stripes and bound with rick rack.
(b) Embroidered bib and sleeves edged in lace.

(c) Motif embroidered on pocket.
(d) and (e) Ideas for pockets.
(f) Pin tucks used to decorate the yoke.

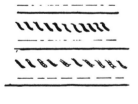

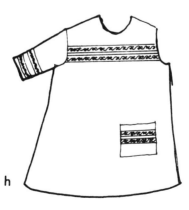

(g) Simple embroidery stitches for use as edgings.
(h) Decorative bindings enhance a simple dress.

g

h

211

A selection of the many kinds of trimmings available.

dle. Replace bent or blunt needles. Do not strain the machine by attempting to work materials such as leather or carpets that are too heavy for a domestic model. Study the book of instructions that is provided with your machine. Don't let the attachments and gadgets remain in their box. Get to know them; they save time and effort.

After having assembled your tools, acquired a sewing machine, mastered the basic processes—what to make? The choice is infinite, but walk before you can run. A simple project completed quickly is better than great things planned but never achieved. The novice dressmaker is wise if she first attempts small, simple garments for a child. Shift dresses for little girls are the simplest of all. Put your faith in a pattern from one of the major pattern companies. Their instructions are detailed and

careful. They want your effort to be a success because they aim to sell more patterns. However, a basic shift pattern gives scope for experiment, and by varying the choice of fabric and trimmings many variations of one theme are possible. The accompanying sketches show a few.

Confidence gained in this manner will help you to progress to adult garments. The pattern companies grade many patterns as "Easy to Make" or "Quick to Sew" or "Only three main pattern pieces." Clothes and home furnishings made by the enthusiastic needleworker are almost always cheaper than those ready made. Frequently they are more carefully constructed and finished and, of course, made to measure; but the compliment that gladdens the heart of the amateur is "Oh, it doesn't look homemade," and this is not difficult to achieve.

Mary Barker

spinning and weaving

BEFORE WEAVING CAN BEGIN, some way must be found to turn fibers into yarn. Our ancestors interwove strips of bark, skins, or reeds to make windbreaks, fish traps, and simple baskets. Although these have perished, early pottery often shows incised patterns reminiscent of twill, herringbone, and other simple weaves. Subsequently, they must have discovered that twisting fibers from wool, fur, or plants would make yarn. Spindle whorls and loom weights are found in excavations of Lake Dwellings and Stone Age remains (Fig. 1 a and b).

All fibers can be made into a thread by drawing them out into a thin line and putting in enough twists per inch to hold them together. Wool is easy to spin because each individual fiber has a certain degree of crimp and, if examined under a microscope, will show a scale structure. Fleeces vary from a soft, full handle to a silky, demi-luster wool or a springy, resilient tweed type.

Before twisting to make a yarn, the fibers must be teased open and separated to form a fluffy mass easy to draw out. With a good fleece this may be all the preparation needed. Otherwise a pair of carders are used to open the fibers. Carders are oblong pieces of wood covered with bent wires. They have handles (Fig. 2), and although the two are the same, it is usual to mark them clearly right-hand and left-hand because the wire teeth wear differently in use. The teased wool is arranged on the left card and then stroked gently by the right card until there is a straight fringe of fibers. These are then transferred from right to left card, and the process repeated. When straightened, the fibers are taken off and rolled into a rolag, ready to be drawn out and the twist put in.

Spinning consists of three processes: drawing out the fibers, putting in the twist, and then winding on the spun yarn.

To spin with a spindle, let the rolag lie over the back of the left hand, and with the right hand, draw out a thin roving. Attach this to a piece of yarn that has been tied to the spindle shaft, then wound below the whorl and fastened by a slip knot to the hook at the top of the shaft. Give the spindle a twirl in a clockwise direction, then pull out some more fibers as twist runs up toward the rolag. Continue drawing and twirling until the spindle hits the floor. It is then time to wind the thread neatly around the spindle.

These three actions take time, so thought was given to speeding up spinning. Leonardo da Vinci shows in his sketch books his idea for solving the problem, but the spinning wheel is thought to have first been made in Rhineland in the 16th century. The advantage of the wheel over the spindle is that all three processes—drawing,

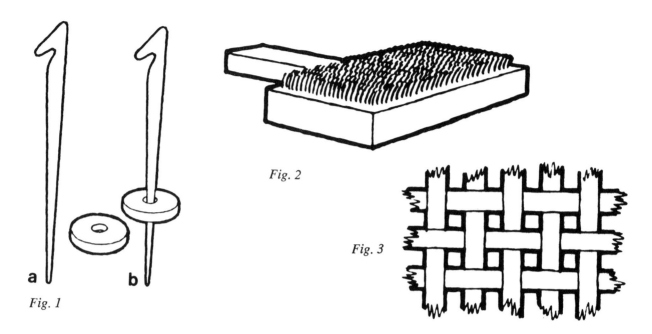

Fig. 2

Fig. 3

a   b

Fig. 1

putting in the twist, and winding on—all take place at once. Early spinning machinery used the same principles and developed slowly into the highly complicated industrial apparatus used today.

Wool is easier to spin when it is in its natural grease as the fleece has been shorn from the sheep. If it is so dirty that it must be washed before spinning, a few drops of oil should be added before teasing the scoured fibers. It is possible to dye either the fibers or the yarn, but in both cases, grease and oil must be washed out first. Dyed fibers can be blended on the carders to give subtle colored thread. By following the instructions on a packet of commercial dyestuff, quite successful results can be obtained. Some general information on natural dyes and dyeing processes will be found in the section on Tie-and-Dye.

Handspinning is slow, so after giving it a trial, it might be best to choose some mill spun yarn. There are special yarns made for weaving, but knitting wool can be used for your first piece of work.

WEAVING

To make cloth, one series of threads, called warp, is held taut from the front to the back of the loom. These threads are divided by some device to make an opening through which a continuous thread, weft, interlaces with the warp at right angles. Plain weave is the simplest interlacement, like darning, under one thread over the next (Fig. 3).

From prehistoric times, weavers have tried to find more convenient ways of separating the warp threads to make a shed for the weft shuttle to traverse. Some early looms consisted of a frame to hold the warp threads taut, with one shed obtained by darning a wide stick under the odd ends and turning it on its side. All the even ends had a loop of string called a leash, put around them individually. These leashes were then tied into bundles or to a rod so that they could be lifted to make the other shed (Fig. 4).

Today, a rigid heddle reed loom that makes plain weave can be purchased. This rigid heddle consists of metal slats with a hole half way, held in a frame. There are usually six slats to an inch with six spaces between. This will give twelve ends per inch. When the rigid heddle is raised, all the threads through the holes are lifted; when the heddle is depressed, all these ends are pushed down. By this simple means the two sheds giving plain weave are made.

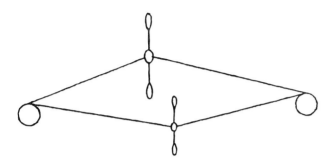

Fig. 4

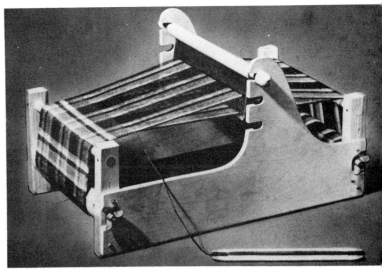

Dryad two-way rigid heddle loom.

Four harness Harris table loom.

When extra decoration is needed, the threads have to be lifted almost like embroidery. It is possible to make delightful patterns in this way, although of course it takes time.

A four harness table loom can weave pattern according to the way the threads are entered through its four harnesses. This is called the draft. After the heddles are threaded, the ends must be pulled through the reed to space them out to the correct number of ends per inch. The harnesses are raised to form the shed, and with four harnesses there are fourteen different combinations of lifts.

A treadle loom has the harnesses attached to pedals. There can be more than four harnesses, but the loom becomes awkward to use with more than eight.

Design

Before the warp can be wound, an accurate plan must be made for the finished article. In a way, you work backward by visualizing the end product and then analyzing it. To weave a scarf on a heddle reed loom, first decide how long and how wide it is to be, whether striped vertically, horizontally, checked, or just a plain color warp with a contrasting color weft. When these decisions have been made, plan it out as follows:

Scarf: finished dimensions—54 in. by 8 in., knotted fringe 3 in. each end.

Warp length	54 in.
Take up and shrinkage	5 in.
(3 in. per yard)	
Waste	18 in.
Total:	77 in. (2¼ yds. approx.)

Width	8 in.
Sett	12 ends per in.
Total number of ends 8 by 12	96
Double outside two ends for selvage	4
Total:	100

The plan is to make a black and white scarf with check border at the edges and horizontal stripes. Color order of warp

Black   4. 4. 4. 4.   16
White   2. 4. 4. 64. 4. 4. 2.   84

Total: 100 ends

215

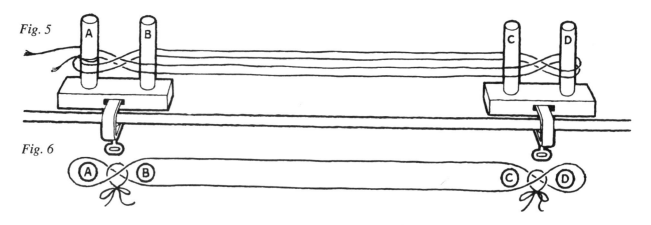

Fig. 5

Fig. 6

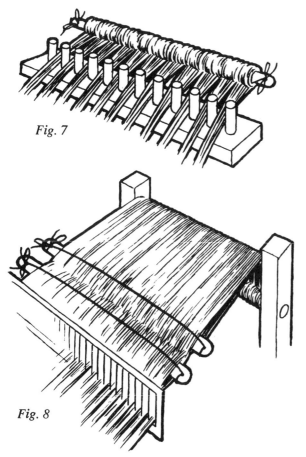

Fig. 7

Fig. 8

Warping

The warp has to be wound with a cross at each end so that the threads are kept in order. To do this, clamp two pegs about 6 inches apart at each end of a table, A.B.C.D. The distance between A. and D. must be the length of the warp. Tie the thread to peg A. then wind in front of B. and C. and behind D.; on the return

journey, the wool passes in front of D. and behind C. and B., in front of A. and so on (Fig. 5). From A. to D. is counted as one thread, back to A. the second end. Take care to follow the color plan exactly. It is possible to upturn chairs on the table and use the legs instead of posts for warping. For long warps, there are special peg boards and warping mills to make this process swift and easy, but there are still pegs each end to make the two crosses. When the correct number of threads has been wound, tie around the crosses with a strong contrast yarn, and remove the warp carefully from pegs A. and B., crocheting it into a chain until it is finally slipped off peg D. This chain keeps the warp even (Fig. 6).

Rolling on warp

The next stage is to spread the warp out to the correct width. A piece of apparatus called a raddle is useful for this (Fig. 7). It consists of a bar of wood with pegs or nails at one inch intervals or even half or quarter inch apart. The rod from the back of the loom is put through the loop of cross C.D. and the strong cord through the other loop C.B. Take care to check that this end of the crochet warp unchains. The threads are then divided into the spaces of the raddle in correct order of the cross. If the sett of the cloth is 12 ends per inch, 12 threads are put into each inch division, and so on. Tie the back rod to the canvas apron on

216

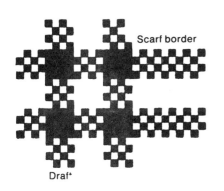

Scarf border

Draft

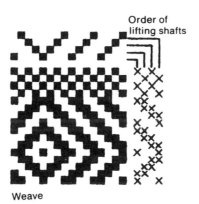

Weave

Order of lifting shafts

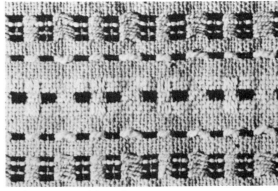

Enlargement of four harness weave.

the back roller of the loom, spacing out the cords so that they are straight. The warp chain is then held firm in the left hand and given a few sharp taps with the side of the right hand. Any threads that have been loosened during raddling should be picked up here. It is most important to roll on the warp at even tension. Holding the warp chain firmly with one hand, turn the back roller with the other. A sheet of firm brown paper, one inch wider on each side than the warp, is rolled in to prevent subsequent layers of threads bedding down on each other. Thin sticks can be used instead. As the warp unchains, repeat the shake and tap routine, keeping a watch for any loose ends.

When the second cross of the warp is reached, shed sticks are fastened on each side with cords (Fig. 8); then the cross tie is undone and the warp loops tied by half bows in about one inch sections to keep them tidy. Looms vary in design, and some way of supporting the shed sticks conveniently must be found. With the rigid heddle reed, the loops of the warp are cut and the ends threaded first through a slit then through a hole, taking the next in order of the cross each time. The selvage is made by entering double ends through the first slit and hole, then threading ends singly until the last two, which are doubled for the other selvage. The next step is to tie the threads in inch-wide sections around the rod attached to the front roller, taking

extreme care that the tension is even.

To begin weaving, raise the heddle reed, and pass the shuttle through the shed, leaving two inches of weft outside the web. This weft end is then tucked around the outside selvage thread into the same shed. Always begin and end the weft thread in this way. If you put the end into the next opposite shed, the finishing off will show. To return to the original scarf design, the color order of the weft must be first four white and then four black picks (the name for weft threads). This weft plan will give white, black, and mixed checks at the borders with white and mixed stripes across.

Difference of four harness loom

In four harness loom not only does the reed have to be entered as a separate process, but also there are many alternative ways of threading the heddles. They can be arranged 4.3.2.1. or any other way to experiment, for instance, 4.3.2.1.2.3.4.1. The order in which the shafts are lifted will give pattern to the cloth. The squared paper diagram shows that when harnesses one and three are raised alternately with harnesses two and four, plain weave is obtained just like that made by the rigid heddle. However, lift the harnesses in the following order in pairs, one and two, two and three, three and four, four and one; these two different ways of entering the heddles will give very different patterns. There are three choices to be made in designing for four harnesses.

217

Horsehair and wool rug woven in harness-switching method.

Peter Collingwood.

First, the order of threading the heddles, called the draft; second, the size of reed and how many ends to put through each dent, called ends per inch, or sett; and third, the order of lifting the harnesses. The best way to understand all this is to set up the loom with a narrow sample, three inches in straight draft and three inches in a different draft, and then try weaving with different lifting plans.

There are infinite variations on four harnesses, but at first the rigid heddle seems limited to plain weave. But this need not be dull; besides all the color combinations of stripes and checks, here are some ideas to try.

Vary the thickness of the warp by putting four ends through the slit and then only one through the hole. Try this in stripes.

Fill half an inch of the heddle reed as usual, then leave half an inch empty. After weaving half an inch, put in a stick instead of the weft. Carry on weaving and then remove the stick. This will make an open lacy scarf.

Embroidery on the loom. With one color warp, weave two inches in self color weft, then use one pick of doubled weft, four picks of fine thread, say silk across wool. Thread a needle with a length of the doubled weft, put this through half inch of the open shed, then make a blanket stitch around the first thick weft, pulling all the fine threads together. Repeat this stitch at intervals across the warp.

Pick up. Weave one inch as usual; then, with a stick in front of the heddle, pick up four threads, leave four threads, right across the warp. Turn the stick on end

and put the weft through. Pull out the stick and repeat the process, lifting up the four threads that were left down last time. Repeated several times, this will make a block pattern. The difficulty is that the take up of weft yarn will be different and tend to pull in the sides of the cloth. To avoid this, try using a row of plain weave between each pick up weft. This is called using a tabby binder, *tabby* being the nickname for plain weave, and this tabby binder is often used when weaving an elaborate draft on a four harness loom.

Great progress has been made in industrial textiles during the past decade. Mass production brings standardization of things to buy, but it is precisely this standardization that will encourage people to create something of their own and find the pleasure the craftsman has in using his hands.

At first the fun of weaving is enough, but soon proper pride in work well done will develop skill. This skill is needed for quality of textile—all important in an age of change and rapid technological invention. Besides the hand weaver making original and beautiful things for himself, there must be the designer-craftsman creating ideas that will influence the whole field of textiles.

These are only a few suggestions because I do not want to spoil anyone's fun in exploring his own ideas. It can be discouraging when one of these ideas does not work, but try to find out what went wrong. Sometimes the difference between success and failure in weaving is very small; change the size of yarn, double up the sett, put in a few spaces, or vary the beat; any one of these factors might make all the difference.

Anne Maile

tie-and-dye

TIE-AND-DYE is a fascinating and practical craft suitable for skilled and unskilled people of all ages. Cloth (usually white) is knotted, folded, bound, sewn, or manipulated in various ways so that during the dyeing process certain parts resist the dye. The skill lies in planning these dyed and undyed areas to form pleasing patterns and color schemes. After the dyeing is finished, whether with one, two, or more colors, the sample is untied and ironed out flat. With the first dyeing, the original white cloth is reserved in the resist pattern. The first color is reserved if extra binding or sewing is added before dyeing the second color, and so on.

ORIGINS

The origins of tie-and-dye, also known as Plangi in some countries, as Bandhana in India, Shibori in Japan, and Adire in Nigeria, are obscure. Tritik is the term given to the sewing methods in many countries. At different times, tie-and-dye has been practiced in most parts of the world, except Australasia. The earliest known records of the craft come from China, India, and Japan (approx. 6th–10th centuries A.D.). Knowledge of the craft spread along the old "Silk Road" and the old caravan routes from the Far East to the Mediterranean countries. It was a flourishing craft in Peru at the time of the ancient Incas, before the Spanish conquest in the 15th century A.D. Early peoples of Mexico and many countries in South America and the Southwest region of the United States also practiced the craft, possibly from the time of the Middle Ages. Today, very beautiful Adire cloths come from Nigeria in West Africa, but when these were first produced is not known.

The basic principle of tie-and-dye, with its dyed and undyed sections of cloth, could have been discovered accidentally and then developed independently in various parts of the world. In the past, the craft was carried out within the family circle or tribe, using

"Daybreak," cotton wall hanging. Author.

the type of handwoven cloth made in the district. Colors for the dyes were obtained from local plants, such as indigo, cutch, lichens, etc.; from roots such as madder; from barks came fustic, logwood, etc.; some dyes from beetles and insects, for instance, lac, kermes, and cochineal; and purple from the Purpura shellfish. Minerals also provided coloring matter.

TOOLS AND EQUIPMENT

Tie-and-dye is a craft that can easily be carried out at home or in the classroom as the basic needs are simple. Dyes and dyebath are of course essential. All receptacles of enamel, stainless steel, and galvanized ware are suitable for both hot and cold dyeing, but for cold dyeing it is possible to use plastic, glass, and pottery vessels. Fabrics: all kinds of cotton cloths, especially

219

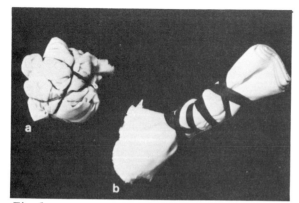

Fig. 1

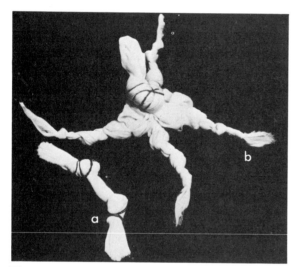

Fig. 2

"February Fill-Dyke," another silk wall hanging by the author.

Rubber bands can also be used. These are easier for young children to work with.

BASIC PROCEDURE

Tie-dyeing consists of the following basic procedure:

1. Wash and iron cloth.
2. Mark out pattern if necessary and tie up the cloth according to the methods chosen.
3. Wet out tied-up sample if required and dye.
4. Rinse and dry.
5. Add more binding or sewing, or completely untie the sample and then rearrange it and retie it before dyeing the next color.
6. After the final dyeing, rinse well and dry.
7. Untie.
8. Rinse again. Dry partially and iron while still damp.

Tying-up Methods

In tie-and-dye the way in which the fabric is dyed is all important. Various methods for tying are:

Marbling. Bunch up the cloth into a ball or a longer length into a roll and bind

mercerized, dye well. Cambric, calico (bleached), drill, lawn, muslin, organdy, sheeting, toweling, cotton, velvet, and velveteen are all good for tie-and-dye. Unbleached calico should be washed several times in the washing machine or boiled with soda and soap powder or detergent before dyeing. Leave cloth to cool in this liquid then rinse thoroughly. Linens, viscose rayons, pure silks, and chlorinated woolens also are excellent for tie-and-dye. However, avoid all crease-resistant cloths.

Some of the dyes will color the man-made fibers, but as a rule man-made fibers require different dyes than the ones to be discussed here.

All strong cotton and linen threads, yarn, twine, fine string, raffia, etc. can be used.

220

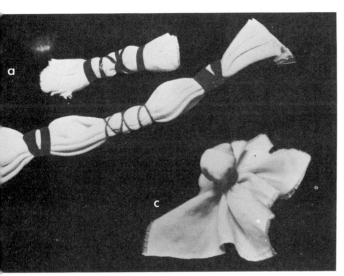

Fig. 3

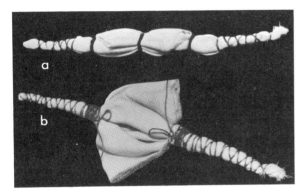

Fig. 4

"Industry." A wall hanging in wool, dyed by the author. Compare this bold effect with the more delicate silk and cotton hangings.

firmly in all directions (Fig. 1a). A small amount of binding will allow more dye to penetrate; a more densely bound sample retains more white cloth. After the first dyeing, untie (Fig. 1b), then retie the cloth, bringing the undyed areas to the outside of the bundle. Dye the second color. Repeat until a satisfactory texture has been achieved.

Binding. This must be done firmly so that the dye does not penetrate too easily and fastened off securely by tying two ends of thread together with a slip knot. A narrow binding produces a resist line, a solid band keeps out most of the dye in that area, and crisscross binding gives a texture on the cloth.

Knotting. Fine fabrics are most suitable for this technique. All knotted patterns are improved if, after the first dyeing, the knots are untied, then tied up again as before and dyed the next color. The knots can be tied loose enough for trouble-free untying, but they will then need a little reinforcing with binding or rubber rings to make sure of getting a resist.

Fold cloth in half lengthwise and tie into knots at intervals, twisting the cloth before tying (Fig. 2a). Pick up the central point of a square of fine cloth, twist it, and tie it into a knot. Pull out each corner in turn and tie into smaller knots (Fig. 2b). For a repeat pattern over a length of cloth pick up points where planned and tie into knots.

Clump tying. Bind small objects, such as stones, beads, buttons, marbles, corks, peas, beans, and rice, into the cloth at ran-

221

dom or to form some prearranged design. Do not cut the binding thread between each object, but bind with a continuous thread; it is easier to untie (Fig. 3c).

Stripes. Gather, pleat, or roll the cloth into a tube lengthwise and bind at intervals. This will give resist stripes across the fabric, with bands of color in between (Fig. 3a and 3b). Change some of the bindings before dyeing the second color. For diagonal stripes, pleat the sample into a tube diagonally and bind it at intervals.

Folded squares. Fold a square of fine cloth into quarters, then across diagonally to form a triangle. Add binding. Dye the first color. Untie and rearrange before dyeing the second color. Innumerable ways of folding squares can be devised, giving a wide range of exciting designs (Figs. 4a and 4b).

Circles. Pick up a point of cloth and smooth it down to look like a closed umbrella. Begin the binding near the point for a small circle and farther away for a larger circle.

Spots. For tiny spots pick up a minute point of cloth on a needle and bind just below it. Remove needle. A multi-spot is formed by picking up and binding several points of cloth together.

Sewing. For sewing techniques, the thread must be very strong or used double. Begin by making a good-sized knot at the end of the sewing thread and always knot any ends when the thread is cut, during the pulling up. Complete all the sewing on each sample before pulling up the threads, bunching the fabric as closely as possible and fastening off without slackening the thread. When untying, cut the thread at the fastening-off knot and the fabric will be released.

Running stitches. Whether you have one, two, or more rows on a single cloth, running stitches can be used to create bands of texture resembling smocking or to outline any shape drawn on the cloth. Stitches should be approximately ⅜ to 1 inch.

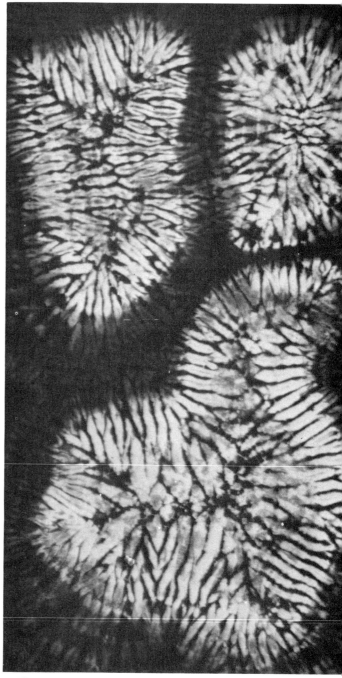

"Alluvion." Cotton wall hanging. Author.

Small stitches do not give definite resist patterns.

Running stitches on double cloth can be used to form bands of texture across the fabric or to outline any symmetrical shape, half of which is drawn against the fold of the cloth.

"In Full Bloom," an example of sewing and dyeing.

"Around and About," a pleated shape dyed on silk and used as a wall hanging. Author.

Oversewing. This can be used across a fold or roll of cloth to give a most interesting band of pattern.

The outline of any shape drawn on the cloth can be oversewn, the size and density of the stitches determining the effect of the resist line so produced. The area within any sewn shape can be bound or can have small objects tied into it.

Pleated shapes. Almost any symmetrical shape can be formed by pleating on double cloth. Draw half the shape against a fold of cloth. Pleat up the cloth along the pencil line. Add a binding to hold the pleats in place, then add further binding where required. This method is effective for large circles, diamonds, ovals, etc. If preferred, the pleating of the cloth can be done by weaving a safety pin in and out along the pencil line. Close the pin when the shape is enclosed. Put a binding below the pin, then remove it. Repeat for each shape.

It is advisable to wear an apron or overalls and rubber gloves when dyeing. Newspaper can be spread over any areas that might get splashed with dye. Drain dyed samples on newspaper before rinsing. Also, newspaper can be used to squeeze out excess water from rinsed samples.

A sample that is "wetted out" (dipped in cold water, then squeezed) before being dyed produces a much more definite resist than if put into the dye dry. Longer dyeing usually gives a deeper color. Aim to get good strong colors. These show up the resist pattern to advantage. Allow for the color being much paler when the sample is dry. Always move the sample about in the dye during dyeing.

In the following procedures light fastness, or the degree to which the dyes are liable to fade in sunlight, is denoted by:
Fair—will fade somewhat after a while
Good—may fade slightly
Very good—should not fade

The materials indicated in each dyeing procedure are coded: A — cottons, B—linen and viscose rayons, C—pure silks and chlorinated woolens.

Leveled off spoon "scoop" measures have been used for amounts given in the dye recipes. Decide how much dye liquid

223

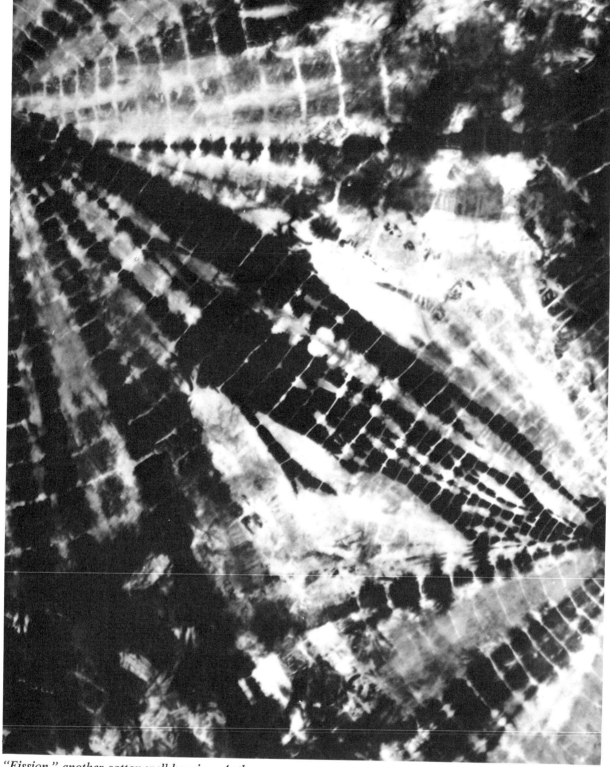

"Fission," another cotton wall hanging. Author.

is required to cover the sample, then work out the quantities of dyes and chemicals from the following standard recipes.

Dylon, Rit, Tintex, etc. will dye fabrics A, B, C, and a few man-made fibers. Light fastness—fair. Varies for different fabrics.

Paste dye from 1 packet of dye (which dyes ½ pound dry weight of cloth) with a little water, add 1 tablespoon salt, vinegar as directed, and 2 to 3 pints boiling water. Use 1 cap measure of liquid dye, plus salt or vinegar to 2 pints boiling water.

Direct dyes for fabrics A and B. Some will dye C fabrics. Light fastness—varies from fair to very good for the best brands.

Paste 1 teaspoon dye with a little cold water, add 1 pint hot water and 2 tablespoons salt. Dye just below boiling for 5 to 60 minutes, according to depth of color required and thickness of the bundle. Rinse. Repeat for each color.

Acid dyes for fabrics C. Light fastness varies from fair to very good for the best brands of dye. Paste ½ teaspoon dye with a little cold water. Add 1 pint of hot water, 1 to 2 tablespoons dye salts, and 1 teaspoon acetic acid 30 percent (or 1 tablespoon vinegar). Dye just below boiling for 5 to 45 minutes, according to thickness of the bundle and depth of color required.

The dyes preceding can be dyed cold, but the colors are much paler than when dyed hot. Use less water for cold dyeing. After mixing, bring dye liquid to a boil to make sure all the dye powder has been dissolved. Then, allow mixture to cool for cold dyeing. Alternatively, after pasting, mix dyes with boiling water. Rinse fabric well after dyeing until water is clear, or resists will become stained after the sample is untied.

Whether dyed hot or cold, when all the dyeing is completed, rinse fabric thoroughly. Dry. Untie. Rinse and dry quickly. Iron fabric while damp, covered with newspaper so that the color does not spread. The samples can be untied while they are still wet, but there is a danger of the resists becoming stained.

When laundering fabrics dyed with these dyes, give them a warm wash only, plus a little soap powder or detergent and dry quickly.

Reactive dyes are for fabrics A and B. Paler colors on C. Light fastness good to very good. Fabrics dyed with these dyes can be boiled.

In the dyebath dissolve 1 to 2 teaspoons dye with 1 pint warm water. In a separate bowl dissolve 4 level tablespoons salt and 1 level tablespoon soda in 1 to 2 pints hot water. When the sample is ready, and not before this, combine the two solutions, stir, and begin dyeing immediately. Dye for ½ to 1 hour, moving the fabric about constantly for the first 15 minutes and then at intervals. Rinse the sample until the water clears. Place in boiling water, plus a little detergent, for 5 minutes, moving sample about occasionally. Rinse well. Untie the sample when wet or when it is dry. Rinse after untying and if possible give the sample a hot wash and final rinse.

When two or more colors are being dyed, give a very hot wash or very hot rinse in between each if possible; otherwise leave the sample to soak in the rinse water, changing it occasionally. The unfixed dye should be removed in order to get the full yield of the next color. Exciting effects are produced if the sample is untied after each color, rearranged, and tied up again before dyeing the next color. Each dyeing remains intact. This enables the pattern to be built up in different sections of the cloth with successive dyeings. Once the soda has been added, the dye becomes ineffective in a very short time. Use dye immediately after adding the soda.

To store, place any mixed up dye in one bottle and the salt/soda solution in another. To use, take equal quantities of each as required. The dye can be used after a week or even longer if the bottles are tightly corked.

Indigo is excellent for tie-and-dye, but because it is insoluble in water, it needs to be vatted before it can be used to dye fabric.

Permanganate of potash and iron rust (ferrous sulfate) are cheap to buy and can be used as dyes. Tie-dyed fabrics are personal and unique. They are particularly distinctive made up into all kinds of garments and articles for the home.

225

Michael Laxton

wood

TREES SERVE AS THE NATURAL SOURCE of wood. Everyone knows this, but it is easy to forget when making a simple stool that what we are looking at once grew, was once alive! That wood is an organic material is probably the most significant factor in its subsequent use by man, for the disciplines that wood dictates stem from its own structural organization. It has determined the shape of woodworking tools and even the manner in which we can manipulate and form wood.

WOOD AS A MATERIAL

The characteristics of wood are unique and individual even to itself, for no two specimens are identical. In visual terms alone, wood surpasses any other material in its beauty of color and endless array of grain and figure marks. The combination of color and figure—determined by species, locality, and rate of growth — has stimulated craftsmen and artists alike to create some of the finest furniture and sculpture that man can claim. In Fig. 1 some of the visual qualities of the more commonly used woods are recorded.

Wood has served man as a structural material for thousands of years because in wood, he found a strong material yet relatively light and fairly easy to work with. The strength of wood is related to its cellular composition. If we liken a tree to a closely packed column of drinking straws, with little mechanical cohesion between the longitudinal straws, we can appreciate that the strength of a piece of wood is related to the direction of the grain. Wood, then, is strong across the grain and weak along or parallel to its grain.

The relative strength of different species of wood is too complex to consider here, except to state that generally, the heavier the sample of wood, the stronger the sample will probably prove to be. For example, weights of oak and pine offer an indication as to their respective strength. The durability of wood—its resistance to de-

"Elegy III," hollow form with white. Barbara Hepworth.

cay from atmosphere and insects—broadly matches its weight/strength ratio; that is, the stronger, the heavier, the more likely the sample will resist decay. For example, oak will resist attack from moisture and insects far longer than common pine. Par-

a

b

c

Fig. 1 (a) oak, (b) teak, and
(c) Columbian pine.

ticular species do have special qualities of resistance; for example, teak—the oily texture of which will resist water and is thus commonly used in boat construction and as draining boards. It is therefore possible to select a particular wood for your specific use. By carefully considering the qualities required and relating these to durability and future situation, wood can be seen as an extremely versatile material.

The last property that must be considered is the tendency of wood to take up moisture—to swell and to shrink. When a tree is felled, a large percentage of its weight is made up of water. Gradually, by being open to the air or being artificially dried in a kiln, the original amount of water is reduced. By this process, wood becomes more stable and permits its successful use in a domestic situation. However, the tendency of wood to absorb moisture still remains, even after many years. If you move a piece of wood from your workshop indoors to a centrally heated environment, that piece of wood will shrink and maybe develop cracks. Basically, any sample piece of wood will eventually assume the level of moisture that is evident in the im-

mediate atmosphere. Thus, an outside door will shrink and swell according to the time of the year.

Availability

The conversion of the tree into usable and convenient planks and bulks of timber follows a fairly standard practice. The tree is sawed as in either of the two manners shown in Fig. 2 and then allowed to season, that is, to dry out. In the case of some special hardwoods or when a particular usage of wood requires a low moisture content, the wood is kiln dried. In any event the sawed sizes are set as actual measurements, that is 1 inch, 1½ inch, 2 inches, etc. After drying, the timber may be planed

227

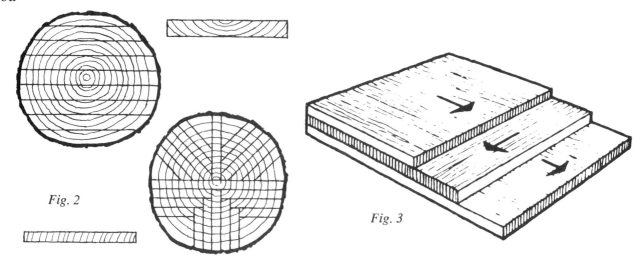

Fig. 2

Fig. 3

before reaching its destination. In the case of a 1 inch sawed plank, this will be reduced to nearer ¾ inch but will still be classed and sold as 1 inch. This is one of several points to remember when buying prepared timber and when designing.

Man-made boards

One of the most significant developments of recent years has been the employment of man-made boards. These are all based on wood, and all in some way increase the value or potential of wood. We can usefully group these boards into two kinds. First, that group in which we find plywood, blockboard, and laminated board. Here, thin layers of wood are glued together, with each successive layer having its direction of grain at right angles to the previous one (Fig. 3). By this process, not only can large sheets of varying thickness be produced, but by making use of the directional strength of timber, boards of great strength can be achieved. Another advantage of building up a board is that, as a result of the construction, these boards will resist to a large extent any movement through shrinkage, and finally they can be faced with a high-class veneer or even a plastic laminate, thus increasing considerably their visual, or surface, value.

The appropriate use of these boards will largely depend on the expected location and permitted expense. However, plywood is primarily used in thicknesses from ⅛ inch to ½ inch as door panels, backs of cabinets, and drawer bottoms, though its potential as a three-dimensional construction material in chair forms, etc. will be seen later. Blockboard and laminated board, coming usually in thicknesses from ½ inch to 1 inch, are used more as a construction material in cabinets, shelves and table tops. The disadvantage here, as with all boards, is the rather unsatisfactory edge that is exposed on cutting. Some provision, therefore, must be made to apply an edging or facing. The normal sheet sizes of plywood, etc. range up to 8 feet by 4 feet and are available as interior, exterior, or special marine qualities.

The second group of wood-based materials that we recognize as man-made boards is seen in the form of hardboard and chipboard, or particle board. Here the wood is shredded or chipped into small pieces, which are then resin-glued under pressure to form sheets, the usual size being 8 feet by 4 feet and ⅛ inch thick for hardboard and from ⅜ inch to 1 inch for chipboard. These boards offer some of the same advantages as plywood and blockboard, except that they are unsuitable for outside use, do not have the same attractive appearance, and need more care in their use as a construction material. They do, however, serve as a cheaper base and can, as such, be used to great advantage.

WOOD IN CONSTRUCTION

There are special tools and techniques to consider before beginning wood construction.

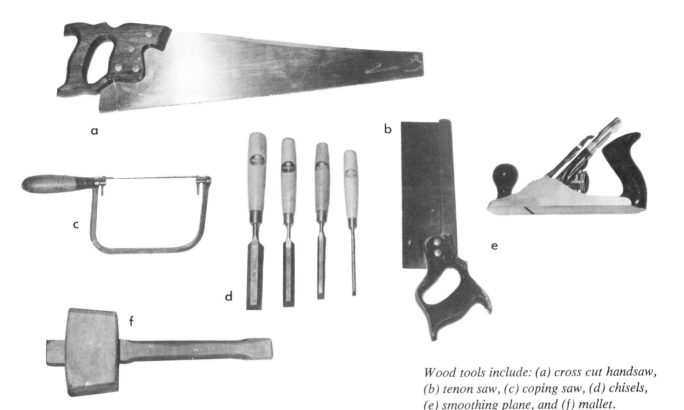

Wood tools include: (a) cross cut handsaw, (b) tenon saw, (c) coping saw, (d) chisels, (e) smoothing plane, and (f) mallet.

Tools

It is wrong to suppose that it is impossible to produce fine pieces of woodwork without an extensive kit of tools. There are, however, a number of essential tools that we must account for. A basic kit might therefore comprise:

1. Cross cut handsaw — used for cutting across boards and general purpose work (12-16 teeth per inch).
2. Tenon, or dovetail, saw—used for general benchwork, cutting of joints, etc.
3. Coping saw—for various curved work and particular joint cutting. Saw blade can be set at any angle.
4. Chisels—beveled edge 1 inch, ¾ inch, ½ inch, ¼ inch for joint work and general removal of waste wood.
5. Wooden mallet—for use in conjunction with most chisel work.
6. Smoothing plane—used for achieving a fine, flat finish on basic woods. For larger work a jack plane may be needed.
7. Other basic tools would include a hammer, ruler, T-square, hand drill and a screwdriver, rasp and file, several clamps, oilstone.

What is more essential than an exhaustive kit of tools is that those you have are used correctly and kept in good order. All manufacturers' instructions and advice should be carefully observed.

With a basic kit of tools available, the next essential requirement is a bench or sound surface on which to work, a surface that can take a standard woodworker's vise or one of the various devices that are available and can be used in place of a vise.

The position in regard to power tools has changed dramatically in recent years, and there is now available a wide selection to choose from, offering a range of attachments for particular uses. By far the most useful is the basic power drill, which can in turn, with attachment, be used for drilling, sanding, sawing, etc. Here again one cannot emphasize enough the necessity to read fully the manufacturer's instructions and act accordingly. Never try to overload or overwork power tools. This is the time when accidents can occur. Well used, however, power tools can be a great asset to the woodworker, both in speed of production and in the quality of work that can be achieved.

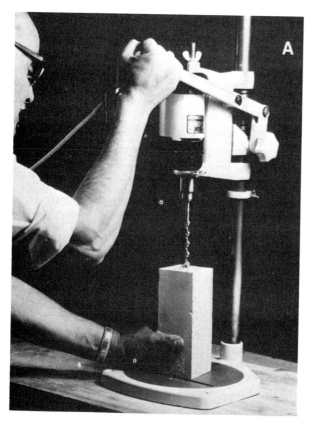

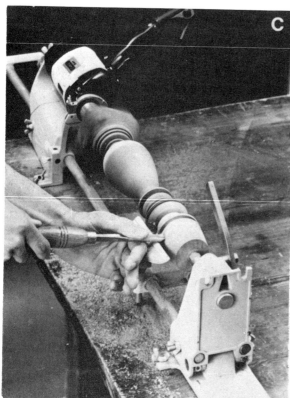
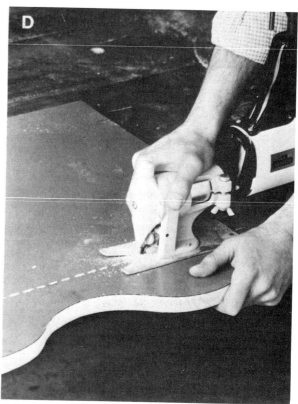

The basic drill with attachments for (a) drilling, (b) sanding, (c) turning, and (d) sawing.

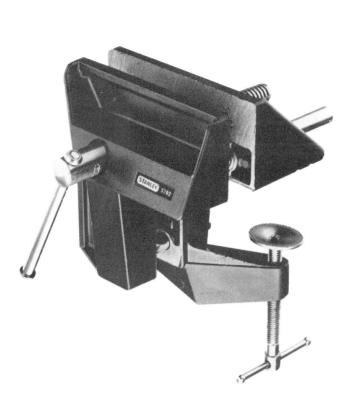

Stanley vise No. 5702 can be fitted to a bench or any flat working surface.

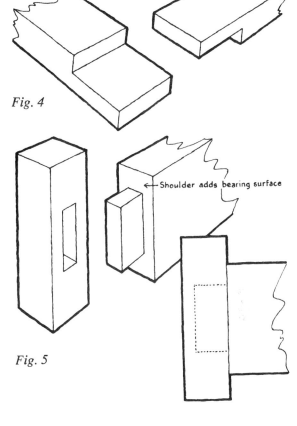

Fig. 4

←Shoulder adds bearing surface

Fig. 5

Adhesives

The advent of plastics and their introduction into the glue industry has produced many new adhesives, many of remarkable strength and ease of use. Two of these glues stand out and are worthy of note.

1. Contact cements are thick liquids ready for use, white in color and changing to colorless on evaporation and being set. Easy to use, strong, clean and leaving no waste, contact cements usually require about 4 hours to achieve full strength.

2. Synthetic epoxy resin glues—available as (a) a thick, clear liquid and a liquid hardener; (b) a powder that is mixed with water. Here, again, these glues are remarkably strong, can be used for exterior or marine use, are fairly easy to work with, and also are clean.

The traditional animal glue, sold as beads, which have in turn to be dissolved and heated, still remains a powerful and versatile glue but cannot compete with the new adhesives in terms of convenience and ease of use.

The process of "gluing up" a job is one of the most important phases of making an item in woodwork. Always assemble and clamp up the structure dry, that is, without glue, and insure that the joints go together without undue pressure. Have clamping blocks ready, clamps available and set to correct length, and also a piece of clean, damp rag to wipe off excess glue. Go through the whole procedure first as a run through and make sure you are organized and really ready to start gluing.

Methods of joining

Since his first interest in the use of wood, man has been confronted with the necessity of having to join separate pieces of wood in order to produce the desired item or structure. The development of joints, as we call them, has been a slow and deliberate process based on a sound and intelligent

231

understanding of the very nature of wood itself. The basic requirement of any joint is to provide a strong and durable fixing, and from our knowledge of wood as a material, we can also say that:

1. Any joint or construction must take account of the direction of grain of the pieces of wood. In order to do this the pieces are mated together. That is, a section from one piece of wood is removed so that the second piece can fit or mate into it. The resulting joint is then glued or fixed in some way, such as by screwing or nailing.

2. The proportion of any particular half of a joint should not be such as to weaken its counterpart. Each mate of the joint should therefore be approximately equal in the amount of wood to be removed and should present equal surface for gluing (Fig. 4).

3. Where possible a joint should add to its own strength and bearing capacity by the introduction of shoulders (Fig. 5).

If we look at the basic construction forms, we usually group these as follows:

(a) Flat frame construction — doors, picture frames, etc.

(b) Open frame construction — tables, chairs, etc.

(c) Carcass or cabinet constructions.

Flat frame construction. The procedure for the jointing of frame structures is the simplest and quickest of all joint making. The common joints used are the lap joint, cross halving, the bridle joint, and possibly the miter joint (See Fig. 6). Most of these joints can be achieved with the use of the tenon saw alone. If a chisel has to be used, as it might in a bridle joint, be sure to work from both sides, and take a little out at a time. All framing joints mentioned will need some form of fixing, by gluing, nailing or screwing, or even doweling—a simple process of drilling through the assembled joint and inserting a locking peg or dowel.

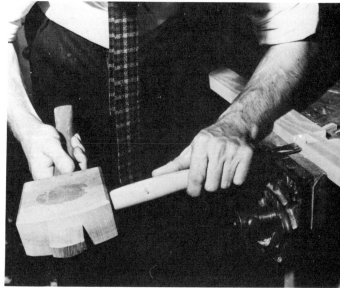

Cutting a bridle joint.

A very important factor to consider in respect of frame construction is to insure you have assembled them square, that is, that all corners register as a right angle. A very quick and efficient way to insure this is to measure the diagonals and, if different, adjust until they read the same.

Open frame construction. The most common and widely used joint in open frame construction is the mortise and tenon. There are many variations on this versatile joint, some of which are shown (Fig. 6). The making of this joint is distinct from those previously mentioned in that a mortise, or hole, has to be made in order to accept the tenon. The easiest way to do this is first to remove as much wood as possible with a series of drilled holes—then clean out the hole with a beveled edge chisel.

A problem that often arises in open construction is the necessity, for instance, of having to join two rails to one leg in order to achieve a three-dimensional corner. The problem is to make a strong joint without taking too much wood away from the leg. Two convenient ways of overcoming this are shown in Fig. 7, but by far the most satisfactory solution is to offset, or stagger, the rails.

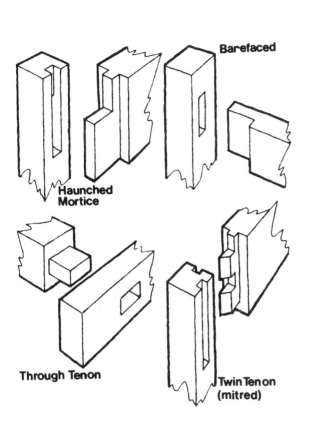

Barefaced

Haunched Mortice

Through Tenon

Twin Tenon (mitred)

Fig. 6

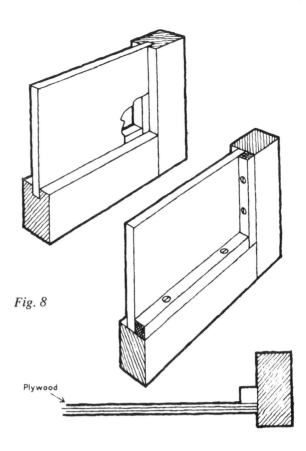

Fig. 8

Plywood

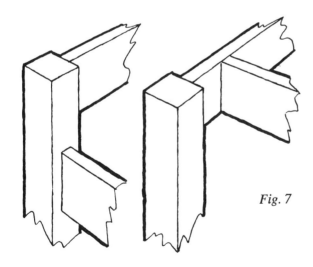

Fig. 7

Apart from the large family of mortise and tenon joints, a very useful joint for open frames is the already mentioned doweled joint. This time the dowels, or pegs, act in lieu of a tenon. Two dowels are necessary to achieve sufficient gluing area and to stop any tendency to twist. Although at first sight this joint would appear an easy

one, the problem of accurate drilling to insure that the dowels and holes are correctly placed requires careful marking out. Here a very useful addition to your tool kit might well be a dowel jig.

Cabinet construction

Probably the most difficult woodwork construction is that of building a cabinet. Here, the very real problem of shrinkage and warping of timber can cause considerable frustration. Provided, however, one recognizes what might happen and takes evading action, cabinets can be built quite satisfactorily. The obvious way to build a cabinet might appear to be simply to join four planks of sufficient width. However, the shrinkage across the width of a board will give trouble, and, unless you have considerable experience, to build a cabinet using solid boards wider than 9 inches is inadvisable.

There are, however, two methods that can be employed to build cabinets of some depth. The first is, in effect, to build up a skeleton frame using either flat frame or

233

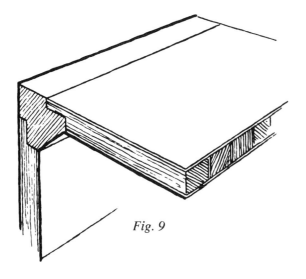

Fig. 9

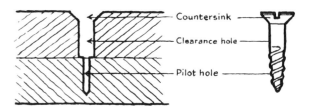

- Countersink
- Clearance hole
- Pilot hole

Fig. 10

open frame construction and then to in-fill the open sides with plywood or hardboard. The best way to insert the panel is to form a groove around the frame. If you have not the facilities to do this, it is quite adequate to lay the panel on fillets, as shown in Fig. 8.

A second method of building a cabinet of some width is to use man-made boards, that is, plywood or blockboard or even chipboard. Here the process of jointing can be fairly simple. By using a corner piece, suitably shaped to take the appropriate size of board, a pleasant looking and very effective cabinet can be made quite quickly (Fig. 9).

The other way of using man-made boards would be to use K/D fitting (knock down). These are easily fitted and do have in their favor the facility that allows the cabinet to be taken apart at any time and reassembled, maybe in a different form.

Joining by fixing

Nails and screws are widely used in constructional woodwork and, correctly applied, can be a most useful asset to the woodworker. In the use of either nails or screws their placing in relation to the edge of the wood is very important — too near and splitting will occur. In the instance of screwing, always drill a clearance hole through the top piece of wood. This allows the screw to pull the pieces together and be effective as a fixing method (Fig. 10).

Methods of forming

The fact that wood is flexible to a certain degree and that under certain conditions can be bent allows the use of wood to extend into curved work. Normally, to cut a curved member out of the solid plank implies weakness, because at some point short grain must be evident; whereas by steam bending or lamination (the two methods of forming) the direction of grain still follows the actual form.

Steam bending. When wood is subjected to a source of steam, the fibers of the timber become supple and able to flex. At this point the specimen is removed from the steam and quickly bent and held in position by a jig until the sample has dried out. After drying, the wooden rail or chair back will remain in the bent form.

Lamination. As well as giving a curved form, lamination, by virtue of the glue lines, insures an extremely strong member. The process here is to cut thin strips of wood, usually 1/8 inch thick, which by themselves are flexible enough to take up the required bend. These strips are then glued and pressed together in a mold of the desired shape. When the glue is set, the lamination can be removed and the mold used again.

Finishing

Although modern technology has given us many excellent finishes, such as polyurethane varnish and cellulose, which in themselves have removed much of the tedious

Steam bending wood around mold. Note steel strip used to pull wood onto mold.

Laminated wood being removed from mold after gluing.

work usually associated with finishing and polishing, it is the preparation of the wood surface prior to applying the finish that is the all-important factor in achieving a good final surface.

Once the job has been assembled and glued up, the first step is to remove any surplus glue and to level off any jointing that needs attention. Next, a firm rub with a fine sandpaper is needed, making sure to rub along the direction of the grain. Finally, remove surplus dust with a soft brush or rag.

Cellulose lacquer. Cellulose is a quick drying, clear lacquer that can be applied by brush. Several thin coats are better than one thick one. You must rub down lightly with steel wool or a very fine sandpaper after each coat of lacquer. After the final coat, cut down with steel wool again and rub in a thin coat of wax.

Polyurethane. Recent advances in plastics and their introduction into the paint industry have produced some first-class finishes that are easy to apply, clear, and have a final hard surface, resistant to scratches and staining. Polyurethane is one of these that is applied by brush and allowed to dry for about four hours. Always rub down in between coats and apply wax on final coat

if desired. Polyurethane is available not only in gloss but in a matte and satin finish.

Painting. Any item of woodwork can also be painted if desired, and in fact much contemporary furniture is painted in bright, pure colors. Here, as with clear finishes, the preparation is all important, and a good coat of primer and undercoat are essential before applying the top coat. The virtue of the matte and satin finishes that are currently available is that they do not show up the blemishes or dust as the gloss finishes do, and they give a softer and less clinical surface.

WOOD IN USE

The extraordinary variety of uses to which man has employed wood is clear evidence both of the versatile nature of wood and of man's own innate ingenuity. Man's use of wood is a study in itself; here we can only outline some of the considerations and possibilities that are relevant today and confine our comments to the domestic use of wood—furniture, with a brief mention of the use of wood in the construction of children's toys.

Design considerations

The importance of thoughtful organiza-

This kitchen interior shows how wood in a domestic setting gains interest through color, texture, and pattern.

tion and careful planning in design work cannot be overstressed. An ill-considered step or a lack of thought in design not only can cause frustration and annoyance but can cost a considerable amount of money and waste of material. We can usefully group the essential design considerations as:

1. Utilitarian application—the use to which the item is intended.
2. Intended situation—the actual position or environment into which the piece of furniture will be placed.
3. Available resources—tools and work facilities that can be expected; level of experience and skill available.
4. Cost—level of expenditure that can be allotted to project; purchase of materials, etc.

Utilitarian application. At first sight, it may seem obvious that a chair is to be sat on and that a china cupboard will have to house cups and saucers. However, the stated use of the project must be examined further. How will it be used? Who will use it? For how long will it be used? How often? Once you begin to question in some detail the very nature and *implications* of the project, it will be seen that a number of important factors emerge that may at first seem unimportant or, maybe, are not even considered. From these questions will come a series of essential requirements, a specification in terms of measurements, basic form, and they may even suggest materials to be used. For instance, a necessity to withstand the effects of heat and spilt alcohol will indicate a special surface.

Intended situation. As any piece of furniture will ultimately reside within a domestic environment, due consideration of

Occasional table made from one standard section of wood.

Modular furniture, such as these storage units, is practical and versatile.

the structure and organization of that situation seems advisable. What relationship will the new piece have to form with the existing furniture? Does it have to "fit in" or can it serve as a contrast? What sort of room and how big is it? What is the decor? Once again, the answers to our question will give us additional information and conditions that will help to formulate a design.

Available resources. As the ideas begin to grow, it is as well to consider early on to what extent your design must be disciplined in order to match up to your workshop facilities, your own experience, and the time you have available. Always plan within your capacity and be sure of success. This in turn will increase your experience and confidence, thus allowing you to be more ambitious with the next project. Better to be simple and succeed than complicated and fail.

Cost. The estimation of the cost must also be an early consideration as well as the local availability of the required material. The contemporary fashionable use of teak as a furniture timber may present problems of availability as well as being high in price. However, the use of afromosia or even iroko will give a similar ap-

pearance at a much reduced price and will be more readily obtainable. There is also a current trend to use the lighter woods such as ash, beech, and oak, all of which are good timbers to work with and are reasonable in price. Some of the softwoods, such as Columbian pine and even a good quality white or red deal, given a suitable hard finish such as polyurethane, can also become very effective as a timber for furniture making. Whatever the wood, think well about your cutting list. Is there another way to prevent waste? This is a particularly relevant point in the use of plywood or blockboard. Lastly, do not forget to add a percentage for finishing materials.

Current trends

In order to appreciate the developing trends in furniture, it is necessary at least to recognize the basic factors that influ-

237

Building bricks are simple, attractive, and easy to make.

This wooden duck on castors could be made easily.

ence and are instrumental in change. One of these, architecture, has always had a very marked influence on furniture and rightly so, for furniture ultimately serves within the environment of architecture. Architecture in turn serves society, its needs, and its patterns of behavior. From this we recognize that the manner in which we live will to a large extent determine that which we need and use in our daily life. Today, we lead a less formal life, in which relaxation and comfort are important considerations. Our demands on furniture are different from yesterday, and therefore new forms are developed as a natural process. Emphasis is shifted, and even our expectations of furniture change. Today we expect our furniture to be compact, light, and versatile, capable of rearrangement.

While we see the influence of architecture on the style and configuration of contemporary furniture, we must also recognize the significance of the progress in its industrial production. The economic need to produce furniture in quantity has assisted the rationalization of construction. The simplicity in form and lack of ostentatious decoration that we uphold today as virtues of good design are largely compatible with large scale commercial production in which handwork must be kept to a minimum.

Some of the most interesting develop-

ments in contemporary furniture are the growing use of color, the interplay of textures, and wide use of new materials.

An obvious post-war development in domestic achitecture has been the building of smaller and more compact houses. This has in turn produced the need for furniture that is not only compact but versatile. Modular/unit furniture is an expression of this need, and today a growing percentage of furniture is produced using some element of modular construction. Here, the exercise is to produce furniture that can interrelate or build up by using a common unit, measurement, or proportion. One of the most important assets of this system is that furniture can be extended or added to, such as storage units, as and when required.

While the exploitation of new materials continues to grow in the furniture industry, wood will still continue to be its basic material. It is interesting to observe how the challenge of new materials has in turn brought about not only a new interest in certain woods but also the enterprising use of plywood in chair forms—a development very worthy of further examination.

Wood in toys

The use of wood as a suitable material from which to build toys goes back to the early civilizations when small handcarved

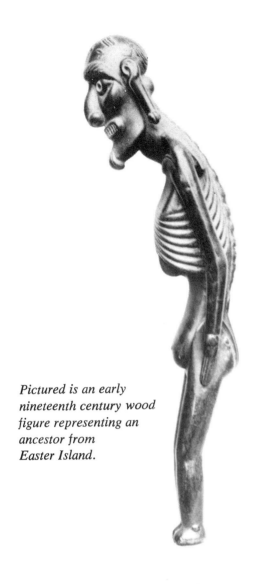

*Pictured is an early
nineteenth century wood
figure representing an
ancestor from
Easter Island.*

Touch forms.

wooden figures and animals were used not only in play by children but also as symbols in various rituals and religious activities. Through the ages, a select number of wooden toys has remained popular such as the rocking horse, Noah's ark, and the dolls' house, as well as the traditional wooden dolls of Austria and Scandinavia. More recently, the garage, the wheelbarrow, and an endless array of vehicles of transport have been introduced.

The making of wooden toys is a comparatively easy procedure, needing few joints and little elaborate construction. The intelligent use of nails, screws, and glue, in relation to plywood and small scraps of wood, can result in toys that give immense pleasure to children. Painted in bright colors (nontoxic paints!) and free from needless detail, toys are best when simple, strong, and stable.

WOOD IN SCULPTURE

While the utilitarian use of wood has dominated man's application of this versatile material, he learned to appreciate very early the suitability of wood as a material through which he could express himself and his ideas. From the moment tools were available, men have whittled, carved, and formed images, impressions, and expressions of their way of life. The natural warmth and beauty of wood are enough in themselves to inspire many men. When coupled with its relative ease of working, this makes wood one of the most stimulating and suitable materials for sculpture.

Undoubtedly the success that artists have had in using wood in sculptural form can be attributed to their ability to understand and appreciate the very nature of wood, its disciplines, and its character. Once this recognition is made, a *rapport* and sympathy grows between artist and his material. From this point his sculpture, whether abstract or realistic, will retain that relationship—the quality of wood.

The newcomer must learn quickly to accept and develop the suggestions made to him by his wood. He must learn to develop its grain and use its variations in texture and color. Therefore, before attemping to carve a definite image, spend the time you would otherwise invest in your first

239

Sculpture composed of natural forms.

attempts at carving in getting to know the character of wood. One way of introducing yourself is through the sense of touch. Here the resultant form is suggested by the wood while you, the tool of its execution, react to the grain, texture, and color. The simple objective is to create a form sympathetic to handling, exposing as far as possible the natural interest and inherent qualities of the wood. Confine your first attempts to convex form; in other words, *shape* rather than carve. Avoid sharp edges and too many changes of direction and keep it simple.

One of the first problems that arises, even in the simple exercise of the touch form, is the difficulty of shaping or carving "in the round." Because we can only work on one side or facet of our sculpture at a time, it is all too easy to forget the hidden surfaces. But because our form is three dimensional, we should always be aware of the unseen relationships if we hope to form a sculpture that has unity rather than four independent sides. To overcome this problem in the initial stages, keep moving the wood around to avoid overworking any one part.

Though the professional woodcarver may possess an impressive array of gouges and carving chisels, much excellent work can be achieved using a very modest collection of tools. Select only two or three gouges to start with: 1½ inch, 1 inch and a shallow ½ inch. These will be the most useful, and it is surprising how versatile you will find them. One or two good rasps and files are also essential.

Nonfigurative

If by nonfigurative we mean abstract, namely, not representational, we have only to examine samples of driftwood, old trees in decay, or even large root formations to appreciate that nature itself can be an effective sculpture. Through the natural process of erosion or decay wood is often wasted or shaped, leaving forms that, though we may hesitate to refer to them as sculpture, do have a sculptural meaning and are worth our observation. Nature illustrates how the weaker wood is wasted or worn away, how small and inappropriate forms are broken off or integrated into the basic shape; she appreciates the character of timber.

If abstract wood carving is to have a

Sculpture assembled from identically shaped units.

meaning, then the quality of the wood you expose by the chosen sculptural form is a prime consideration: for why else carve in wood? The wood is your inspiration; it gives you an idea that you take up and develop or, just as valid, the wood seems suitable for an idea already formed.

Figurative

Representational or figurative wood carving differs considerably from that of abstract work. In abstract work a compromise and balance are achieved between idea and material. In representational carving, however, there exists a third and very powerful consideration—the image. The strength of the image, whether it be of a bird, a fish, or human form, can, because it is so familiar, overcome and dominate our attention. Thus, wood can become incidental and often even inappropriate as a sculptural material.

Subject matter should be chosen with utmost care and due understanding of the selected wood. Avoid figures, whether animal or human, that have exaggerated, flamboyant, or extended form. For example, while a seated squirrel or rabbit might be an appropriate subject, it is doubtful whether a giraffe or standing stork would make a satisfactory wood carving. Even with a suitably chosen subject, the danger of dominance by the image can remain if a reconciliation is not made between subject and material. Forms will have to adjust and accommodate the material, as the image has to be compromised to fit the character and nature of the wood. Never force an image onto the wood because it will surely reject it or wear it very unhappily.

Sculpture by assembly

The concept of sculpture by assembly revolves around the idea of "building up" or "putting together" a number of independent units to concentrate attention on the relationship of those forms, whether joined or separate. The opportunities for an imaginative and individual expression in wood grow because now woods can be interchanged, and colors and textures used to counterbalance or complement.

Just as with the newcomer to carving, where the touch form provides a useful initial project, so an appropriate introduction to sculpture by construction or assembly is to examine the potential of a number of identical units. To observe the wide variety of form and spatial interest that can be achieved by the use of a simple repetitive unit is a rewarding experience. This can gradually be extended until a whole range of forms can be used with confidence.

The excitement and satisfaction of using wood in sculpture can in the final analysis be appreciated by the artist himself only when he grasps that simple and rewarding understanding of the quality of wood.

index